Bilingual development and literacy learning

Bilingual development and literacy learning

East Asian and international perspectives

Norbert FRANCIS

City University of Hong Kong Press

ISBN: 978-962-937-205-7

Published by

City University of Hong Kong Press
Tat Chee Avenue
Kowloon, Hong Kong
Website: www.cityu.edu.hk/upress
E-mail: upress@cityu.edu.hk

Printed in Hong Kong

Table of Contents

Detailed Chapter Contents

Preface

In East Asia, as in all regions of the world, second language learning and bilingualism have always been important academic objectives, as far back in history as is possible to record events reliably. But only until more recently have these objectives, including first and second language literacy, been within reach of the broad majority of learners enrolled in school. In the not too distant past, the possibility of attaining bilingualism of this kind had been the privilege of a select few. We could say that today it is still restricted to a fortunate minority; but new conditions have laid the groundwork for changing this state of affairs. Globalization is one of the reasons. Digital technology is another.

Without a doubt, the growing attention to research about different kinds of bilingualism is related to the rapidly growing interest in learning English, evidenced in all but the most isolated societies. Of course, English has not always been in this position. Historically, other languages have served the function of lingua franca across borders and cultures: each in its time, Arabic and Latin in the lands of the Mediterranean and Europe, the languages of the great indigenous empires of the Americas, Chinese throughout East Asia, to mention only a few examples. Today, however, the potential and promise of intercultural communication is different: the "franca" aspect of the current international language of wider communication is global in the true sense, for the first time in history. At the same time, we should not forget that around the world a number of regional lingua francas are also expanding, all of this making the scientific study of bilingualism more important than ever before.

Increasingly, learners face complex and demanding language learning objectives; and choices about major commitments to language learning that are not always optional. This is because the relationships among the national, regional and international languages in each country, and in each community of speakers, are complex and demanding in the same proportion. Complicating matters of this developing bilingualism and multilingualism is the parallel pressure on many languages resulting in their displacement, by an expanding language, and even in their extinction. Often, learning a second language results in losing proficiency in one's first language. Related to this phenomenon of "learning and forgetting," is the common outcome of bilingualism in which there is an imbalance in proficiency between one language system and the other. This kind of unequal distribution of competence and ability, in fact, is the most common outcome of bilingual development and second language learning. Understanding these different kinds of language interaction is important for fields of study such as linguistics and psychology and for resolving a number of practical problems in education, to take one example.

One may ask: what is special about bilingualism and literacy in East Asia that it came to be included in the subtitle of this book? In regard to the interaction between two grammatical systems (reading and writing aside for now), and the way that young children acquire them to become bilingual, and the way that adults learn second languages, there is nothing peculiar in the languages of East Asia. There is probably nothing exceptional in this case, from a cognitive point of view, compared to bilingual development in any other part of the world. Rather, it is in the domain of literacy where cross-language/cross-writing system and bilingual/biliterate comparisons are truly interesting. Here it is fair to say that the contrasts among the writing systems in question are exceptional in some important ways. The morphosyllabic characters of Chinese writing, incorporated into and adapted by Japanese writing, have no parallel in any modern orthographic system. They may not have any other true historical parallel either (although this claim is likely to be controversial). Most interesting, however, is the suggestion by recent research that despite the differences in the design of writing systems, common processes of literacy learning and use are shared across all literate cultures.

Today, in part because of the speed and efficiency of word processing, and the rapidly increasing access to it by literacy learners, new interest has emerged among linguists and psychologists in the comparison among writing systems. In the not too distant past, access to portable computers was also the privilege of a select few. How do both native speakers and second language beginners learn the morphosyllabic system, how are the subcomponent skills represented mentally, and how are they put to use in performance (e.g., in terms of comparisons and contrasts with alphabetic systems)? In bilingualism and biliteracy, what are the interfaces, mechanisms of transfer, and mutual influences among systems and subsystems? What aspects of literacy knowledge and processing are the same across orthographies, and which aspects are different? In short, the research problems in these areas are unique and special.

Other aspects of bilingualism and literacy addressed in the coming chapters are not specific to any language or writing system. These correspond to the "international perspectives" in the title. In fact, we should be wary of arguments about language and writing that emphasize at every turn particular and peculiar, culture-bound and "local," and highly context-dependent properties. Alongside exceptional and unique aspects of literacy ability there is reason to assume universal foundations as well.

Two aspects of bilingualism and multilingualism, both related to the notion of uneven development mentioned above, are especially important from the language policy and planning point of view because they involve issues of social inequality.

1. Speakers of minority languages and speakers of national languages face different, in many ways unequal, requirements, opportunities and conditions of use, for example: knowledge of a language that is optional versus obligatory, access to resources tied to languages of wider communication, prospects of the very survival of a community language into future generations.

2. For many minority language students who have not yet learned the national or official language, disproportionately unfavorable learning conditions result, on

> average, in reduced attainment of academic language objectives in school (literacy above all). A factor that contributes to these unfavorable conditions could be the mismatch between the language of instruction in school and the language that children understand. For example, some children learn how to read and write in the language they understand completely; others face the challenge of literacy learning in a language that they understand incompletely, or not at all.

This book is not about inequality in society and the unequal distribution of language learning resources, and offers no direct solutions for policy makers on this score. But the linguistic/cognitive research problems of imbalance and asymmetry (in the bilingual mind) are important to discuss because they are part of the solution.

My sincerest thanks are owed to colleagues and friends for their valuable consultations, critical comments and suggestions, and interesting discussions on the topics in this book: Kerim Friedman, Scott Hadley, Xue-ping Hu, Kent Johnson, Panay Kumod and the students and faculty of the College of Indigenous Studies at the National Dong Hua University, Melissa Shih-hui Lin, Judith Oller Badenas, Akiyo Pahalaan (Tung-Chiou Huang), Charles Perfetti, Jiang Xia, Jin Xue, and especially Chih-Hsiung Tu for his help in analyzing the writing sample in Chapter 5. Thank you to Natalia and Zoraida for the interesting discussions on a number of the important topics in Chapters 5, 6 and 7. I am especially grateful for the many helpful comments and suggestions offered by managing editor Edmund Chan and anonymous reviewers of earlier versions of the final manuscript.

Acknowledgement is granted to the following publications. Portions of earlier versions of chapters 2, 3, 4, 5, 6, 7 and 8 appeared in Applied Linguistics, International Journal of Bilingualism, Journal of Child Language, Language in Society, Language Learning, Language Sciences, Tamkang Studies of Foreign Languages and Literatures, and proceedings from symposia on English teaching published by the English Teachers Association of the Republic of China.

Abbreviations

AoA	Age of Acquisition	28
CALL	Computer Assisted Language Learning	6
CBI	Content-based Instruction	124
CF	corrective feedback	111
CLI	cross-language influence	156
DL	disfavored language	23
EAP	English for Academic Purposes	129
ESL	English as a Second Language	124
FFI	Form-focused instruction	90
FL	foreign language	2
FTFA	Full Transfer Full Access	32
IL	indigenous language	8
L1	first language	2
L2	second language	2
2L1	two first languages (early childhood balanced bilingualism)	27
L_a and L_b	two languages of a bilingual speaker (no indication of which is L1 or L2)	17
LAD	Language Acquisition Device	20
LIC	language of international communication	8
LLSD	Language Learner Sensitive Discourse	126
LTH	Language Threshold Hypothesis	65
MoI	medium of instruction	142
MT	mother tongue	5
NL	national language	5
PLD	Primary Linguistic Data	23

PoS	Poverty of Stimulus	21
RL	Replacing Language	22
SL	sign language	50
SLA	Second Language Acquisition	4
SLI	Specific Language Impairment	42
SpL	spoken language	50
TL	target language	106
ToM	Theory of Mind	47
UG	Universal Grammar	18
UPP	Universal Phonological Principle	61
WL	weaker language	19

Chapter 1

Introduction — Problems of bilingualism and second language literacy in today's globalized learning spaces

1.1 Four themes — From theory to practice

Around the world, one of the interesting differences from one country to another in how people think about bilingualism is how conscious (and self-conscious sometimes) they are of it. At one extreme, knowledge and use of two languages is cause for controversy and conflict. At the other extreme, the casual observer is often surprised at how similar problems, potentially controversial and conflictive in the same proportion, appear to be taken for granted. This book will examine the central research problems in bilingualism and second language (L2) learning from the point of view that they should not be taken for granted. Properly understood from the perspective of the cognitive sciences, none of these problems, ultimately, should be the source of social and political conflict either.

For investigators, our increasingly globalized societies are continuously multiplying opportunities for research, and for all of us, opportunities for greater intercultural understanding. For educators, these changes actually present interesting challenges, even though sometimes the challenges seem to be overwhelming. The rapid social and economic transformations in Asia pose some of the most interesting opportunities and challenges in recent times. To take one example, among many other important ones: the dramatic expansion of learning English as a second or foreign language (FL) in the region, not only in quantitative terms but also in regard to diversification, will soon prove to be historically unprecedented (Cheng, 2008; Evans, 2011; Rajagopalan, 2009). The learning of "English as FL" has increasingly given way to the *appropriation of English* with the emergence of new variants, the result of extensive bilingualism and cross-linguistic influence.

At the same time, we have witnessed the growing importance of learning Mandarin Chinese as L2 (in countries where it is an official or national language), and the continued importance of learning the Chinese writing system in the greater East Asia region, and a new interest in Chinese as FL or heritage language internationally (Yip and Matthews, 2010). The learning and teaching contexts vary widely, as well as in their complexity. To give just a few examples: all children in Japan learn the Chinese characters that historically have been incorporated into their writing system, and simultaneously learn the alphabetic writing system as a part of L2 learning of English, and for writing in Japanese for some purposes. First language (L1) Cantonese-speaking children in Hong Kong learn two L2s, Mandarin and English, along with their respective writing systems. A similar trilingual learning task is a challenge for many Taiwanese elementary school students. Different bilingual and biliteracy learning situations present themselves in Singapore, and all of South East Asia, Korea, in minority language speaking regions of Mainland China, and so forth (Clothey, 2005; Yu, 2008; Zhao and Liu, 2010).

As should be evident from this brief survey of language use, in the study of bilingualism it is difficult to separate out the problems of second language reading and writing, in particular when L2 literacy involves a different writing system, not just a variant of the same kind of orthography. Bilingual and L2 literacy thus present special opportunities to understand bilingualism in general, especially when the cross-writing system comparison involves design features that are maximally different.

Considering the many research problems that have presented themselves in recent years, the following chapters will be organized around four themes. The first two themes (Sections 1.1.1 and 1.1.2) examine what research has suggested about bilingual development and how bilingual ability is structured into systems and subsystems. The second two themes (Sections 1.1.3 and 1.1.4) consider how bilingualism is related to literacy, an important consideration in the teaching of second languages in school.

1.1.1 Imbalances in bilingual development

What is the impact of intensive second language learning on the development, and even continued viability in some cases, of minority and indigenous languages? Such is the problem that Lin and Man (2009) address from a language policy and planning perspective in their wide-ranging study of bilingual education in Southeast Asia. How can young people appropriate an international language for academic purposes, perfect their abilities in the national language, and preserve — even continue to develop — their mother tongue/primary language, if, for example, it's not the same as the national language? Closely related to the problem of competing language learning demands is that of first language attrition and imbalanced bilingualism in situations of both second language learning and simultaneous bilingual development. This might appear to be an unusual way to begin a discussion of dual-language development. But, to fully understand bilingualism it is important to not only study cases of balanced proficiency, where the two language systems have attained an equilibrium in use and competence. To be sure, the equal distribution of linguistic knowledge and ability is often viewed as an ideal standard against which bilingual proficiency of the unequal kind is compared. However, a moment's reflection reminds us that it is imbalanced bilingualism, worldwide (especially considering all cases of second language learning), that is the most typical, probably among both children and adults. Such a view of knowledge and ability assumes that some components are "specialized" to some degree and others are "shared," the latter sometimes called "cognitive-general." This idea leads us to the second theme.

1.1.2 Systems and subsystems

How is competence and ability in two languages structured mentally? Relevant to this issue is whether or not the two linguistic subsystems (parts of a larger language system) are represented separately. Then, are there domains of knowledge that are shared in common (not specialized or bound to either linguistic subsystem)? What are the other components of bilingual proficiency, and what is the nature of the interaction among them? Or alternatively, might the idea of a componential mental architecture for bilingualism (and by extension, for monolingualism) be incorrect? Should we instead conceive of language abilities as internally homogeneous and holistic?

1.1.3 Cross-language and cross-writing system literacy

Of the many research problems in bilingualism and second language learning is bilingual literacy or literacy in a second language — it's one of the most important for educators. Here, the most interesting questions are related to comparisons between L1 literacy and L2 literacy when the writing systems contrast to some degree. The sharpest contrast involves alphabetic writing and morphosyllabic Chinese writing. For example, in what way are reading skills deployed differently in alphabetic and morphosyllabic systems? What might be some of the universal underpinnings of written language processing and literacy learning, common to all orthographic systems, acquired in all literate cultures? From this point of view, the sharpest contrast is the most interesting.

1.1.4 Language and literacy teaching

What are the most effective and efficient approaches to Second Language Acquisition (SLA)? Similar to pedagogical issues in literacy learning, an important controversy has persisted in the field of second language teaching, opposing what are sometimes called *natural approach methods* on the one hand and so-called *instructed SLA* on the other. What is the role of grammar learning, different kinds of focus on form in SLA, and metalinguistic awareness? Readers will notice that this debate is parallel to a similar one in literacy teaching, opposing whole-language and direct instruction approaches.

1.2 Looking ahead to the upcoming chapters

Chapter 2 begins our discussion of the first theme, a consideration of the two possibilities in bilingual development: the early balanced and the imbalanced kinds. Contrary to popular conception, the imbalanced kind can be either sequential (a L2 that begins to develop after L1) or simultaneous (two languages that develop together from birth). As we will see, studying how the language subsystems of bilinguals can develop unevenly not only helps us understand why one language comes to be stronger and the other weaker, but also opens a window onto the inner workings of the Faculty of Language. The idea here is that what we call "language" is internally diverse; bilingualism adds another dimension of diversity.

The unique insights of the study of (typically) imbalanced bilingualism lead us to consider, in Chapter 3, cases of imbalance that are extreme, or exceptional, in some way. This survey of the research picks up on the discussion of the second theme of the book — the mental architecture of bilingualism. Interestingly, asymmetries (typical, atypical and extreme) reveal more clearly the internal structure of complex abilities and faculties. The difficult question then is — in what way can these abilities and faculties be considered to be componential? The difficulty resides in the stubborn fact that all the evidence so far that might help us sort out the different hypotheses among researchers is indirect — it will be so for some time to come.

Chapter 4 considers one field of study where the different proposals regarding the componential structure of language abilities might be tested — reading in different languages and different writing systems. Reading ability is complex and multifaceted, and should therefore lend itself ideally to considering the idea of interacting cognitive components. The relevant concept, introduced in Chapters 2 and 3, which has punctuated a number of important ongoing debates in the cognitive sciences is *modularity*. The field of literacy studies is only one example among many where this discussion is important. This notion, in fact, is the overarching conception that will tie together the four themes of the book. Understanding the components of reading ability takes us to the third theme of the book. Taking literacy as a good example of a complex ability, some of the points of controversy might be pertinent to the study of other cognitive networks and what researchers sometimes call faculties "in the broad sense." For example, hypothetically, the Faculty of Language (broad), contains a subcomponent that we could think of as the Faculty of Language (narrow). For an introduction to the debate, see Fitch *et al.* (2005), Kinsella and Marcus (2009), Pinker and Jackendoff (2005).

Beginning in Chapter 5, attention is shifted more toward applied research problems, of concern mainly to educators, following up on the topic of the previous chapter on bilingual literacy learning. Together with Chapters 6 and 7, this section of the book will round out the discussion of theme #4 — effective and efficient approaches to second language teaching, which now in the 21st century almost always include teaching of L2 literacy. In school, the core objectives of this kind of program also include *advanced* L2 literacy, for higher-order academic purposes. Recall from the above-mentioned examples of trilingual learning that the tasks language learners face have become more complex over the years. For example, in the case of minority language speakers in Mainland China, Hong Kong, Macau, and Taiwan, two second languages, the national language (NL) and an international language, are now both subject and medium of instruction in the elementary school curriculum. Learning space and opportunity need to be optimal for all students; otherwise, advanced literacy in the NL and English (the now required international language) will continue to be only within reach of a select elite. If literacy development in children's mother tongue/first language (MT/L1) is a viable option, this goal would become even more remote under less than optimal instructional conditions. In bilingual and second language teaching, crucially, optimal implies the implementation of the most effective and terminally efficient methods; this is the underlying main idea of theme #4. Parenthetically, the same three-tiered language-learning panorama presented above, born of the new globalization of the late 20th century and current millennium, is not peculiar to East Asia; see discussion in Mohanty *et al.* (2010) and Seidel and Moritz (2009). Most immediately and forcefully, it is presented to the new generations in the African countries, the Indian sub-continent, and parts of Latin America and Europe.

Chapter 5 follows up on the topic of literacy from the previous chapter, now zeroing in on an aspect of bilingual writing ability, and likewise ends with a proposal for future comparative writing system research — a comparison between alphabetic and non-alphabetic writing in how learners focus attention on language and orthographic forms. The central concept here will be the role of negative evidence in language learning, specifically in this case on the development of writing ability (corrective feedback, for example, is a kind of negative evidence). A clear example of focus on form that involves negative evidence is that of self-correction by beginning writers. In fact, as will be shown in the report of a current bilingual literacy project, studying self-correction in two languages turns out to be highly productive from a methodological point of view. Parallel to the questions that we asked in the previous chapter, here we ask: how might focus on form strategies differ between Chinese and an alphabetic script that is also highly regular (sometimes called "transparent" or "shallow"), such as Spanish? On the other hand, what basic processing universals might support self-correction strategies that provide learners with usable negative evidence?

A wider lens on negative evidence, and on positive evidence now, is set in Chapter 6 where we ask about corrective feedback in SLA in general. A number of interesting and difficult questions come up regarding the effectiveness of corrective feedback, problems that are not easily sorted out by "proponents" and "opponents" in the on-going debate. It also happens that recent advances in e-learning, specifically in Computer Assisted Language Learning (CALL), are casting old controversies into a new light on the question of how positive and negative evidence can be harnessed by learners. In particular, research in an area that was touched upon in Chapter 3, language learning exceptionality, has suggested an application of CALL to a very difficult problem — the convergence of critical learning resources when they are severely scarce, concentrating them when learners do not have access to adequate instruction or to reliable sources of language input.

Chapter 7 gathers the different threads of discussion together in a review of a currently popular instructional model in bilingual and second language education — *immersion*. It begins by clearing up an especially unfortunate misunderstanding. Defined, as it properly should be, as content-based L2 teaching, immersion methods are equally applicable to both bilingual education and second language programs (that are not bilingual in the sense that learners do not receive systematic instruction in their L1). Examining two contrasting models of immersion will bring back into the spotlight the concepts that were covered in the previous chapters — positive and negative evidence in SLA (e.g., in contrast to L1 acquisition), the role of deliberate learning strategies and metalinguistic awareness, and the componential nature of language ability.

Chapter 8 will review a selection of recent studies that students of bilingualism should take up, preferably to be read before beginning this book. It begins with a logical starting point — the brain (where knowledge of two languages resides), in a survey of the neurolinguistics of bilingualism (Paradis, 2004). From this narrow (in the positive sense) starting point, I recommend a broad introduction to the field that uniquely combines psycholinguistic and sociolinguistic perspectives (Myers-Scotton, 2006). The following studies return to the important topic of imbalanced bilingualism in childhood, one that for many years has been badly neglected (Yip and Matthews, 2007; Montrul, 2008). The research on bilingual first language acquisition (De Houwer, 2009) takes a step back from the particular examples of bilingual asymmetry and provides a broader perspective. Again, it's surprising what all the possibilities actually are when children are exposed to two languages from birth. *Bilingual development and literacy learning: International and East Asian perspectives* (this book) is a sequel to my recent study of child bilingualism (Francis, 2012) that takes the circumstance of minority and indigenous language bilingualism as a conceptual framework. It introduces and defines the basic concepts; and as such it might be useful to consult for background.

The concluding chapter will revisit and summarize the themes of this book and contrast them to a different perspective on second language learning and bilingual development. In a series of papers given some years ago by Stephen Krashen (2003), known as the *Taipei lectures*, he outlined a theory that calls into question much of the recent research in the field. Thus, a critical review of this debate should help readers better understand the issues at hand.

The reader will notice that the review of the research on bilingualism in the upcoming chapters also argues for a point of view. An example was just given. The arguments and claims that will be proposed for discussion coalesce around the four themes presented above, and come together in the end. At the same time, throughout the discussions of research, it should be kept in mind that the arguments and claims should be taken as proposals, because the emerging evidence in all four areas of investigation is still only pointing us toward interesting hypotheses, some with more initial support than others. As the final and conclusive proofs are not yet around the corner, the point of view presented for consideration should be understood as a modest contribution to the task of formulating workable hypotheses that can be compared side by side. Testing them will build upon the impressive advances in this line of work that have already been made.

1.3 The concept of diglossia (or triglossia) [1] applied to language learning

Returning to the theme of trilingual language education policy, multiethnic China, and more broadly East Asia, presents the same panorama that many countries face whose national language (NL) is not a widely spoken international language. It indeed seems contradictory to make such an assertion about a language with so many speakers. In any case, it is important to emphasize that this three-tiered language learning condition is not exclusive to developing countries. As was mentioned earlier, in many countries of Europe, for example, such a three-language panorama is one that language learners must consider, depending on the specific domain of language use for academic purposes in each case. But, the Asian examples are especially illustrative, given the degree of diversity (among languages and dialects) and scale, in purely quantitative terms, that is involved. Just to take one example, the number of intermediate and advanced English language learners in China and India alone, will probably soon surpass, if it hasn't already, the number of native speakers of English world wide.

A simple and straightforward three-way hierarchy frames the learning problem that in one way or another students, educators, and policy makers converge upon to a greater or lesser degree (see Figure 1.1). Language learning needs follow from the different purposes and functions that each language serves. Language learning curriculum and allocation of language learning resources should respond to these needs, purposes and functions, all this related to the concept of diglossia that we can now expand to triglossia.

Figure 1.1
Access to information: A triglossic hierarchy

For young people whose mother tongue/primary language is at the same time a language of international communication (LIC) and the national language of their country, by and large, learning a second or foreign language represents an enrichment option. For the great majority enrolled in secondary and college level FL programs, typically of widely varying rigor and intensity, the stakes are relatively low on average, relative, that is, to the following two cases.

Proficient speakers of (and fully literate in) the national language, e.g., Mandarin Chinese, in Mainland China or Taiwan, are presented with a different set of options. If it is also their MT/L1, learning a foreign, *non-LIC*, language is an enrichment, similar to the way it is in the first case. Mastery of a minority or indigenous language (IL) of their country would also be enriching. Such mastery could be highly enriching and motivating in regions where a non-NL or non-official language is the most widely spoken, maybe even by an absolute majority. For example, in a given autonomous region or province the primary MT/L1 of the majority of speakers may not be the national language (e.g., Tibet, Taiwan, Xinjiang Autonomous Region). At the same time, a growing segment of the population is bilingual, having learned the NL as a second language (as would typically be the case for all young people who have attended school). Among these young people, many now speak the NL as their stronger, now primary, language, and have lost proficiency in their IL (what previously was their primary MT/L1) — this is the topic of the next chapter. For them, relearning the IL is an enrichment that can be highly motivating.

But for tertiary level studies, if neither the IL nor the NL cannot completely serve the functions of international language of science and academic exchange, the mastery of a LIC is no longer simply an enrichment, but a requirement. On average, the stakes are much higher than in the first scenario (FL learning when MT/L1 coincides with the NL and a LIC); see Lin and Morrison (2010) for a discussion of one aspect of this issue — access to academic vocabulary tied to the demands of higher education. There are, of course, some important exceptions to this requirement, in the arts and humanities, for example. Note also that tertiary level education is only the most typical example of this information access problem; some level of proficiency in a LIC, depending on information access circumstances, is required today in a wide range of endeavors and professions, not just for academic purposes.

The same set of requirements and enrichment opportunities must apply to speakers of minority and indigenous languages, for whom the stakes are now the highest. This includes the added requirement, for them, of acquisition of the basic platform of NL grammatical competence for advanced mastery of the NL for academic purposes. While today, when fewer and fewer communities remain isolated from their respective national culture, many bilingual students are fully proficient in the NL, for all practical purposes, from an early age. But for IL speakers who are beginner learners of the NL as a L2, they have the greatest interest in the most productive trilingual learning environment. For them, the IL represents an important resource, a linguistic/cognitive support system, for the development of higher-order language abilities and for effective L2 learning of the NL (Adamson and Feng, 2009; Wan and Zhang, 2007). In communities where IL preservation is still viable and remains among the historical and cultural commitments of the IL-speaking population, the language is much more than a learning resource. The goal of language teaching, then, should be an "additive trilingualism," as Lai (2011) aptly projects. Consider the contrasting circumstances of:

- deeply rooted minority languages with millions of speakers (Beaser, 2006; Groves, 2010) versus
- weaker and endangered languages (Adamson and Feng, 2009; Chen, 2010; Zuo, 2007).

The problems of language preservation in situations of significant asymmetry and progressive displacement by a majority language are complex and difficult. Understanding how these tendencies of IL erosion are related to NL expansion (even when the IL is numerically "majority" within a region or province) involves the study of how language subsystems interact in development, especially bilingual child development. This is the topic of the next chapter on balanced and imbalanced bilingualism.

Among the 55 officially recognized minority ethnic groups (approximately 104.5 million, 8.4% of the population) many more minority languages are included among them, spoken by about 6% of the Chinese people (Zuo, 2007). Complicating matters greatly, however, is the recognition of speech communities as speaking a "language" or a "dialect" (of a language), as among the varieties of what could be considered as Chinese in the broader sense. They are sometimes not mutually intelligible, and on mainly linguistic criteria distant varieties would be normally considered separate languages. Sometimes these are termed the "Sinitic languages," e.g., Mandarin,[2] Wu (spoken in the region of Shanghai), Yue (Guangdong, Guangxi, Hong Kong, Macau), Min (Taiwan and Fujian province), and so forth. Speakers of the last three alone, together, easily number over 200 million. Thus, in many cases the designation of "dialect" or "language" is given with political or language policy considerations in mind; see, for example, the discussion in Groves (2010) on the relationship between Cantonese and Mandarin and how their status is perceived by both speakers and non-speakers.[3]

For minority language speakers, the three-tiered diglossia imposes special conditions of language learning. For these speakers, one of the critical policy questions revolves around the decision of when during children's progress through the grades does the second language NL become a *medium of instruction*, as opposed to a *subject*. Conversely, for how long should the MT/L1 be the sole or predominant medium of instruction? The question then is posed: can the indigenous or minority language remain as a medium of instruction in some subjects, even after the bilingual L2 learners have mastered the NL? Implicit in this discussion is the (correct) assumption that introducing a second language as medium of instruction (immersion) marks a transition to the most effective set of language teaching approaches, if implemented correctly. On the other hand, in a well-designed bilingual instructional program, the L2 can be the medium of instruction in some subjects from the very beginning — on this view, there is no "transition" from one method to another. Lastly, it is important to emphasize that immersion does not imply in any way that the L2 must be the sole medium of instruction. In well-designed bilingual instructional models, immersion methods are applied to the second language component of the program.

Crucially, the debate on medium of instruction and bilingual instruction happens to coincide with the observation of growing tendencies of language shift toward Mandarin among young people. Language shift results in the loss of the minority language by an entire generation of speakers. The dilemma, very often, is viewed by minority language speakers as a difficult choice:

- earlier and more robust immersion in the NL, in the way it is often implemented, can result in weakening even more the minority language, while
- postponing NL immersion later and later into the upper grades leaves students unprepared for the demands of academic literacy in secondary school, demands that must be complied with in the NL.

Equal access to English for academic purposes for minority language speaking students looms in the background in all these debates. The interesting problem of selecting an orthographic system for each language intervenes as a parallel dimension of controversy. Both the NL and the LIC are represented by writing systems that are completely standardized, in the case of the former, the establishment of Modern Standard Written Chinese, based on Putonghua/Mandarin. With few exceptions, no consistent access to advanced content knowledge in the academic disciples is possible without mastery of one of these writing systems. That is, as students progress through the grades they need more and more access to texts written in these languages of wider communication. On the other hand, preservation of a minority language in the medium and long term, in the modern day, seems to depend on the adoption of a writing system (an alphabet, syllabary, or a morphosyllabic character orthography) and standardization along similar lines. Minority peoples who strive to preserve and consolidate their autonomy have an interest in promoting IL-medium instruction in some reasonable proportion, developing a standardized IL writing system, and establishing realms of authentic literacy use (even in the extreme case, for archival purposes, of a moribund language). The nation, by all accounts, can share these same objectives for the purpose of achieving stability through a recognition of diversity and greater democracy in language choice. This, by the way, is the official stated policy of the Peoples Republic of China. The most immediate language choice is that of ensuring the most favorable conditions for early linguistic and academic development of school-age children who do not yet speak or understand the NL (Adamson and Feng, 2009; Klöter, 2004; Wan and Zhang, 2007; Zuo, 2007). The proposal in this book is that the most favorable conditions for academic language development of L2 learners imply the inclusion, to some degree, of their L1 in the curriculum.

A different perspective on bilingual education in China, and presumably by extension, in other countries of the greater East Asian region, is the strong opposition expressed by Hu (2008) to the emerging language teaching policy that emphasizes English as the most important of the languages of international communication. According to this view, the promotion of this policy within the educational system is fundamentally akin to "acting as an accomplice to linguistic imperialism." As if English proficiency has become "one of the most defining characteristics of talent in contemporary society" it is now in the service of elites, fueling the "tendency to devalue Chinese as a language of development and modernization" and even a "weakening identification with the heritage of Chinese culture" (p. 220). The critique goes further by questioning the rationale of bilingual education models internationally and casting doubt on findings of research that have pointed to beneficial learning outcomes of different variants of dual-language instruction. One bilingual model in particular is singled out for negative assessment (in part because it has been considered for widespread application in Chinese elementary school level foreign language programs): content-based second language teaching, or bilingual immersion, based on the example of French immersion in Canada. This particular aspect of the critique we will consider in Chapter 7.

Many readers may find somewhat puzzling the prediction that English FL/bilingual education might result in the weakening of Chinese culture and a devaluation of its language, of deeper roots by thousands of years, today in ascendency once again. No such devalorization has been evidenced in other regions of East Asia (of Japanese in Japan, of Chinese in Taiwan, of Vietnamese in Vietnam, and so forth). In countries with a long-standing established national language, which have shifted to similarly ambitious FL learning programs, no weakening of the national language has been demonstrated. The strong European languages, in the same way, have maintained their dominant NL-status within the borders of their respective nations, unaffected by expanding bilingual instruction, similarly for Spanish and Portuguese in the Americas. That specifically advanced academic literacy in Chinese might suffer erosion (p. 213) under the influence of learning English for academic purposes is a concern that isn't supported by evidence either, judging from similar applications of bilingual educational policy elsewhere. The possibility seems far-fetched from every plausible point of view. It should be kept in mind that the relevant comparison is not to a situation pitting an indigenous language lacking a standardized writing system and literary tradition, on the one hand, against a dominant colonial language imposed by a superior occupying power of many years, on the other. Advances in character processing technology, coupled with the continuing expansion of access to portable computing, to take just one example, in fact, point in the opposite direction. Neither the writing system nor the (national/official) language is in decline today, digitization having definitively laid to rest the idea that *pinyin*, for example, could replace morphosyllabic writing. In the United States, the nervous humor has it that "in Beijing they are learning English today so that we can learn Chinese tomorrow."

Before picking up again on this theme in Chapter 7, we will start with theories of bilingualism as they inform a difficult research problem — explaining how language subsystems develop unevenly most of the time. Uneven development in bilingualism is the rule, even though it is often useful to think in terms of ideal conditions in which domains of linguistic competence are distributed in a balanced way. For this reason Chapter 2 starts with problems of incomplete language development and attrition of knowledge. Chapter 3 takes this a step further, where imbalances are no longer of the typical kind. Together, both kinds, each in its own way, help us better understand how the "bilingual mind" (an overused term) is structured and how it is used for actual comprehension and expression. The research summarized in these two chapters will clarify under what exceptional conditions a foreign language might actually come to displace a national language. In addition, getting a better understanding of the psycholinguistics of bilingualism will be important for work on a number of (less hypothetical) practical applications. The biggest subfield of applied linguistics is about learning and teaching applications in school. This implies language learning for the special demands of academic achievement.

Bilingualism in school, especially when second language learning is involved, includes the objectives of L2 literacy learning. For this reason Chapter 4 begins the transition from theory to practice. The remaining chapters keep the focus on applications, problems in the applied disciplines associated with language and literacy teaching. Theoreticians shouldn't put the book down in Chapter 5, because real world classroom issues in language learning still present difficult challenges of concept and explanation. Educators shouldn't skip the first half because it's impossible to make sense of the debates about teaching methods and materials without thinking about plausible explanations for why language learners respond the way they do — why they are successful, when they are, and why when they are not successful.

Notes

1. Tridiglossia is an extension of the term diglossia (see Glossary entry). Authors who have described the three tiered hierarchy of language use discussed in Chapter 1 have in mind a distribution of language functions and purposes, and how speakers perceive them, on three levels. A rough and simple example is: (1) regional or local, (2) national and (3) international. When the term "trilingualism" is used in this book, it simply refers to the interaction of three languages (e.g., in learning situations) without any necessary implication of a relationship of hierarchy or that the languages are distributed according to specific social function or communicative purpose. In that way it is a more general term. It is also used interchangeably with "bilingualism" in most contexts.

2. Mandarin, overwhelmingly, is the Chinese language with the largest number of speakers, spoken as a mother tongue by more people than any other language in the world. Modern Standard Chinese, the national language of "Greater China" (Li, 2006) is based on Mandarin (Modern Standard Chinese is known as Putonghua in Mainland China, Hong Kong and Macau, Guoyu in Taiwan); see Glossary entry for Putonghua.

3. An example of a politically biased use of the terms "language" and "dialect" would be Tse *et al.* (2007). In their study of the influence of the language that Hong Kong primary students speak at home on their Chinese reading ability, Cantonese is described as a "mere dialect" (p. 401). Children's minority dialect or first language competence is viewed as a problem, such that the Chinese proficiency of successful readers has not been "contaminated by Cantonese" (p. 405). The way Tam (2011) explains the relationship between Putonghua and other languages and dialects (of a language) is more helpful: "[Cantonese] is a branch of the spoken Chinese language representing the culture of southern China" (p. 414). It is more precise than the formulation in Tse *et al.* (2007) in their characterization of Modern Standard Written Chinese as: "the written equivalent of Putonghua, the spoken language of the people of China" (p. 400). See Glossary entry for Putonghua.

Chapter 2

Balanced and imbalanced bilingualism

2.1 The problem of explaining the role of experience in language development

In recent years, investigators of early bilingualism, first language attrition, and child second language learning have begun to find common ground on a number of important research problems. This chapter will survey the research and will show that the study of unevenness in the development of two languages reveals more clearly how the critical problems for future research on bilingualism should be framed. The convergence of these three fields of study will contribute greatly to this reflection and re-assessment. In addition, clarity on the question of balanced and non-balanced bilingual development is important for understanding how the Faculty of Language guides acquisition in all circumstances. For example, in non-balanced bilingualism, a weaker language emerges in the face of the normally developing stronger language. Usually, the explanation for this divergence is that there must have been a difference in the amount and/or quality of input to one language subsystem over the other. But a closer examination of the many bilingual case studies now available suggests that this account cannot be the whole story.

Getting the bigger picture, and thinking about a more complete explanation, is also important for understanding accelerated language shift, the loss of a language to an entire speech community that has become bilingual. Language shift is the sociolinguistic counterpart to the psycholinguistic process involved in language attrition as it affects competence in an individual speaker. Language shift, at the community level, sometimes shows itself to be remarkably rapid, also not completely explained by what would seem to be the obvious societal factors. Languages with a relatively large a population base, a writing system and established literary heritage, having been a medium of higher education and occupying high social status have undergone sharp decline and replacement; Janhunen (2004) provides an interesting example. Today, when the incentives, and pressures, for minority language speakers to learn the national language are greater than ever before (Wei and Hua, 2010), the study of asymmetry in language development, especially among child bilingual speakers, promises to help explain broadly based sociolinguistic trends.

For minority language communities that seek to preserve their linguistic heritage, understanding the relationship between individual and collective tendencies in language replacement takes on an immediate practical importance. Indigenous and minority language communities have the right to pursue the goal of preservation; this principle is widely recognized and even constitutionally guaranteed in many countries. Thus, a clearer understanding of the forces of language maintenance and erosion when opportunities and limitations for the different languages in bilingual/trilingual contact are unequal will provide families and community policy makers with the tools to chart the most effective way forward. Interested readers should consult the *Handbook of descriptive linguistic fieldwork* (Chelliah and de Reuse, 2011) for recent advances in the science of documentation and language revitalization.

2.2 Child development in two languages

Cross-linguistic interaction and the different kinds of asymmetry in bilingual development have come to the forefront in the research on child language. The study of how the language knowledge subsystems interact and the study of the differential effects of this interaction on language-A (L_a) and language-B (L_b) touch on virtually all important research questions in the field of bilingualism. These areas of study are closely related in many ways. In a special issue of *Applied Psycholinguistics* on bilingual development, two articles directly addressed central issues related to this area of work (de Houwer, 2007; Meisel, 2007). A third (Mayberry, 2007), while appearing to address it indirectly, presented a line of research and conceptual framework that points toward resolving the most important problems posed by the first two.

In an extensive survey of parental language input patterns in bilingual families, de Houwer calls attention to a persistent imbalance in child bilingual ability — an apparent puzzle, one that we could tentatively describe as a Paradox of Bilingual Acquisition. While child monolingual development achieves a success rate of 100% (related to the notion of "completeness"), exceptional cases of impairment aside, only a fraction of children (perhaps a large fraction) raised in families in which there is active bilingual socialization attain complete native-speaker mastery in both languages. Results of the study indicated an estimated success rate of 75% for two languages. Most interesting was the finding that widely commented approaches to promoting child bilingualism (e.g., the one-parent-one-language rule) were neither necessary nor sufficient for native-speaker ultimate attainment in two languages. Even the most ambitious approaches of favoring the minority language, for example, fell short of expectations — in 3 to 6.5% of families in the sample in which there was evidence of exclusive or predominant use of the "home language," children did not speak it (de Houwer, 2007, p. 421). In other words, it seems that completeness may be attained in L_a and L_b, or in only one or the other. These results are consistent with studies of rapid language shift, where a majority language quickly becomes dominant among the school-age bilingual population even under conditions of daily predominant home use of the eroding minority language (Oller *et al.*, 2010).

Meisel's discussion of conceptual problems in the research on uneven child bilingual development is an important recent contribution to our understanding of this many-faceted question. Relevant it is as well to some of the critical debates in the broader field of first and second language acquisition. Four closely related points in particular deserve our careful consideration, each of which will be taken up in turn:

- Given exposure to L_a and L_b, are manifestations of the developmentally delayed or weaker language the result of imbalances in competence or performance?
- What explains early differentiation between the language subsystems of the bilingual? At first glance, it appears that this cross-language differentiation is tied to the concept of an endowment for bilingualism/multilingualism (Genesee, 2003; Pettito *et al.*, 2001).

- The first two points lead to an assessment of the Weaker Language Hypothesis (Schlyter, 1993). Under what circumstances might the weaker or non-dominant language of simultaneous bilingual acquisition come to resemble a second language — or — is this even possible? Part of the discussion here concerns the different proposals among researchers on the more fundamental issue of how first language and second language competence differ.
- What are the research prospects on gaining a better understanding of the possible external factors (and "internal," we might add) that are causally related to either processing imbalances ("performance factors") or to the development of partial competence (representational, or knowledge-of-language factors)? Specifically, which domains of language ability or grammar knowledge are likely to be affected?

In the discussion of these four points, for argument's sake, the same basic assumptions made by Meisel about the nature of the Faculty of Language and the theoretical framework of Universal Grammar (UG) will be accepted. At the same time, these research problems of imbalance and differentiation may lead us to question some of the proposals of mainstream Universal Grammar in the field of bilingualism. But much discussion still lies ahead before the lines of debate can be clearly drawn.

2.3 Use of language or knowledge of language

One way to approach the problem of the distinction between performance and competence is to think of the different kinds of language ability as comprised, in each case, of a complex of knowledge structures and processing interconnections.[1] In uneven bilingual development the emergence of a weaker/non-dominant language can be attributed to two different kinds of imbalance involving: (1) component mechanisms of language and information processing, unrelated to or apart from competence, or (2) competence itself, keeping in mind that processing and competence factors, together, may affect ability. Under #1, the non-dominant language might be subject to a temporary lag in the rate of development. How the language subsystems influence each other in actual comprehension and expression may result in an inhibition of processing interfaces and other types of operation that act upon the competence modules. In some way, a limitation is imposed on how all these components are put to use in the performance of abilities (consideration of the other logical possibility, that of a "permanent inhibition," will be deferred to Section 2.4). In contrast to this temporary processing-induced delay, diminished competence in the non-dominant language (imbalance #2) assumes a delay in the growth of actual language knowledge. In regard to a competence imbalance, the two logical possibilities, in this case, should also be accepted as plausible outcomes: an attenuated initial advance in the construction of grammatical knowledge or one that results in a definitive non-native ultimate attainment in either L_a or L_b.

According to Meisel's distinction between these two kinds of imbalance, in explaining processing factors of asymmetry (imbalance #1), *system inhibition* figures as the most prominent causal factor. On the other hand, imbalanced competence would be characterized by or described as acquisition failure or *incomplete acquisition* of the non-dominant language. The former is a quantitative tendency in development, of usage and proficiency; the latter is qualitative, about the properties of linguistic knowledge. In attempting to distinguish between the two, one could examine performance errors in bilingual child speech that might reflect incomplete acquisition. For example, the appearance of null subjects or objects, null articles, and so forth, not permitted in the target language, at higher frequencies than expected, might be evidenced in some contexts but not in others. This would indicate that the deficit at issue might not be one of grammatical knowledge, but rather a problem of consistent usage. In addition, it would be necessary to demonstrate somehow that omission patterns in the weaker language (WL) are qualitatively different from those of monolingual children; and even if such evidence were to be presented, what importance would we attribute even to a significant delay in the emergence of a given grammatical pattern if at some later point in development it eventually does emerge?

Dussias (2004) discusses the kind of evidence that would be necessary to be able to distinguish, in adult bilinguals, between erosion that has "occurred at the source of knowledge" (p. 368) as opposed to interference and control of processing phenomena. Regarding the latter, in an interesting study of the role of inhibitory control of L1 structures, Levy *et al.* (2007) argue that such inhibition helps learners overcome interference during early L2 learning. These effects were demonstrated in short-term L2 learning tasks on subjects whose rudimentary mastery of the L2 categorically excluded any possibility of L1 competence erosion. At a "deeper" level involving more than just processing imbalances, given that there are finite memory and processing resources available to the bilingual (conceivably more limited in young children), there ensues a competition for these resources. As a result, some components and subsystems may come to be favored at the expense of others (Köpke, 2004). The less frequently activated subsystems and structures are thus inhibited under the influence of the competitor language, for example an expanding L2 (Gürel, 2004). Initial (even seemingly minor) usage preferences raise the activation threshold for lexical entries, for example, in the "dispreferred" subsystem. For preschool age bilinguals, control mechanisms that regulate the use of the two grammars might respond to even slight imbalances, more so than in the case of mature bilingual speakers. We will return to the question of the effects of interlinguistic competition in Section 2.6.

While it is arguable that the processing-competence distinction is necessary to maintain, making a clear demarcation in early child bilingualism may turn out to be exceedingly difficult, if not impossible by any method. One approach to the conceptual problem, at least, might be to work "backwards" longitudinally, taking as a starting point two contrasting distributions of bilingual ability, for example, in late childhood:

1. in a population of balanced bilinguals, that fraction whose early bilingual ability was marked by a relationship of dominant-nondominant L_a and L_b. That is, delay in

the WL was temporary; and

2. older child bilinguals (and former bilinguals) whose imbalanced ability has stabilized or become more pronounced.

For #1, evidence could be marshaled that points to a processing explanation in some cases, without excluding definitively a competence differential in others. On the other hand, in #2, it would seem that the older the bilingual and the more stabilized the non-dominant or attrited language, the less likely it would be that the underlying cause can be traced to processing factors alone.

In some ways, it is the second scenario that is more interesting — an early/premature stabilization at an incomplete grammar in the WL, or outright L1 attrition. One question that is raised is whether the WL, in this case, has taken on a status, a mental representation, similar to that of a second language. In temporary delay, with the benefit of hindsight, the answer is obvious. What sense would there be even to try to distinguish between a three-year-old's immature L1 grammar and a hypothetical "L2" grammar — temporary WL of early childhood bilingualism? However, in long term/permanent delay, the question cannot be dispensed with so easily; among normal children, only second language development undergoes stabilization short of the target language (often termed "fossilization"). A first approximation to this problem requires a consideration of the "UG in L2" question: are second languages UG-constrained, and does L2 development depend, at least in part, on recourse to the Language Acquisition Device? Sorace (2003) and White (2003) offer one set of considerations for discussion. From this point of view, what exactly might "acquisition failure" mean? In terminal L1 attrition, one could argue that there is a language-specific failure, confined strictly to the attrited language subsystem ("language" with a lower-case "l"), similarly for sharply insufficient input conditions for L_a or L_b. Deprivation in primary language development results in actual impairment of the acquisition mechanisms (and defective "Language" with a capital "L"). But should the term "failure" also apply to a WL that begins to develop and stabilizes in the manner of a L2?

Meisel (2007) agrees that the Language Acquisition Device (LAD) will not be able to be fully deployed if "acquisition conditions deteriorate" below a minimum level of usable Primary Linguistic Data. The defect in the research on this question so far, as he points out, is coming up with a principled approach for determining what that threshold might be in the case of a WL, and if in fact it is a question of a threshold at all. Admittedly, among UG-oriented researchers the problem of minimum acquisition conditions hasn't been given the attention it deserves. It comes up when we consider L2 learning, L1 attrition, and separately, in language input deprivation; and the problem is actually quite difficult and complex. The important point is that "amount of exposure is unlikely to suffice as an account of the phenomena" at issue here (p. 511). This is one of the key topics of the next section.

2.4 The Paradox of Bilingual Acquisition meets the Logical Problem of Bilingual Acquisition

For now we will set aside the factors discussed in the previous section related to processing and attend to knowledge of language in each grammatical subsystem of bilingual development — how competence comes to be represented, in particular how it comes to be represented unequally, when comparing L_a and L_b. One starting point would be the proposed Logical Problem of Bilingual Acquisition outlined by Yip and Matthews (2007) in their study of developmental asynchrony and cross-linguistic influence between dominant and non-dominant languages. Compared to the challenge faced by children in acquiring one language (that competence is underdetermined by language experience), exposure to two grammars should impose an even greater burden on the acquisition capacities. Faced with more varied and more subtle input ambiguity (now cross-linguistically), why isn't bilingual acquisition marked by significant delay and defective mastery across both languages? The child is faced with the task of categorizing linguistic data into two sets, more conflicting evidence, and with opportunities to test hypotheses divided. Rather, parallel and equivalent attainment of native-speaker developmental milestones, or the same in one language or the other, by young bilinguals suggests that the acquisition mechanisms of the Faculty of Language are grossly under-exploited in monolingualism. Yip and Matthews portray the learnability problem of two languages in terms of a Poverty of Dual Stimulus.

Part of the overall problem of the Poverty of Dual Stimulus (PoS_D) is what we could call the Subset-Superset problem in language acquisition, common to both L1 and L2. Figure 2.1 presents an adaptation (Francis, 2007) of Pinker's (1990) version of the same basic idea. In both child language development and second language learning, a rudimentary grammar forms around a set of "hypotheses" that have been confirmed (the inner circle "H"). The language acquirer/learner (henceforth "learner" for short) is faced with the task of expanding the incipient subsystem outward toward the complete target language (the intermediate circle). Incorrect hypotheses, formed in the outer ring (overgeneralization, transfer/interference from the bilingual's other language, etc.) come to form part of the developing grammar, and the learner must find a way of retreating (the centripetal arrow) from the hypothesized grammar that is "too large." In this instance of the PoS problem, the child learner's task consists in discarding structures that have been "over-generated" (in the outer-H ring) without the benefit of negative evidence, which is not available in processible form to young children.

Especially in child bilingual acquisition we can see how "dual poverty" does not mean "too little." According to one view, a fully engaged and unfettered, domain-specific, LAD makes it possible for young children to be able to converge on the target, overcoming the severe limitations, especially for them, of domain-general learning, such as systematic reflection on erroneous hypotheses, corrective feedback, and other kinds of attention to language form. Acquisition, therefore, must be subject to prior constraints on the "hypothesis space" that learners depend on for convergence toward the target (Anderson and Lightfoot, 2002; Crain *et al.*, 2006; Meisel, 2004; Pinker, 2004). For second language

Figure 2.1
The subset-superset problem in language acquisition

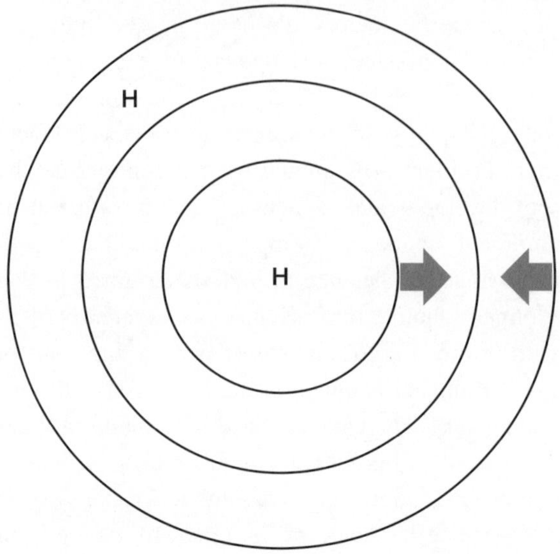

learners, in theory, negative evidence, metalinguistic awareness, domain-general cognitive strategies and deliberate learning help compensate for a LAD that is inhibited, blocked or filtered to one degree or another. Parenthetically, the approach to the PoS problem taken in this discussion is somewhat different from that of many mainstream generative models. For example, the Poverty of Stimulus should not imply that domain-general learning plays a marginal role in L1 acquisition.

In Replacing Language (RL) development (that coincides with L1 attrition), analogous processes unfold in which a fully-formed or immature, but well-formed and normally developing, native-speaker child grammar is subject to erosion or delay under the displacing force of an expanding linguistic subsystem:

1. The attriting L1 retreats now to a more rudimentary grammar (or undergoes a premature stabilization/delay). The learner, of course, requires no negative evidence for the formation of new structures in the weaker or disfavored language;
2. New (interlanguage) grammar will come from both the smaller hypothesis set (inner-H) and the outer-H ring, based on positive evidence alone. Negative evidence is neither typically forthcoming nor necessary if attrition is progressive (convergence on the target language no longer an issue);
3. The RL also advances on the back of positive evidence. Having appropriated a fully engaged and unfettered LAD (because RLs are epistemologically equivalent to L1s; see Francis, 2012, for why in principle they must be), negative evidence, metalinguistic awareness, and the application of explicit learning strategies, again,

are superfluous for the construction of a complete and mature native-speaker core grammar.

In other words, replacement/attrition is also subject to the Logical Problem of Bilingual Acquisition. In particular we shall see how the "attrition" aspect of RL development suffers from a Poverty of Stimulus condition of its own, a kind of "PoS in reverse."

2.4.1 How much positive evidence does the LAD require?

Even the strongest version of a parameter-setting/triggering model of language acquisition must assume a minimum amount of usable Primary Linguistic Data to the UG-constrained acquisition processing mechanisms of the Faculty of Language. All children overcome the problem of stimulus poverty, but input cannot be too inconsistent or overly restricted (Pinker, 2004). Interestingly, in the case of bilingual acquisition, evidence from studies of early L1 attrition strongly suggests that this threshold, all other factors remaining equal, will tend to be higher, on average, in the Disfavored Language (DL) of the L_a–L_b pair. "Disfavored" here refers to either the L_a or L_b in early bilingual development where an external (e.g., sociolinguistic) or internal (to the Faculty of Language) factor might channel it toward becoming the weaker language. Bilingual development would then proceed toward a differentiation between one dominant or stronger language and one non-dominant/subordinate or weaker language.[2] Montrul (2006, p. 354) argues along similar lines: "input appears to play an even more decisive role in bilingual acquisition than in monolingual acquisition, particularly if bilingual children are to develop balanced proficiency or maintain the two languages to some degree." Stronger/dominant and weaker/non-dominant, imply actual measurable categories of ability or knowledge. In the following hypothetical continuum (Table 2.1), for our purposes, the critical interval or range is where the exposure to each language in bilingual acquisition should be sufficient for native-speaker ultimate attainment even in the Disfavored Language — threshold conditions 7–10.

The very idea of a requisite "threshold" is still not clearly defined, in theory accepted by all researchers, but difficult to specify and even more difficult to test empirically. The most compelling findings are of examples of input deprivation of one kind or another and the degree of success that child learners have had in overcoming it (Goldin-Meadow, 2005; Senghas et al., 2008). Nevertheless, the intriguing question here is how the notion of input threshold needs to be considered separately in monolingual development and bilingual development, as was pointed out by de Houwer. The hypothetical examples in Table 2.1 attempt to portray what should be considered as two different issues, two different kinds of "threshold" in which different conditions and constraints apply, even though informally we are comparing the PLD thresholds for completeness in monolingualism and in bilingualism.

Table 2.1

Threshold of received Primary Linguistic Data to (1) make possible or (2) assure complete native-speaker ultimate attainment

Threshold 1 (makes possible) + + + + + + + + + +
Threshold 2 (assures) ~ ~ ~ ~ ~ ~ ~ ~ ~ ~

In the L1 of monolingual development

1. Total deprivation, minimal contact with processible input (wild children).
2. Severe deprivation but sufficient exposure to allow for the emergence of a rudimentary pidgin (primitive home sign).
3. Less severe language deprivation (late L1 learning; e.g., deaf sign language after Critical Period).

~ ~

4. Restricted input, but with conditions given that allow for complete creolization by child language learners (first generation of fully competent Nicaraguan Sign Language signers, in Senghas *et al.*, 2006).

In the DL of bilingual development

5. Sporadic and minimal contact with disfavored language (visits to the home by a DL-speaking relative whose conversations with parents are overheard by children).
6. Highly restricted input in the Disfavored Language, equivalent to #2 or #3 above, at a level that would be insufficient even for normal L1 monolingual acquisition.

\+ +

7. Restricted input in the Disfavored Language equivalent to #4 above.
8. Imbalance in exposure for L_a and L_b, but input in the Disfavored Language is sufficient for normal and typical acquisition (i.e., native-speaker ultimate attainment would be assured in the case of monolingual acquisition).
9. Minimal imbalance between L_a and L_b.
10. Equal exposure to L_a and L_b under completely balanced input conditions.

What immediately is suggested in this schema is:

1. whatever conditions apply to the threshold in the L1 of monolingual development apply unambiguously to the dominant language of bilingual development. That is, all conditions at #4 and any other level of exposure to a more complete language model assure complete native-speaker ultimate attainment for the dominant language. Corollary to this stipulation is the exclusion of "semilingualism" (language impairment aside), even in all cases of subtractive bilingualism/L1 attrition in which a L2 replaces the former L1 as primary language.[3]

2. A discontinuity appears between conditions 1–4 and 5–10, which at first glance appears unjustified, at best highly speculative. While beyond monolingual condition #3 (~ ~ ~ ~) native-speaker completeness is assured, beyond bilingual condition #6 (+ + + +) native speaker completeness in both languages is only made possible, up to an including condition #10 (corresponding to de Houwer's 3–6.5% of children

who might show evidence of a diminished ability in the "favored" ambient family language).

This seemingly imprudent working proposal, in fact, is supported by findings from a growing body of research that has directly examined bilingual child L1 attrition/early stabilization under conditions 8, 9 or 10:

- Anderson (2001) — English–Spanish,
- Bolonyai (1998, 2007) — English–Hungarian,
- Kaufman (1998, 2001) — English–Hebrew,
- Schmitt (2000) and Bar-Shalom and Zaretsky (2008) — English–Russian,
- Wei and Hua (2006) — English–Chinese, and studies summarized in
- Montrul (2008) and De Houwer (2009).

Allen *et al.* (2006), Pfaff (1999), and Silva-Corvalán (2003) while not explicitly focused on unambiguous instances of equivalent input distribution between L_a and L_b resulting in imbalanced ability, present cases in which there is a strong supposition that at least some of the study participants fell into the above three categories of attrition or delay, condition 8, 9 or 10. Working under the assumption that attrition of a L_a can only proceed concurrently with its replacement by a L_b, (or vice versa), studies have shown that stabilization and decline in the weaker language undergo a more rapid onset and a deeper erosion the younger the child. In other words, even a slightly weaker immature grammar, for example, is more susceptible to the effects of "competition" from a slightly stronger and more actively developing grammar (Köpke and Schmid, 2004) than would be the case in an older bilingual with mature fully formed grammars in L_a and L_b.

We can now return to the idea of how the Logical Problem of Bilingual Acquisition applies to L1 attrition. Assuming an epistemological equivalence between L1 and RL development, the logical problem must be the same for both (by extension, as will be discussed in Section 2.5.3, we can propose that the same logic, with a difference, applies to L2 learning). What is usually overlooked, however, is that the underdetermination of the course of development by input received is a logical problem not only for the Replacing Language but also for the receding (attriting) language. For example, investigators of imbalanced child bilingualism often attribute the early stabilization (and in some cases "decline") of the non-dominant language to an imbalance in the external conditions of language acquisition: one language tends to be slightly, or more substantively, disfavored in actual day-to-day use, subject to sociolinguistic inequalities of prestige value, communicative utility, outright discrimination and public disfavor, reflected, in turn, in negative perceptions on the part of the child bilingual, and so forth.

Here now, the problem (the PoS paradox in reverse) consists in the widely accepted principle that none of these external conditions (short of Threshold #3 in Table 2.1) results in the deterioration of core grammatical competence in monolingual development. For example, regardless of how ashamed a child is made to feel about his or her native language, the development of grammar knowledge stays its course, to native-speaker completeness. The same impermeability would conceivably apply to the strongly dominant language of child bilingualism if the non-dominant language is significantly less developed.[4] External input conditions corresponding to the Disfavored Language appear to facilitate the actual fossilization and decline of grammatical competence *only in* bilingualism and *only if* a dominant language subsystem begins to follow the developmental course of a RL. An apt metaphor for this reciprocal relationship is that L1 attrition is the "flip side of the L2 acquisition coin" (Montrul, 2005, p. 201). This seems to be the conclusion that one might be able to draw from the above cited studies of L1 attrition: if the DL had been, hypothetically, the only language of early socialization it would have clearly fallen into a category at Threshold #4 or above, input sufficient to ensure native-speaker completeness. Again, the difficult but important question of input conditions comes to the fore, one that linguists should no longer set aside. What is interesting is that in child bilingualism additional factors need to be taken into account to get the big picture.

Meisel (2007) emphasizes the importance of the findings of early separation of the bilingual's language subsystems. Indeed, the absence of a prolonged, or even transitory, "fusion" of grammars, and the evidence for how early some of the subsystems begin to differentiate (Bosch and Sebastián-Gallés, 2001; Pettito *et al.*, 2001) should be surprising to us, representing a compelling case for the PoS_D problem, more so even than in monolingual acquisition. A number of aspects of bilingual ability such as equal conversational skill in both languages, pragmatically appropriate alternation, inhibition in performance of the non-selected language, and systematic codeswitching would be impossible to account for within a holistic and integrativist framework that rejects the separate subsystems model; also see relevant studies by Paradis, *et al.* (2005) and Pettito and Holowka (2002). But the early and spontaneous autonomy of L_a and L_b also goes hand in hand with the other kind of differentiation under consideration in this section. The general consensus from studies of early bilingual asymmetry (Yip and Matthews, 2007) appears to be that the effects of "delay" in the non-dominant language do not significantly penetrate the competence of the dominant language (superficial and transient transfer effects aside), the latter's course of development remaining sealing off and on track. That is, "delay" in bilingual acquisition, impairment and pathology aside, corresponds not to Language (with a capital "L") but rather only to one or the other instantiation of it.

A more specific account of what the "endowment for multilingualism" entails can now be proposed for further research, in four parts, outlined below.

i. The capacity for bilingual acquisition

Provided with sufficient input (above Threshold #6 in Table 2.1) children are capable of acquiring more than one language (up to and including native-speaker competence) with no additional or special input conditions beyond those that monolingual children receive.

ii. Native-speaker ultimate attainment is ensured

Exposure to more than one language during the critical period does not compromise any aspect of Language development (with a capital "L"). Native-speaker competence is ensured in one language subsystem (The Provision of No-semilingualism), and may be attained in more than one (two primary languages — 2L1), again with no additional or special input conditions (such as direct instruction). The emergence of a non-dominant/weaker/attriting language subsystem from among the child's "early L1s" does not affect the overall course of development of the remaining dominant language (Autonomy of Linguistic Systems). N.B.: this hypothesis differs from a widely held informal version of the "endowment for multilingualism" — that given adequate input conditions in two languages 2L1 development is ensured.

iii. General cognitive development ensured

No negative impact on any aspect of intellectual development or general information processing skill results from any variety of early bilingualism; see Bialystok (2007) for a review of the research on "cognitive effects."

iv. Child second language learning is part of the biological endowment for multilingualism

Children provided with normal and typical exposure to language during the critical period are capable of learning and attaining high levels of proficiency in a second language (up to and including native-speaker levels). The completeness of Replacing Language development in L1 attrition and untutored near-native L2 attainment indicate that no sub-component or aspect of the LAD is lost during initial L1 acquisition; all of UG remains intact and continues to be a resource (subject to filtering/blocking from an unattrited L1 subsystem) for L2 learning.

Readers are encouraged to consider an alternative model of bilingual development to the one presented in this section. The Competition Model (MacWhinney, 2005) does not assume a specialized LAD or the design features of UG. But interestingly it accounts for the L1–L2 attainment difference in a way that is analogous and parallel. Also, the Competition Model's application of the concept of "interference" in explaining shifts in dominance from L1 to L2 is consistent in large part with the RL development hypothesis.

2.5 How can we describe different kinds of imbalanced bilingualism?

At first glance, Meisel's critique of the Weaker Language Hypothesis (WLH), attributed to Schlyter (1993), appears to be centered on a relatively narrow issue — whether the grammar of the weaker language of early bilingualism might come to be represented and develop in the same way as a second language. Secondly, what evidence would support a claim that a WL is of the same kind as a L2 (and different in kind from a L1, specifically, the dominant pair of 2L1 bilingualism)? A moment's reflection, however, prompts us to realize that the critique opens the door to a broader set of related questions:

- In the first place how can we describe the difference between development in L1 and L2?
- How might the nature of this difference be related to the difference between the dominant and non-dominant languages of early bilingualism?
- What is the role of UG in L2 learning, and
- how should we evaluate Age of Acquisition (AoA) effects?

Together, these questions provide another example of how bilingualism, especially in its peculiar asymmetries, allows for a privileged perspective on long-standing issues in the language sciences, as we saw in the previous section regarding evidence that contributes to a better understanding of the PoS problem.

2.5.1 A fundamental difference between L1 and L2

On the one hand, broadly recognized divergences between L1 and L2, acknowledged by researchers from equally divergent theoretical perspectives, point to a rough outline of a consensus: uniformity and spontaneity in the first (Gleitman *et al.*, 2005; Lust, 2010), wide variation in the second, most notably in regard to ultimate attainment (DeKeyser, 2005; Domínguez, 2007; Han, 2004). On the other hand, the view that a qualitative decline in language acquisition capacity, a marked offset, occurs around puberty seems to have been largely discarded. As proposals for a "L2 sensitive period" end point are pushed further and further back for different grammatical modules, it appears that for *second languages* no such maturational offset age will be possible to identify (Hakuta *et al.*, 2003, MacSwan and Pray, 2005), strongly suggesting what the fundamental dichotomy may actually turn out to be: for L2, no critical age, *per se*, but rather a qualitative difference between L1 and L2, including for children (i.e., L1 acquisition, which can only proceed normally in early childhood, versus child L2 learning). Crucially, the No-critical-period-for-L2 hypothesis should not be confused with the different issue of a critical period for first language development. Clark (2003) presents an opposing view, dispensing entirely with the notion of a biologically programmed critical period, even for L1.

Now, the problem that presents itself is how, among bilingual children, can we draw a distinction between a L1 (the unambiguous mother tongue that manifests all the defining features of primary language, including automatic and spontaneous emergence and uniform native-speaker ultimate attainment) and a L2. What makes the problem important in the case of L2, as Meisel suggests, is that perhaps there is *no age cut-off* that can serve as a reliable marker; that is, "onset of acquisition during sensitive phases…is a necessary but not sufficient condition for native language acquisition" (2007, p. 496). Even more suggestive is the possibility that the factor of "sufficient exposure" to the target language (even during the pre-school years) does not suffice to explain why one language subsystem of early simultaneous bilingualism emerges as a complete L1 and the others might diverge from native-speaker completeness. Could this weaker/nondominant language evolve toward a representation characterized by a L2-type linguistic competence?

2.5.2 Could the difference between the dominant and non-dominant languages of early bilingualism be fundamental?

The critique of the studies of delay in the WL speaks to this question directly, the counter-arguments presented by Meisel regarding findings of interlinguistic discrepancies being certainly well founded. Among young children the evidence for "acquisition failure" in L_a or L_b is rarely conclusive. An early differentiation in rate of grammatical development, even a significant delay in the WL is difficult to assess. Even notably deviant features, contrasting sharply with monolingual age norms, do not prove the case for the emergence of a non-primary language type knowledge representation. But on the other hand, the findings from studies of delayed L_a or L_b development are necessary to account for. In regard to this research problem, it would be incorrect or misleading, impairment/trauma aside, to refer to "delayed bilingual development." This is because of the two linguistic subsystems only one is subject to inhibition and delay.

While during the period of early bilingualism even evidence of extreme delay may be inconclusive, the emergence of a weaker, nondominant, and attrited/prematurely fossilized language subsystem cannot be excluded. To do so would be tantamount to denying the possibility of such a competence asymmetry, restricting explanations of imbalance to processing factors alone. Recall also, that quantitative measures of (equivalent) "amounts of exposure" are neither reliable nor are they ironclad guarantees of balanced 2L1 competence. Clearly, for the many studies of imbalanced early bilingualism cited so far, longitudinal data at points during middle and later childhood will be required to then evaluate the initial findings retrospectively. In any case, as was suggested earlier, the implication of "acquisition failure" appears to be too categorical, except in the clear-cut instances of insufficient input conditions (in Table 2.1, at or below threshold #3 for monolinguals) and terminal L1 attrition (one of the topics of the next section).

2.5.3 The role of UG in second language learning

To say that the WL of early bilingualism patterns like a L2, or that its development resembles L2 acquisition, is only interesting if what is meant is that a qualitative competence difference distinguishes it from the primary dominant subsystem. The WLH is more interesting if the detour the weaker language takes from the course of the dominant primary language is not temporary. To begin with and to be clear, the WLH does not make the claim that child L2s (or adult L2s either) are formed by a different kind of knowledge (see Bernardini and Schlyter, 2004); that the primary L1 is UG-constrained, subserved by encapsulated language-specific structures and second languages are not, or that L2s are subserved by defective knowledge structures. This would be especially difficult to sustain in the case of early child language development.

To the extent that "acquisition failure" in a WL implies such a deterioration or unavailability, it is not the best way to describe imbalanced competence. Rather, the proposal being made here is that there is no reduction in the language acquisition capacity. No "failure" of the LAD occurs when the growth of competence does not mark the typical milestones on schedule, even in the case of extreme delay, precursor to premature stabilization. Then according to this approach, claiming that the WL resembles L2 becomes less controversial. If we came to the conclusion that it is possible for a WL or non-dominant language to begin to develop like a L2, this would not imply a failure of the LAD for the WL, or that only the stronger language is UG-constrained.

This view differs from the hypothesis that UG comes to be deteriorated or eroded as a consequence of setting parameters to L1 values, and that the acquisition capacity of the LAD is diminished in L2 learning (Bley-Vroman, 1996; Clahsen and Muysken, 1996; Schachter, 1996). However, the difference in approaches to the UG-in-L2 problem may not be as deep-seated as appears at first, as more recent studies seem to have suggested, e.g., Clahsen and Felser (2006). The idea that is favored in this chapter, that the UG acquisition mechanisms come to be "blocked" or "filtered" implies that they are still potentially available to the L2 learner (i.e., still intact, in their entirety):

1. variably accessible when a fully formed and stable L1 mediates L2 learning, or
2. completely and uniformly accessible in RL development, as they were in L1 development, because they were never subject to deterioration.

Thus, if the nonavailablity-of-UG-in-L2 position could contemplate the possibility of blocking/filtering/inhibition, instead of *loss* of language acquisition capacity, then the models would be more similar than different. The proposal of Herschensohn (2010, pp. 281–283) appears to offer the possibility of a reconciliation on this point (L2 development is always different from L1 development because L2 learners are "already language endowed"). For example, L1-mediated L2 learning often gives rise to rule systems that are deficient (varying widely from early fossilized to near-native). Non-native L2 competence is not constrained in the same way that native grammars are constrained as evidenced in diminished L2 ability (Clahsen and Felser, 2006); i.e., competence is incomplete, not just different. But saying that non-native grammars are not constrained in the same way does not imply that L2 learning does not require the resources of the LAD, because the Poverty of Stimulus problem still applies (Montrul, 2006), near-native and advanced L2 competence providing the most compelling examples (Sorace, 2003; White, 2003). In addition, since RLs *are* constrained in the same way as native grammars (attaining L1-category completeness), over the course of their development they must have had full access to an integral and undiminished LAD. The UG-guided language-specific acquisition mechanisms are unlikely to ever have suffered deterioration, then to be subsequently regenerated for the purpose of replacing an attriting language subsystem. See Francis (2012) for a more complete exposition of the L1-filter/RL-development research proposal.

Perhaps some of the resistance to the idea that UG remains intact, and that it participates in L2 learning, stems from the wide variation in L2 mastery (very unlike that in all typical L1 acquisition); Liceras (2010) provides arguments for why interlanguages are still natural languages and why, therefore, they are constrained by Universal Grammar. The objection would be — how could early fossilization, final states at the low end, at the opposite extreme from near-native, be the product of an undiminished LAD and UG? Part of the answer to this question can be found in the findings from research on child second language acquisition. Does it proceed more like the L2 of older learners (tending to share the properties of *second languages*) or more like first language development (sharing the *mother tongue* acquisition circumstances of their younger counterparts)? This point leads us to the last topic of this section.

2.5.4 How should we understand Age of Acquisition effects?

Recall that while they are related, the issue of AoA effects in L2 must be clearly separated from AoA in L1. Investigations of child L2 acquisition show why this separation is necessary. The studies of Herschensohn *et al.* (2005) and Schwartz (2003) revealed some important differences between adult L2 and child L2 learning. However, overall, it is the resemblance that is most notable, surprising if middle childhood is considered to still be within a critical or sensitive period for L2 acquisition. For example, unlike in L1, child L2 acquisition is marked by a dissociation between syntax and inflectional morphology, related, as it might be, to other instances of uneven development in second languages, again, not observed in L1. If further research shows child L2 ultimate attainment to vary in a similar way that adult L2 mastery is distributed, the L1–L2 dichotomy would be confirmed across all ages. In passing, this would also serve to undermine the idea of a critical period for L2, potentially, even, for any age range. Montrul (2006) makes a related suggestion. Importantly for this research question, a distinction needs to be drawn between child L2 learners whose L1 has undergone attrition and child L2 learners who have maintained their mother tongue as primary L1. In the former scenario the L2 is in effect a RL, sharing all the essential properties of a first/primary language.

All of the above is central to the discussion on the role of UG in second language acquisition. If the L2 development of children, even young children, shares characteristics in common with all L2 learning, this suggests a fundamental commonality between L1 and L2: access to UG in both. The divergences from L1 developmental patterns and the variation in ultimate attainment that characterize second languages then can be accounted for by the influence of the first language subsystem, a proposal known as Full Transfer Full Access (FTFA). The effects of L1 transfer vary widely from one learner to another, up to and including permanent effects on interlanguage representations of the L2 (White, 2011). The FTFA hypothesis is similar in its essential aspects to the proposal outlined in the previous section for further research on imbalanced early bilingualism and L1 attrition. The L1-filter/RL-development hypothesis introduces one nuance to FTFA: that FA (full access) should be thought of as complete "availability" of UG, because none of it erodes during or after L1 acquisition. But the formation of L2 grammatical structures ("setting of L2 parameters") is filtered or blocked by the L1 subsystem (restricting access). These restrictions, or conditions, correspond to the FT part of FTFA.

2.6 Research prospects — Uncovering the factors that contribute to imbalanced bilingual development

Current approaches to the research on imbalanced bilingual development point toward future directions along three lines: (1) applying a componential approach to bilingualism (Francis, 2008) that seeks to understand how imbalance and attrition are selective and systematic, for example in relation to vulnerable components and subsystems; (2) untangling the factors of processing and competence (Köpke, 2004), especially in relation to the notion of inhibition; and (3) achieving precision on the question of AoA effects, following the proposals of Mayberry (2007) on the essential developmental function of first language acquisition and the related question of how L_a and L_b subsystems (theoretically balanced) might differentiate into L1 (or stronger language) and L2 (or weaker language).

2.6.1 Vulnerable domains in the weaker or attriting language

Attrition is not haphazard forgetting (Seliger, 1996) and non-dominant languages appear to develop predictably, just like L2 acquisition is considered to be systematic. None of these three language development outcomes are based on a "wild grammar." This idea underlies an important line of research that seeks to identify the linguistic components that tend to be affected when a diminished competence or ability (in a non-dominant, attriting or second language) diverges from the expected course of native-speaker development. Such a goal corresponds to the need to "formulate theoretically motivated and empirically testable claims about the grammatical domains affected and the external factors causing such effects" (Meisel, 2007, p. 512).

If vulnerable domains, and their more resistant counterparts, are revealed selectively, this result implies systematicity, and the possibility that universal principles are at play. One line of research that has attracted a good deal of attention identifies the interface between so-called "narrow syntax" and semantic/discourse knowledge as the source of instability in response to cross-linguistic influence. In child bilinguals, the non-dominant subsystem appears to be especially prone to dominant subsystem-induced attrition/replacement if the divergence begins to widen before the non-dominant language subsystem has been consolidated. In this case, the interface domains may be more prone to such interference from the dominant subsystem (Bolonyai, 2007; Sánchez *et al.*, 2010; Sorace, 2005). For example, in Italian and Spanish, learners must acquire (or preserve) the syntactic structures that license null subjects, and at the same time learn the conditions of discourse and pragmatics that constrain the use of this grammatical option. The conditions are complex and subtle, contrary to some accounts, involving more than just [+/-topic shift]. Interface domains have in fact been shown to be more vulnerable, for one, perhaps, because they require the integration of competencies from different components, a factor related to "complexity" (Sorace, 2005). While it would be too categorical to claim that "narrow syntax" is uniformly and persistently spared, for example in attrition, the finding of a tendency for greater degrees of vulnerability at interfaces is important to investigate further. It would bring up again two important issues from related work: whether deficient performance can be explained completely by processing factors, and whether L1s, L2s, RLs, non-dominant L_bs, and attriting language subsystems all share the same kind of mental representation (e.g., UG-constrained) or not. Above all, and of major theoretical implication, is the question of what exactly are the properties of interfaces that maintain interactivity among the competence modules.

In an important study, Argyri and Sorace (2007) hint at how difficult this problem will turn out to be. Setting out to test among child Greek-English bilinguals the relative vulnerability of "narrow syntax" and the syntax-pragmatics interface, the results should prompt us to back away from the strongest claims regarding how robust and impermeable the "hard constraints" in "narrow syntax" are in imbalanced child bilingualism, and conversely in regard to the hypothetically inherent instability of the interface structures. Findings were mixed with assessments showing that one syntax-pragmatics interface construction not to be open to cross-linguistic influence and one of the "purely syntactic" constructions found to be vulnerable.

Stepping back from the fine details of the language-specific analysis in each bilingual situation, the authors seem to be in favor of a discussion on what is an interface in the first place; for example, between what types of linguistic component are different kinds of interface implemented, and what kinds of structure in each case do they place into correspondence? In addition, from the many examples in the bilingual research literature it is possible to consider two categories of interface — one in which the relevant correspondences are effected completely below awareness and are not accessible to monitoring, in contrast to the kind that is subject to varying degrees of introspection and reflection in everyday language use. (Election of null-subject in Spanish and Italian and metalinguistic knowledge on the part of a bilingual child of cross-language variation involving transitive-intransitive patterns in Spanish and English, for example, come to mind.) An interesting alternative approach to this important research problem might be that of Allen (2006) and Jackendoff (2007) — in regard to the interaction within grammar between form and meaning, develop a model that cedes some of the language components to semantics and discourse/pragmatics that have been traditionally (depending on one's theory) considered to be within the realm of syntax, all of syntax then becoming much more "narrow."

2.6.2 Two kinds of cross-language inhibition

As we saw in Section 2.3, the idea of concurrent activation and inhibition has appealed to investigators as a way to explain asymmetries in bilinguals' expressive and receptive abilities. Assuming that in normal language use access cannot be completely denied to either language subsystem, that neither can be hermetically pre-selected out and kept out, the exercise of some kind of inhibitory control explains grammatically well-formed performance in one language or the other, and even in codeswitching. Importantly, language mixing in young bilinguals is not necessarily evidence of attrition of a weaker language or failure of inhibitory control (Halmari, 2005); in fact, the claim is that it usually is not. A breakdown (partial or temporary) or attenuation of this kind of cross-linguistic interface that controls interference might explain dominant language-induced errors and significant delays in the attainment of expected developmental milestones. A dominant language might be able to more easily and more often surmount the hypothetically less developed and more permeable processing/control mechanisms of this kind in young children.

So far so good. But, if we take language ability to be formed by a composite of competence modules and processing components (e.g., interfaces), we should hesitate to maintain a hard and fast non-interactive separation between competence and processing. In other words, the effects of processing and use might impact on actual linguistic knowledge, especially in an immature still-developing grammar. This hypothesis assumes that neither language subsystem of the bilingual child is in place at the early stages of development (including the possibility that they are in place "under the surface" simply waiting for the respective sets of detailed and highly specific parameters to be fixed). It also assumes that acquired (language-specific) knowledge structures are not permanent, sealed off and impermeable to erosion. For example, perhaps, a dominant subsystem may even begin to inhibit the emergence of structures of the slightly less robustly developing subsystem if the onset of divergence between the two occurs early enough. Of course, all of the above speculation awaits a proper formulation, then to be eventually discarded or confirmed empirically.

In any case, this speculation is not new to the field. Sharwood-Smith and Van Buren (1991) used the general idea of parameter-setting and resetting to first reject the notion of a completely encapsulated language-specific grammatical competence that is resistant to erosion; this would presumably include the purportedly "hard constraints" of "narrow syntax." Thus, L1 attrition may proceed both within the domains of processing *and* knowledge of language. Second, since the core grammar of the attriting L1 is not closed off, air-tight, initial stages of attrition/replacement restricted to the complementary forces of activation and inhibition between L_a and L_b may be a precursor to an actual erosion of competence in one or the other. Recall, the proposal in this chapter is that only in brain damage or other kind of pathology would erosion of competence occur in both. Köpke (2004, p. 4) summarizes Sharwood-Smith's earlier work on this proposal that presents itself still today as a framework for a research program on important unresolved problems of imbalanced child bilingualism. A three-stage development is proposed:

1. Performance deviations in the WL can be attributed to imbalances ("failure" is too strong) in processing related to the activation and inhibition mechanisms. Growth of competence remains undeterred;
2. a transitional stage in which the dominant language exercises significant influence on the WL, but the bilingual is still able to switch back to well-formed and age-appropriate native-speaker forms;
3. restructuring of the grammar — the emergence of a new modified competence. Following this approach, inhibition begins to act upon the actual construction of new grammar in the WL/attriting language, going beyond just inhibition on access to an intact grammar of a typically developing (non-attriting) WL.

2.6.3 The essentiality of L1

The research by Mayberry and associates on delayed L1 learning in deaf signers prompts us to narrow the application of the concept of the critical period, resulting in a very important clarification about how the Language Acquisition Device is deployed in different circumstances of development. Whereas AoA effects for L1 have been found to be robust and consistent, they are mixed and not consistent for L2, suggesting again that for L2 acquisition different questions need to be asked, in addition to some of the same ones. Mayberry's findings provide an important clue to the question of under what conditions, precisely, does an actual deterioration of the LAD occur: in the case of late deaf learners, clear evidence that in delayed L1 development (outside the window of opportunity bounded by the critical period) the LAD suffers a material degradation, affecting all subsequent language development in both L1 and L2. Not only do late L1 learners typically not recover from initial stages of deficient L1 acquisition, they also appear to be handicapped in their attempt to master second languages. In contrast, normal L1 exposure equips the language acquisition mechanisms for successful L2 learning. This conclusion is based on findings from the assessment of L1 and L2 learners in both modalities, sign and spoken, and of early learners and late learners (Mayberry, 2007; Boudreault and Mayberry,

2006). Corroborating evidence for the essential/foundational status of early L1 comes from reports of rapid RL development in young children abruptly separated from their L1 environment (Nicoladis and Grabois, 2002). All of these findings are consistent with the hypothesis presented earlier from a number of investigators, that the LAD is maintained undiminished upon attainment of L1 completeness. Actual loss of the language acquisition capacity would be then restricted to the aftermath of late, abnormal, L1 learning (or other type of trauma); only under this condition would it be rendered defective (presumably, in part).

In their study of brain imaging of language plasticity, Pallier, Colomé and Sebastián-Gallés (2003) ask: Can a second language replace the first? Their subsequent discussion of AoA effects and the concept of a critical period links Mayberry's results from the study of *impaired* development to the situation of *normal* child L1 attrition, the latter always concurrent with replacement. The Pallier *et al.* findings also represent an antecedent to the L1-filter/RL-development hypothesis, elaborated upon in this chapter. In regard to replacement, two proposals are counterposed — the "crystallization hypothesis" and the "interference hypothesis," the latter implying that brain circuits programmed for language acquisition remain "plastic." Plasticity, in this sense, allows a new language subsystem to be able to "completely [override] the traces laid down by the first," (p. 155); for example, in L1 attrition the RL comes to be represented in the same domains in which the first language was represented. A parallel can be drawn between this "interference hypothesis" and the proposal that RLs take on the status of primary language, attaining completeness. If replacement continues its course, the networks of linguistic knowledge are "reset" (Ventureyra *et al.*, 2004) clearing the way, so to speak, for full acquisition, again — a second time around.

Evidence against "crystallization" is also consistent with the position that UG remains intact after L1 acquisition and that it participates in L2 acquisition (because of "plasticity"), corollary to the proposal that RLs require full access to the specialized language acquisition mechanisms if they are to attain primary language type completeness. Short of replacement, in successful L2 acquisition, what accounts for the characteristically wide variation in second language ultimate attainment is the "presence of processes and representations attuned to the first language [that act] as a filter" (p. 160), a kind of "interference." Conversely, as replacement proceeds in L1 attrition, the expanding language subsystem "interferes" with the maintenance of the attriting subsystem.

The Pallier *et al.* study forms part of a larger project that has focused attention on the subtle imbalances in child bilingualism (Bosch and Sebastián-Gallés, 2001; Navarra *et al.*, 2005; Pallier *et al.*, 2001; Sebastián-Gallés and Bosch, 2001), presenting findings central to the present discussion, and now its conclusion. Beginning with a confirmation of previous conclusions of research on early separation of the language subsystems in child bilinguals, assessments of infants found no significant delay in discrimination capacities.[5] From this, we can also put into perspective two different categories of delay:

1. sustained failure to mark developmental milestones and major imbalances that indicate impairment, and

2. lesser asymmetries within the range of normal variation in language acquisition that might be related, for example, to greater processing demands associated with two languages instead of one.

The latter are of great theoretical interest, but do not indicate impairment or arrested development. In addition, the question of the existence of #2 type asymmetries (e.g., the early divergence between dominant and non-dominant languages) should be independent of the question of early separation of L_a and L_b. That is, these imbalances do not stand as evidence against the autonomous representation of each language in young children; for further discussion, see Bosch and Sebastián-Gallés (2001) and also Yip and Mathews (2007).

Working with Spanish-Catalan bilinguals, the factor of the L1-filter, or L1 "sieve" (Navarra *et al.*, 2005), presents itself as an important model-building concept for future research. Even in highly proficient adult bilinguals with early intensive childhood exposure to Catalan, Spanish dominance can be revealed in the way that the speech signal is segmented, similarly to the way that Spanish monolinguals perceive Catalan contrasts (Pallier *et al.*, 2001). Crucially, among bilingual infants there is also a tendency for some measure of priority to be given to a dominant subsystem. Catalan-dominant infants show the same preference pattern as Catalan monolinguals even though there is an important difference, quantitatively, in the amount of exposure to Catalan. In contrast, the relatively small difference in exposure between the Catalan-dominant and Spanish-dominant bilingual children correlated with a qualitatively different pattern of sensitivity to phonotactic patterns (Sebastián-Gallés, 2001, pp. 384–385). The authors suggest that these results pose a challenge to the view that sufficiently intense exposure to a "second language" early enough in early childhood should suffice to ensure the same native-like competence level that characterizes primary languages. The question for future research is: in a given domain of linguistic knowledge, given sufficient exposure in L_a and L_b (see Table 2.1), is native-like competence *ensured* in both or only in one of the bilingual child's languages?

2.7 Uneven development suggests new directions for research

The ideal balanced bilingual speaker is an important and necessary starting point for conceptualizing a research program in child bilingualism and for carrying out the right experiments and other kinds of study. In addition, in real life, many bilingual children actually approach and attain this equilibrium. An interesting theoretical problem in these cases is to explain why, language impairment aside, a balanced bilingualism must also be a dual completeness. On the other hand, it appears that the various conditions of disequilibrium in bilingualism have turned out to be singularly revealing of the underlying structure of the knowledge of two languages and how they develop. In fact, research findings from the sharpest and most profound imbalances in language development (next chapter) seem to have opened the widest window on these objects of study that are normally so hard to observe (Goldin-Meadow, 2005; Law *et al*., 2005; Mayberry, 2007; Paradis, 2004; Senghas *et al*., 2008). In this way, accounting for both balanced and non-balanced bilingualism within the same conceptual framework presents itself as one of the most important goals of future research.

A promising way forward would be to focus in on the interaction between the external imbalances in patterns of language use and the internal developmental imbalances of dual language acquisition. How external (social) factors interact with internal factors, for example, will help us understand the problem of rapid language shift in situations of minority-national language bilingualism. Why is the minority language highly vulnerable to erosion in some cases while being less so in others? See Myers-Scotton (2004, 2006) for one possible framework for this research. The different patterns of language mixing and codeswitching in early childhood, for example, should provide evidence for both balanced and non-balanced development under the different kinds of interaction between sociolinguistic and Faculty of Language-internal factors. This approach to the basic research questions should also lend itself to serving research on the applied problems because neither the external nor the internal factors should be neglected in trying to better understand changes in child and adult bilingual ability.

Notes

1. While the notion of ability as incorporating language knowledge and processing, adopted in this book, differs from the traditional dichotomy between competence and performance, it has nothing in common with any of the various holistic/integrativist views on this question that reject outright any distinction between competence and performance. Holistic/integrativist approaches to the study of bilingualism are often associated with so called "multicompetence" models (Hall *et al*., 2006; Jessner, 2008). As an anonymous reviewer pointed out, the construct of ability as presented here may also be inconsistent with mainstream Universal Grammar (not just differing). This assessment may in fact be correct. Truth be told, I have found many discussions of competence and performance (and of "i-language" and "e-language") to be somewhat confusing, especially as these concepts are applied to bilingualism.
2. Among most authors in the applied fields, and especially among bilingual practitioners, the categories dominant and non-dominant typically assume internal differentiations, actual properties of the bilingual mental architecture that are potentially measurable (indices of either processing/skill or competence). A different sense of "dominance" is used in Argyri and Sorace (2007) in which it appears to refer to differences in language use patterns and exposure. In Chapter 2, the term Disfavored Language refers to the language that children are exposed to less frequently and which is used for communication at a lower level or less often. The idea here is to avoid the implication that balanced or unbalanced

external experiential factors determine actual bilingual ability or competence in a straightforward way. (The intention of Argyri and Sorace was not to imply this either.)

3. The idea of thresholds and interlinguistic imbalance presented in Chapter 2 discards the possibility of a stable "incomplete" competence in both L_a and L_b in normally developing children. For example, it would differ from models of semi-lingual speaker or "incomplete learner" (Montrul, 2004, Figure 1), except in cases of language impairment. True "semi-lingualism," therefore, is proposed to apply only to abnormal L1 learning outside the limits of the critical period (or to trauma/inherent deficit). An example of such highly restricted input conditions would be late exposure to sign language for deaf children who fail to surpass an incomplete and deficient linguistic system in either their spoken or sign languages. For our purposes, in evaluating "completeness" in bilingualism, it is the mental grammar of each linguistic subsystem that should be relevant, not an external "dictionary grammar."

4. The concept of encapsulation of the LAD against non-linguistic external constraints related to social inequalities, language prejudice, etc. (its robustness in the face of even extreme conditions of disfavor), was highlighted for us in our work with bilingual children who speak an indigenous language (Francis and Navarrete Gómez, 2009). The core grammar of the DL is affected, cognitively/linguistically, only under the concurrent influence of an emerging dominant language system (of the RL-type).

5. There is a need here to clarify and reconcile the finding of early separation of the linguistic subsystems and the model of bilingualism in which it is proposed that there is one universal syntax, a single computational system, shared in common between L1/L_a and L2/L_b (Bernardini and Schlyter, 2004, referencing MacSwan, 2000). In what way, precisely, do bilingual children with uneven development "project more syntactic structure in the Stronger Language than in their Weaker Language," and how is it in this imbalance that "the Weaker Language has less developed structure" (Bernardini and Schlyter, 2004, p. 50)? According to the authors, differentiation between the language systems resides in, or derives from, separate lexicons; and separation is the "result of different features in the different syntaxes projected by the lexicons" (p. 52). What is meant then by "different syntaxes"? Are they language-specific (autonomous and separable) or integrated into a single unified structure?

Chapter 3

Bilingual development in exceptional circumstances

Continuing our study of asymmetries in bilingualism from the previous chapter, we now consider examples of clearly atypical and extreme imbalance. The concept that comes to the fore is modularity, or how competence and ability can be thought of as componential. New proposals for rethinking this concept have prompted researchers to increasingly consider the findings from outside their respective fields. A critical discussion of modularity by Marcus (2006) calls for just such a multi-disciplinary reflection.

This chapter reviews recent research from the field of bilingualism with a focus on exceptional circumstances of learning and acquisition (deafness, language impairment, and literacy disorder). Findings from this work bear directly on the new approach to modularity that is being proposed by Marcus. Both exceptionality and bilingualism allow for perspectives on cognitive architecture that may reveal how its components are structured and how they interact in a way that is not as easy to assess in typical language ability and monolingualism. The critical issues appear to be separability (autonomy) of neurophysiologic systems, and whether or not cognitive structures are subserved by domain-specific or domain-general competencies. Resolving these questions will have important implications for the remediation of developmental disorders in language and literacy, and for a better understanding the development of sign language and spoken language-based systems.

3.1 Which aspects of language ability are specialized, and which are not?

We will now examine advances in the research on exceptional circumstances of bilingual development and the use of two languages under atypical circumstances. Exceptionality, a broad category, includes within it the condition of deficit resulting from trauma to the language centers of the brain or from congenital impairment. The resulting breakdown of language ability, as in aphasia and Specific Language Impairment (SLI), has provided researchers with a vantage point from which to study its interacting components not easily obtained from observing the workings of unimpaired nervous system structures. When breakdown is selective, the componential nature of language ability and language knowledge is potentially revealed more clearly. While still controversial in a number of respects, this idea has been a guiding assumption on the part of many students of bilingual and polyglot language impairment — that from selective breakdown we can infer the distinctness, on some level or another, of the modules and mechanisms that underlie linguistic functions; that the functional components of language ability might be shown to be instantiated in separable neurophysiological subsystems (Anderson and Lightfoot, 2002; Goral *et al.*, 2002).

Under the broad category of exceptional circumstances are other conditions, which do not imply a deficiency. Or another way of thinking about this other class of exceptional language ability would be that a given dysfunction might be specific to the performance of certain language tasks, but in other respects, again, it does not imply a fundamental cognitive impairment, strictly speaking. The most instructive example of the second kind of exceptionality is deafness. While it may limit the ability to perform tasks related to speech perception and production, one of the important recent discoveries of linguistic science has been that even the most severe and absolute loss of this sensory channel does not, in and of itself, affect either the integrity of the Faculty of Language or the ability to communicate. Startling at first glance, this conclusion will continue to have far-reaching implications both theoretically and practically. This is especially the case if it is correct that a disabling of such a seemingly fundamental sensory function, by itself, does not degrade linguistic competence or primary communicative ability *to any degree*. It is to the study of bilingualism that the implications are particularly important. Conversely, recent advances in the study of bilingual development have provided researchers and practitioners in the field of deafness and sign language with a more comprehensive perspective for their work.

In addition, it has been argued that a better understanding of the natural sign language systems that children develop should uncover the basic contours of the core grammatical capabilities that are universal to all language acquisition circumstances (Goldin-Meadow, 2005). If these capabilities are part of the constitutive underpinnings of linguistic knowledge, understanding them better should also tell us something about the componential nature of linguistic knowledge and language ability, if they are, in fact, componential. The acquisition mechanisms that purportedly serve to "overcome" insufficient language models, for example in the development sign pidgin and creole systems (Singleton and Newport, 2004), presuppose, according to this view, a biological specialization somewhere within this domain. This is the connection, in the present discussion, to the question of componentiality mentioned above in relation to the study of breakdowns occasioned by damage to the brain's language networks.

Depending on the circumstances, bilingualism may also place a strain, or impose an imbalance, on the integrated language system. Language appears to be integrated in a holistic manner because of its complexity and extreme efficiency in performance. Importantly, not all varieties of bilingualism imply cognitive imbalance; a case in point might be the completely simultaneous and "symmetrical" acquisition of two languages in early childhood (Petitto and Holowka, 2002). On the other hand, asymmetrical early bilingualism (one dominant language instead of two primary languages), first language attrition (i.e., language replacement), and second language learning may induce or be directly related to internal imbalances of one kind or another. Sociolinguistic inequalities, typical of most situations of language contact, introduce external factors that interact with the internal factors. Recall that this was the topic of the previous chapter. Following this introduction, we will review recent research findings related to these asymmetries in three areas of exceptional bilingualism: (1) the problems of sign language development in children, (2) bilingual language disability, and (3) literacy disorders in first and second language.

In regard to the concept of componentiality, oversimplified debates about whether language (knowledge and/or ability) is entirely specialized or entirely cognitive-general have reached a predictable and salutary impasse.[1] Rather, recent proposals have suggested that there might be a greater degree of diversity within the domain of language ability than previously assumed, including the possibility that "language" depends on both specialized and non-specialized faculties, this very dimension of cognitive diversity being an important aspect of its modular architecture. In line with this approach, of the six fields of study mentioned by Jackendoff (2007, pp. 32–33) that appear to bear on the issue of some kind of specialization in language knowledge, five of these are directly related to our topic of exceptional bilingualism:

- the grammatical parallels between spoken and signed language;
- the genesis of creole languages in children, most recently studied in the creation of Nicaraguan Sign Language;
- directly related to the above point, sensitive periods for language acquisition and the consequences of late onset for L1 and for L2;
- characteristic brain localization of language functions as revealed in aphasia, and the parallels in acquisition and aphasia; and
- the genetics of different types of language deficit.

How these circumstances of exceptionality interact with bilingualism will be taken up, in turn, in the next three sections on — Deaf bilingualism (3.2), Bilingual aphasia and SLI (3.3), and Cross-linguistic and cross-writing system dissociations in literacy disorders (3.4).

In an attempt to place a conceptual framework around the evaluation of the concept of modularity, and in how it might apply to the problems of exceptional bilingualism, the models developed by Pinker and Jackendoff (2005), Ullman (2001), Paradis (2004) and Marcus (2006), and their associates, will serve as a rough guide. For their part, Ullman and Paradis have proposed explicit models of bilingual competence, and Towell (2004) and Francis (2012) have tried to apply "representational modularity" (Jackendoff, 1997) to new theoretical approaches in the study of second language learning and bilingualism that might account for the fundamental differences between L1 and L2 development, among other still outstanding problems. Despite some divergence in approach among the above, two proposals will be considered:

- that a significant shared common ground is evident from a first reading of these authors' work, and a convergence on at least some important points should be seriously pursued, and
- that the findings from the research on deafness/sign language, language impairment in bilinguals, and cross-language dyslexia/dysgraphia make for a good test of their respective models.

The overarching question is: are the cognitive systems that subserve the different aspects of language ability domain-specific or domain-general? Assuming that different components of bilingual competence and bilingual ability are isolable, what does it mean, exactly, to claim that they are separate, cognitively? Eventually, this question will need to be answered from the point of view of how they may be separable neurofunctionally.

From their study of infant speech and sign language babbling, Petitto *et al.* (2004, p. 65) pose the question graphically: does the brain possess "specialized tissue that is uniquely sensitive to specific rhythmic patterns at the core of natural language structure?" In what way or to what degree are the components of language ability dissociable one from another? Can separable linguistic components depend on domain-general systems or are they necessarily domain-specific? And how should the widely accepted distinction between declarative and procedural knowledge be understood in relation to competence in two languages? For example, does L2 proficiency rely to a greater degree on declarative knowledge, and is this difference (in relation to L1) an example of how the components of bilingual ability are dissociable? Coltheart's (1999, 2005) influential modularity approach, which proposes a Dual-route model of reading, and which in broad terms appears to take up aspects of the Declarative-Procedural Model (e.g., Words-and-Rules Theory in Pinker and Ullman, 2002), will be necessary to examine when we consider the work on bilingual and cross-language dyslexia in Section 3.4.

The questions of separability and domain-general versus domain-specific systems are closely tied to two other issues in language development. How are claims about the Poverty of Stimulus problem and sensitive (or critical) periods in language acquisition related to the concept of a cognitive specialization in some aspects of language? Both of these issues come up in an important way in the study of deafness and sign language, the topic of the next section.

3.2 Deaf bilingualism

As was suggested in the previous section, research on language acquisition in deaf children has shifted more and more toward the view that the key questions are better understood when they are studied as problems of bilingual development. For example, it appears that the closer the situation approximates the optimal conditions of normal sign language acquisition in early childhood, the closer it corresponds to the typical circumstances of child bilingualism and second language learning, and less so to those of disability remediation. A strong emerging consensus today suggests that with the provision of early access to sign language as L1, and early dual-language instruction (including literacy), deaf children run no greater risk of deficit, neither linguistic nor cognitive, than children in the general population, bilingual or otherwise (Fusellier-Sousa, 2003; Grosjean, 2010, Wilbur, 2001).[2] Conversely, early deprivation of usable sign language during preschool socialization and denial of sign language resources during the first years of schooling significantly increases these risks (Daigle and Armand, 2004; Mayberry and Lock, 2003; Niederberger and Frauenfelder, 2005). Today, unfortunately, most countries still do not adhere to a policy that recognizes sign language alongside other national and minority languages within the framework of an official (or de facto) multilingualism. For example, sign language users would benefit from nation-wide standardization and an educational policy that implements bimodal/bilingual (sign plus spoken language) instruction for deaf students (Lin *et al.*, 2009).

Unlike in the acquisition of spoken languages, sign language development almost obligatorily (rare cases of adult sign language monolingualism aside) involves one type or another of early bilingualism or second language learning typically beginning in elementary school. Some of the most common being:

- for deaf children, early exposure to oral language accompanied by some degree of sign language deprivation, followed by late sign language learning as L2.
- sign language as L1, plus contact with spoken language-based systems such as manually coded spoken language, use of a manual alphabet or non-alphabetic orthography (fingerspelling), and spoken language learning per se as L2 (simultaneously or subsequently).
- any sustained attempt at literacy learning in the majority/official language of schooling (either alphabetic or non-alphabetic writing system).

The next section will examine evidence for componentiality and the domain-specificity of language from studies of how a sign language creole emerged in the multilingual social mosaic of Central America. Both early child bilingualism and child creole creation present closely related problems in the study of the acquisition of first and second languages, problems that lie at the heart of the different controversies about the nature of language knowledge itself.

3.2.1 Language genesis in Nicaragua

The first reports of the rapid construction of a fully formed sign language creole by deaf children in Nicaragua during the 1980s (Kegl *et al.*, 1999) brought forward compelling evidence for two hypotheses in language acquisition related to the ideas of specialization and modularity, albeit still controversial today: Age of Acquisition (AoA) effects and the Poverty of Stimulus (PoS) problem.

Subsequent work has confirmed and refined initial claims about critical period effects (AoA) and how children surpass impoverished language models (the PoS problem). Studies by A. Senghas and associates in particular have identified the key dimensions of language creation in this exceptional situation — how intergenerational ("inter-cohort") transmission interacts with developmental language acquisition mechanisms within individuals. In one series of studies, the properties of discreteness and combinatorial patterning in children's signs was shown to be achieved by successive cohorts of new members of the signing community, each one upgrading the grammar of the emerging Nicaraguan Sign Language (NSL) in a way that is not characteristic of general inductive learning. For example, the transition from holistic gestural representations to linguistic constructions (elements are separated and then recombined grammatically) occurred in a kind of qualitative leap forward by the young children of the second cohort (1984–1993) who grasped the initial but partial advance that the first cohort children (before 1984) had created earlier. The first cohort children built a system that was richer than the primitive homesign that they came with into the school community. In turn, the younger second cohort children (still within the critical period for normal language acquisition) generated a new grammar, which spread "horizontally" among peers of the same age group. Crucially, the now older first cohort children did not fully master the constituent structures and hierarchical combinations of the second cohort's new grammar, new advances in the evolution of NSL for which they had earlier prepared the groundwork. The researchers in one report call particular attention to how this aspect of "vertical" convergence was not obtained, despite the evident superiority of the adolescents in attaining other types of complex learning objective. A similar progression was evident when researchers analyzed the emergence of spatial modulation that serves different grammatical functions (Senghas, 2003).

According to the researchers, among young children with full access to the language acquisition mechanisms, grammatical properties arise naturally, even when these are absent from the input. It is as if they were predisposed to seek out certain basic and essential elements in the gestural representations that have the potential for being reprogrammed as linguistic forms, this predisposition derived from the "unique proclivity of the human mind for structuring a communication system along grammatical lines" (Sandler *et al.*, 2005: 2665). What the researchers found was that these linguistic properties did not arise in the same spontaneous way among the older children (Senghas *et al.*, 2004), most of whom we can assume were subject to early language deprivation during their period of homesign development in isolation. Apparently, impoverished and late L1 learning not only degrades subsequent language processing and acquisition capacity (Mayberry and Lock, 2003; Boudreault and Mayberry, 2006), but also limits the development, at least temporarily, of certain general cognitive abilities that depend on the use of language. Morgan and Kegl (2006) describe the significant difficulties that NSL signers, who had not benefited from early sign acquisition, have with Theory of Mind (ToM) tasks involving deception and lack of knowledge states.

These findings are consistent with the research on "experience-dependent plasticity" in cognitive development. According to Neville (2005), the mental faculties form an interconnected network of systems and subsystems each of which display degrees of specificity in their functional properties. Maturational constraints, like the ones that appear to operate in NSL acquisition, have different effects on the properties of these distinct systems and subsystems. Some domains of knowledge or processing may be more or less susceptible to sensitive period effects; and the developmental "windows of opportunity" may open on schedules that vary from one to another. In contrast, other domains may be permanently open, showing no sensitive period effects. This might explain, at least in part, the uneven profile, even within "language," of children's abilities in atypical and deficient development (e.g., some aspects of syntax versus the semantic component of lexical knowledge). Even within grammar itself some domains may be more vulnerable to the effects of deprivation and others less so, such as the essential/basal linguistic properties that survive in conditions of highly restricted input. In theory, some disorders might be relatively circumscribed and "localized," others more diversified, one of the research questions to be taken up in Sections 3.3 and 3.4.

From all of this so far a relationship can be proposed between the effects of Age of Acquisition and the Poverty of Stimulus problem. The Poverty of Stimulus problem appears to apply in a different way for young children acquiring their L1, normally, than it does for delayed L1 learning after the critical period. That is, both AoA and the PoS problem imply some kind of specialization in language development, both appearing to be associated with particular kinds of knowledge, certain components of linguistic competence in this case. In the development of this competence (or these competencies), in L1, young children are able to easily overcome the PoS only within a closed-ended critical period. In abnormal, late, L1 learning, the PoS cannot be overcome in the same way. What follows is that despite the differences between how L1 and L2 develop, even in children, late L1 learning is not the same as L2 learning. The former proceeds with an impaired Language Acquisition Device, unlike in the development of second languages under normal conditions of prior L1 acquisition during early childhood.

The capacity to "deductively" upgrade impoverished language input and build a grammar spontaneously applies in different ways to different acquisition and learning circumstances. Hypothetically, it applies to normal L1 acquisition in the most natural and unfettered way. For L2 learners, if L1 acquisition had proceeded normally within the genetically programmed AoA parameters, it still applies, access to this capacity "filtered" by L1 "settings" (Francis, 2012; Sebastián and Bosch, 2001). This was the theory proposed in Chapter 2. And for children learning their L1 outside the critical period, the grammar building capacity is now impaired, impaired as well for subsequent L2 learning, according to Mayberry's account. Development still proceeds, but with a defective LAD and with the deployment of unaided inductive strategies and other general purpose learning mechanisms. This explains why both:

- language development can still advance and;
- an atypical variation is manifested in L1 attainment, similar to that in L2 learning, but uncharacteristic of typical L1 acquisition.

Notably, the grammar constructing capacity appears to operate in all cases of language deprivation and insufficient language model, as long as the critical acquisition mechanisms are still intact, or intact to some degree. For example, homesign, a conventionalized gesture system or "rudimentary pidgin" created by young children, shows evidence of being Universal Grammar (UG) compatible, evidenced in the "resilient properties" of language as these are instantiated in the homesign system (Goldin-Meadow, 2005, pp. 217–221). The first cohort of Nicaraguan signers independently boosted it, approaching the construction of a fully formed creole, completeness achieved by a second cohort, again without the benefit of access to a complete model, but with full access to a LAD. In other words neither a reasonably "complete model" nor full access to a LAD, by itself, appears to be sufficient. The homesigners, as young children, only had the latter; the youngest members of the second cohort had both, the usable input they received apparently being complete enough for them.

At the same time, Goldin-Meadow's claim is important for understanding all non-primary and atypical language development, as well as the first stages of normal primary language acquisition in young children. If correct, we can propose that even the earliest stages of child mother-tongue acquisition, all categories of second language learning, and the development of pidgins of the most rudimentary level are UG-constrained. The PoS problem appears starkly evident in the cases of outright restricted input; but the evidence from the wide variety of these situations suggests that it figures in the typical language acquisition scenario as well.

3.2.2 Language in speech and sign

Shifting the lens from development issues to how sign language is cognitively represented and how it is processed, the questions of domain specificity and encapsulation can now be refined with a critical eye (Sandler, 1993). Beginning with the assumption that both spoken and sign language must be based on a foundation of linguistic knowledge of the same kind, the lower-level, or peripheral, mechanisms of input processing (sometimes called "transducers"), for example, cannot be an integrative part of "a language module." Parenthetically, it appears that the auditory and visual channels do not exhaust the possibilities of lower-level input processing for primary language acquisition or language use either. The tactile modality, it seems, can also process primary linguistic input (Reed and Delhorne, 1995). Domain specificity, then, must apply to a much more finer grain of component. Computations would be of a different kind in the periphery — the input and output processors that interface with "external" motor, visual, auditory and tactile mechanisms. In contrast, they would be of the same basic kind in the linguistic modules and their corresponding interfaces upstream, so to speak (syntactic structures, for example). Encapsulation also would have to be considered case-by-case — for each knowledge structure (competence module), what kinds of interface are required for speakers and signers to be able to use all the subsystems automatically and efficiently? In both instances, this includes access to central systems, at the one end, and all interaction beyond the language modules at the other end. For example, a problem similar to that for signers is posed for spoken language users regarding the interfaces that need to be in place for the learned skills of reading and writing (Jackendoff, 2002). In summary, there cannot be a single integrated "language module."

Related to this issue is the observation that the modality difference between speech and sign is also reflected in structural differences "more internally" within the language faculty proper, not just in the periphery. Sign languages appear to form a single language type, setting them apart from all spoken languages. For example, morphemes in sign are combined simultaneously, and they have a common pattern of verb agreement (Sandler and Lillo-Martin, 2001). The authors raise the possibility that iconicity not only plays a role in the formation of individual lexical items, but also contributes to other grammatical peculiarities of sign language, implying that conceptual structure and spatial relations interact in an important way with syntax and morphology.[3]

We can now return to the specific issue of bilingual/bimodal development and L2 learning that includes a sign language. The study of deaf bilingualism presents a seemingly different separability question from the one that was posed in Section 3.1. Our present concern in regard to separability in the conclusion to this section is about mental representation and processing. Are the languages of bilingual/bimodal signers, a sign language (SL) and a spoken language (SpL), differentiated across two autonomous sets of grammatical systems, with separate lexicons, each with its own rules of organization? At first glance, it might appear that the argument for separate representations (Paradis, 2004) might be stronger or more obvious than it is for bilingualism within the same modality (two SLs or two SpLs). But two unique features of deaf bilingualism make the problem interesting, and potentially relevant to all cases:

1. SpLs for deaf signers include manually coded speech-based systems, fingerspelling, and what is termed "contact signing," and
2. One of the most important sources of relevant empirical evidence in this area, code-mixing, includes the possibility of simultaneous use of two language systems, in addition to the standard sequential type to which speech bilingualism is restricted.

And in studying SL-SpL mixing, we should always keep in mind that there is an important distinction between native-speakers (children born to deaf parents) and late L1 learners whose first substantial contact with sign language is during later childhood or adulthood.

In relation to the possibility of specialization in language, one way in which certain proposals seem to line up is that if it is admitted that some degree of modularity exists in language (that at least some components are domain-specific), then it is more likely to expect that entire language subsystems (L1, L2, etc.) are separable. In contrast, if all aspects of linguistic knowledge in bilinguals are structured along domain-general lines, it would be expected that L1 and L2 are combined in a homogeneous and integrative manner. In this regard, readers are referred to an interesting discussion by Berent (2004) of the possibility of the creation of a "third system" in contact signing. Briefly summarizing the arguments, this possibility should be dispreferred in favor of applying the traditional analysis of code-mixing to SL-SpL discourse. In other words, we should take advantage of the same analytical procedures since the respective alternative systems are both natural languages. Pointing to the wide variation in contact signing patterns, it would seem to be preferable to first try to sort out the specific circumstances of acquisition and L2 learning, and then see if the standard approaches to language mixing are still applicable. The first observation that would be relevant is that native signers appear to be more effective in code-switching/mode-mixing than late signers. Following Mayberry and Lock (2003), native signers would also have been most successful in L2 learning of a SpL. Based on their study of infant native-signing bilinguals, Petitto and Kovelman (2003) make the case for a strong version of early separation and against any degree of "fusion." Research over the years, in fact, has generally converged on a model that rejects the idea of a "unitary system" in child bilinguals, even at early stages of development (Fabiano and Goldstein, 2005; Meisel, 2001). Further research will need to carefully account for:

- AoA effects,
- ultimate mastery of the SL (keeping in mind that many deaf signers exercise full native command of neither their "L1" or their "L2"),
- level of SpL proficiency; that restricted input is a distinguishing characteristic of sign language bilingualism, setting it apart from spoken language bilingualism, and
- exceptionally complicating contextual and sociolinguistic factors.

In a major study of the influence of English on British Sign Language, Sutton-Spence (1999) points out that in SL-SpL codeswitching the factor of ultimate attainment in each language makes analysis of mixed patterns more difficult than in the case of switching between two spoken languages. For example, we may want to categorize differently the insertion of SpL constituents by young highly proficient native-signers as opposed to insertions by older deaf signers who were late learners and have integrated SpL-based grammatical structures, loan translation, and finger spelling more completely into their mental representation of sign language. In addition, the above considerations are complicated by AoA effects — native signers possess at least one fully formed language system; bilingual/bimodal late L1 learners may have attained completeness in neither.

For a comprehensive discussion of the various "two-level, three component" models (autonomous L1 and L2 lexicons, shared conceptual system) of bilingualism and how they apply to sign language, see Dufour (1997). Of particular interest regarding this model is the finding of spoken language dominance in simultaneous production, for hearing signers and even many deaf signers. The above mentioned complicating variables, particularly AoA effects in sign language proficiency, are critically relevant again. For example, under what special circumstances might the SpL system consistently assign its grammatical frames to mixed utterances for deaf signers? Whatever the results of this line of investigation might be, an emerging consensus among sign language researchers is that SL-SpL language mixing (codeswitching, borrowing, etc.) provides bilingual/bimodal learners with useful learning resources (as is the general view in the field of SpL bilingualism). The "pooling of [language] resources" contributes to a "positive language interaction" (Menéndez, 2010).

Again we can see how this field of study provides the sharpest examples for our theme of exceptional bilingualism, especially for the pending questions of domain-specificity and componentiality of language knowledge. The discussion of how "two-level, three-component" models of bilingual lexical access (see Gollan and Kroll, 2000, for an overview) apply to deafness and sign language is a fitting way to introduce the next section, on impaired bilingualism. In fact, case studies of sign language aphasia have been particularly instructive in understanding how underlying knowledge structures are affected in language disorder overall.

3.3 Bilingual aphasia and Specific Language Impairment

Together with the compelling results supporting significant AoA effects, results from studies of damage to linguistic networks in signers rank among the most important discoveries in the science of language. Most interesting among these is the finding of double dissociation between non-linguistic spatial cognition and linguistic competence in sign language, standing as strong evidence for neural specialization for some components of language. Like hearing aphasics, impaired signers manifest patterns of breakdown that correlate with speech symptoms associated with Broca's aphasia or Wernicke's aphasia, for example, accompanied by intact spatial cognitive abilities. Conversely, deaf patients who suffer from severe (general) spatial defects may show preserved signing ability, even though in sign language the use of space plays an important grammatical function (Sandler and Lillo-Martin, 2001). It should be cause for reflection why it is that we owe these advances to critical investigations on the unique circumstances of language learning and language use that deafness imposes. Indeed, the results from sign language research regarding these central issues are robust and consistent, recent studies confirming earlier conclusions going back more than twenty years (Newport, 1990).

It is also noteworthy why studies of language disability so often take up the issue of how L1 and L2 systems are represented. In a case study of an adult deaf signer who had suffered trauma to the central semantic system, Marshall *et al.* (2005) uncovered dissociations along two different dimensions: (1) between understanding of non-linguistic gesture and sign comprehension. Strikingly, the patient could count on no advantage in her defective sign language performance with iconic signs, confirming the autonomy of each domain in relation to the other. (2) Under the effects of a central semantic disorder, translating (from British Sign Language to English) far outstripped naming ability in both languages, providing further evidence for direct non-semantic connections between L1 and L2 lexicons. In other words, translation does not need to engage in all circumstances the same processing components as naming (Marshall *et al.*, 2005, p. 731). We should expect further research in this area to confirm results from studies of bilingual aphasia between two SpLs. One important line of work focuses on the dysfunction of activation and inhibition of interconnected autonomous language systems in selective impairment and recovery (Ansaldo and Joanette, 2002; de Groot and Christoffels, 2006; Fabbro, 2001; Green, 2002).

This section and the next, on bilingual and cross-language literacy deficits, are closely related, together, setting themselves apart from Section 3.2 on sign language bilingualism for the reasons already mentioned at the beginning of this chapter (two different kinds of exceptionality). One of the key research questions in the fields of language and literacy impairment, one that bears directly upon our topic of specialization and modularity is: Are the performance limitations of aphasia, Specific Language Impairment, and dyslexia/dysgraphia the consequence of domain-specific disorders, or can they be characterized in terms of domain-general deficits (Fletcher, 1999)? A secondary question might be: does the general idea of specialization of components, or the existence of isolable mental domains (perhaps a different issue), necessarily imply domain-specificity? For example, can there be separable cognitive components all of which are subserved by domain-general structures?

Traditionally, and for good reason, language disorders and dyslexia/dysgraphia are studied separately. However, one research problem that they both share in common helps us better understand the specific versus general domains issue. Evidence for all disabilities in question depends on measures of performance, on series of language tasks, oral, sign or written, receptive and expressive. As such, the disability as it is actually manifested can be rooted in a defect in any one or a combination of the following:

1. a linguistic competence module or knowledge representation,
2. a non-linguistic competence structure upon which the ability depends, and
3. an information processing mechanism or interface component.

And within each category, more than one structure might have come to be impaired. Perhaps more apparent in analyses of dyslexia/dysgraphia, language-related disorders that fall under broad categories, such as SLI, are of a wide diversity, etiologically. Each one, it would seem, needs to be considered in turn, case-by-case. An empirical question then becomes, which aspects of a given disability are domain-specific, and in which aspects is there a participation of domain-general deficits? Which of the participating cognitive domains in #1, #2 or #3, that come together in the typical and normal performance of the ability in question may be relatively more autonomous and encapsulated and which are more integrative and non-specific?

From this point of view it would add clarity to the discussion if we distinguished between *disabilities*, evidenced by outward expressions and clusters of symptoms, on the one hand, and impairments or *defects in specific components* from #1, #2 and #3 above, on the other hand. So it appears that researchers interested in studying breakdown in domain-specific systems have formulated their hypotheses more cautiously — it is unlikely, they would contend, that all language disabilities, of the SLI type for example, have as their underlying cause exclusively domain-general dysfunction. This seems to be the approach that van der Lely (2005) favors as a way of sorting out the complexity of SLI, not thought of in recent work, by and large, as a single unified disorder. One case in point would be children afflicted by a relatively uncommon Grammatical-SLI, who show persistent core deficits in specific computational aspects of phonology (independent of problems with articulation, i.e., speech is clear), morphology, and syntax, specific, for example, to certain grammatical computations. For example, among French SLI children, problems have been identified in understanding and producing clitic pronouns but not determiners, e.g., *le*, the same phonological form for both (van der Lely, 2005). Interaction, in development, among the components of grammar with non-linguistic knowledge structures, and the deployment of compensatory bootstrapping strategies, alter the overall disability profile. But if the impairment persists (evidence of "deviance" rather than "delay"), and remains persistently discrete to some degree (some measure of independence from perceptual processing abilities, nonverbal intelligence, vocabulary, etc.), this points to a subtype of SLI specific to grammar, a modular LAD deficit (Fletcher, 1999), specific in turn to the subcomponent or subcomponents that appear to have been corrupted.

Another way of describing this kind of language disorder is to find evidence for the existence of two different kinds of memory system:

- procedural/implicit, underlying "symbol manipulation," and
- declarative/explicit, underlying associative memory (Ullman and Gopnik, 1999; Ullman, 2001),

leading to the possible conclusion that these systems correspond to two distinct types of knowledge structure, each with their own distinct sets of computing and processing mechanism (Paradis, 2004). Ullman's approach, to be clear, differs from the others in certain respects, a topic for the concluding section.

The new field of study on how SLI affects bilingual development allows us to evaluate the different models in a situation of cross-linguistic comparison within the same individual, with the same underlying deficit. Resulting variations across-language have to be compatible with findings from the monolingual condition. With this in mind, Paradis *et al.* (2005) compared a general cognitive/perceptual processing and a language-specific explanation for the results of an assessment of French-English bilinguals with SLI (age 7), Mean Length of Utterance-matched normally-developing bilingual 3-year-olds, and respective groups of monolingual French-speaking children, both SLI and typically-developing. The most interesting finding was related to the comparison between bilingual SLI and monolingual SLI. Overall, the performance of the bilingual SLI children on key measures was not inferior. On some assessments, the bilinguals even appeared to be acquiring the grammatical pattern in question more rapidly than their monolingual SLI peers. Given that bilinguals would have significantly less "time-on-task" to process input in French than monolinguals (as much as 50% less), the finding of equivalent performance is interpreted as contrary to the expectations of a domain-general limitation theory (in this case involving children affected by this sub-type of SLI). In other words, a more severe PoS problem presents itself in bilingual SLI, one that is still overcome by the affected children. According to the authors, constructivist/usage-based models would predict lower levels of attainment relative to monolinguals — Handicapped by domain-general processing and globally slower and less efficient learning mechanisms, the time-on-task factor should be reflected in delays and deficient attainment *to a greater degree*. Clearly, more work, both experimental and theoretical, is needed to explain why this result is not obtained; that is, how do bilingual SLI children overcome PoS under these, more onerous, exceptional circumstances?

In regard to all of the points discussed in this section, Thomas and Karmiloff-Smith (2005) propose a different way of framing the problem of componentiality as it might be revealed in language disorder. Their review of the research deserves a close reading as it challenges a number of conceptions associated with modular approaches to the study of language disability; some of these conceptions may in fact turn out to be misconceived. We are reminded first of all to consider separately the cases of adult acquired aphasia from developmental disorders. For the latter, the processes of interactivity and compensation, together with the greater neurological plasticity in children, unfold under abnormal constraints. Altogether, these account for a fine level of "fractionations" both within and across domains, leading to the question: how specific can innate specifications, under genetic control, be? At what level of "granularity" should we expect to find links between the genetic code and components of language? Plausibly, such links exist, but not at the fine level that actual patterns of disability have suggested. Thomas and Karmiloff-Smith's arguments present the most difficult challenge for theories of "massive modularity" (Sperber and Wilson, 2002), although it should be granted that their questions are directed as well to proponents of weaker versions. Their main idea, that the developmental process itself is an essential aspect of an emerging modularity, is an important part of the discussion, related to the problems posed by sign language, deafness, and AoA effects that were touched upon in the previous section. The research problems include — interactivity among cognitive domains, degree of encapsulation, and the importance of language input on ultimate attainment of linguistic knowledge. The reader will recall that these were raised by Sandler (1993), who also proposed a critical assessment of the some of the earlier conceptions of modularity, interestingly, from a different theoretical point of view than that of Karmiloff-Smith.

3.4 Domain-specific and domain-general domains in language

We can now take up the proposal from Section 3.1 for a discussion of a possible convergence on the question of specialization in language (i.e., that some components of language are specialized). The review of the research on exceptionality and bilingualism has provided findings that might facilitate the search for some limited common ground. Even in a discussion involving widely divergent views (not the case at all in this chapter), a good place to begin is to try to identify points of coincidence. From these points the lines of debate in a proper confrontation of hypotheses and findings can be drawn, distilling out what the essential differences really are. One way to better understand the issues might be to divide the question of specialization between:

1. separability of cognitive capacities – the existence, in the first place, of cognitive domains (e.g., faculties or ability networks) that are underpinned by distinct biocognitive structures, with the capacities in question being autonomous and isolable in some way, and
2. domain-specificity — whether the autonomous and isolable knowledge components and processing mechanisms in a domain in #1 are subserved by substrates that are highly encapsulated and dedicated exclusively to them.

This seems to be the approach to the problem taken by Ullman. The review article by Marcus (2006) on two ways of applying the concept of modularity addresses #2 (domain-specificity) directly.

To start, in regard to the existence of separate and autonomous components (question #1), there appears to be a broad agreement, more or less, among the authors we have studied. In bilingualism, evidence comes from double dissociations, along two different dimensions — On the one hand, differentiations are evident between linguistic and non-linguistic capabilities, (a "vertical dimension"). These contrasts also reveal themselves differently when comparing L1 and L2 (Ullman, 2001). On the other hand, the differentiation "across" the L1 and L2 subsystems (the "horizontal dimension") is evidenced in the separation of the language subsystems in bilingual children. Aside from early separation in childhood, other examples of differentiation along this dimension are:

- selective impairment between L1 and L2 in developmental disorders of literacy, and
- when in selective recovery from acquired aphasia the spared, or less disabled, system is not always L1, not always the dominant language, nor the most recently learned.

See Paradis (2004, pp. 195–203) for an exposition of the "Three-store hypothesis" that addresses this kind of differentiation.

The second aspect of the specialization question (domain-specificity, question #2 above) is more complex. For example, in regard to language development dispositions ("biases"), what kind of component is an input processor that is designed for processing linguistic information for acquisition? The research on the effects of AoA and the PoS problem (critical period effects in deafness, bilingual SLI, in Sections 3.1 and 3.2) suggests that these phenomena are specific to the acquisition of certain kinds of knowledge (e.g., core grammatical competence), and not others. As regards processing in general, Coltheart (1999, p. 118) defines a system as domain-specific (for him, the essential feature of modularity): "if it only responds to stimuli of a particular class." For now, let us set aside these approaches to the problem (recognizing that they are not uncontroversial). Rather, the more contentious issue, in this discussion, is about domain-specificity, and modularity, in relation to how mental structures are represented, one that is related to but somewhat different from the acquisition and processing questions, an observation made by Sharwood-Smith (1991) years ago.

On this point, Ullman (2001) contrasts his Declarative-Procedural Model to "single-mechanism" connectionism, but also to traditional dual-mechanism theories. While the Procedural-Declarative Model accepts that lexicon and grammar are each based on distinct and separate computational systems, it does not assume that the relevant components are dedicated and domain-specific (presumably, in terms of the representation question, meaning "highly encapsulated"). Understanding the difference in this way, it probably would not be consistent with the conclusions, which we reviewed in Section 3.2, drawn by Paradis *et al.* (2005), van der Lely (2005) and Fletcher (1999) regarding specifically grammatical impairments in SLI. Rather, according to Ullman, the separable language systems would be subserved by domain-general structures, predicting associations with non-linguistic functions, among grammar, motor and general cognitive skills, and habits. For example, SLI has been found typically not to be characterized exclusively by syntactic deficits, but also by disabilities in the realm of motor control which affect speech, difficulties with controlling coordinated face and mouth movements (Marcus and Fisher,

2003; Thomas and Karmiloff-Smith, 2005). For their part, van der Lely and colleagues might reply with a question: is there any aspect of language competence that is domain-specific, revealed in certain sub-types of SLI? One needs to keep in mind, the argument would go, that the behavioral assessment of all types of SLI takes measure of *abilities*, something that is bigger than any single competence component. Skills and abilities, being multi-component complexes, bring domain-specific modules and domain-general cognitive structures together in performance.

Fortunately, the way the different proposals and claims seem to line up so far doesn't draw a neat line opposing two clearly discernable camps, a motivation for the original idea of exploring the possibility of finding some common ground. For one, it's not clear which aspects of the traditional "dual-mechanism," e.g., the distinction between lexicon and grammar, are still viable (Jackendoff, 2007). Similarly, the traditional dichotomy between competence and performance has been questioned by linguists seeking to integrate findings from experimental and applied research in language acquisition and from research on the different aspects of language use (Culicover and Jackendoff, 2006; Newmeyer, 2003).

One possible avenue to pursue might be to abandon what Marcus (2006) calls "sui generis" modularity, in which cognitive domains are conceived as entities entirely onto themselves, encapsulated to a degree that does not allow for horizontal and top-down influences from other cognitive domains. Regarding developmental language impairments, genetic defects are not typically associated uniquely with single unambiguously circumscribed disorders, or vice versa. Computations that are implemented in different complex tasks draw from configurations of different arrays of lower-level structures, rather than one wholly integrated and tightly encapsulated circuit. According to Marcus, this helps explain the coincidence of selective impairment and co-morbidity, and why developmental disorders are associated with multiple domains. On the one hand, neither SLI nor dyslexia, *per se*, could be "a modular deficit" because no single component, by itself, corresponds to the configuration of cognitive domains required for normal language or literacy ability. On the other hand, it is unlikely that linguistic competence, to take one example, is preprogrammed at the level of very fine detail.

These arguments against a conception of modularity that depends on "overly specialized devices," and in favor of incorporating a richer interactivity, have been brought forward by a number of authors (Callebaut, 2005; Calabretta and Parisi, 2005, to mention just a few). Along these lines, the idea behind the relationship between knowledge and ability that has been assumed in this chapter, slightly different from the standard competence-performance dichotomy, might help in sorting out some of the issues. Another way forward might involve seeing what can be salvaged from the traditional dual-mechanism approach, and associated theories like Universal Grammar, after critically examining new proposals from within this tradition that have questioned some of its long-standing concepts. The next chapter will follow up on this discussion, applying the same concepts to bilingual literacy and to interesting research problems in the comparison between different writing systems.

Notes

1. In this discussion, language abilities can be thought of as each comprising a different set of linguistic knowledge components and processing mechanism components that have developed and have been "brought together" (e.g., in learning) for the performance of these abilities, and their component sub-skills. Thus, two different but related abilities would typically "share" some of the same knowledge components. In this sense, "knowledge" refers to competence. Ability (synonymous with proficiency) corresponds roughly to the traditional notion of performance, how the competence components and relevant processing mechanisms are put to use in comprehension and expression.

2. The one qualification that might apply to the "no inherent deficit" claim for deafness (understood as profound deafness) is in regard to full and complete mastery of the secondary language ability of literacy in a spoken language-based writing system. Even assuming the optimal conditions of native sign language development from birth and early L2 learning of a spoken language, the attainment of higher-order reading and writing abilities may present a greater level of difficulty, on average, for literacy learners who have restricted access to the phoneme-grapheme correspondences of the spoken L2 orthography in question. Related to this possibility is the fact that, overall, deaf children's literacy achievement lags significantly behind their hearing age peers, persisting through to the end of secondary schooling. Estimates are that as many as half of all deaf high school graduates read at an elementary grade level (Mayer, 2007). The interesting research question here is whether non-alphabetic writing systems offer deaf literacy learners a measure of relative advantage in some aspect of reading or writing.

3. A reviewer called our attention to the fact that iconicity is not a dominant feature in any fully formed sign language. For discussion of this complex issue, and more generally about how some of the differences between sign and spoken language correlate with modality, see Pietrandra (2002), Sandler and Lillo-Martin (2001) and Vermeerbergen (2006).

Chapter 4

Bilingual literacy and comparative research on writing systems

This chapter begins the discussion of writing and literacy, specifically when readers know a first and a second language. Comparing different writing systems and how speakers of different languages put them to use is another way to study bilingualism and reading. In particular, the circumstances of bilingual and second language literacy learning offer investigators and educators an important additional vantage point from which to better understand the *components of reading ability*. Cross-writing system comparisons complement this perspective. Comparing writing systems, and how children learn to read through the medium of each system provides for tests of a number of hypotheses currently being considered by researchers. One particularly instructive series of tests involves the contrast between alphabetic and non-alphabetic writing systems.

This examination of the research will examine proposals related to the role of phonology in word identification with a special focus on the morphosyllabic Chinese orthography. A componential, or modular, approach to the study of reading ability will be evaluated in relation to claims made from different perspectives on the question of the activation of phonological representations in reading. Notice that we are picking up the discussion from the last chapter on what it means to say that language abilities can be decomposed into components. In this chapter, the question before us is the following: is the Universal Phonological Principle, proposed by C. Perfetti, compatible with a modular approach to the study of reading ability? Recall that *modularity* was the overarching theme of Chapter 3, this now being a good opportunity for readers, if they haven't already, to check the Glossary entry for this important concept, along with those for — *ability, aphasia, metalinguistic awareness, competence, dyslexia, top-down, and Universal Writing System Constraint.*

4.1 Are there constraints on writing systems that are universal?

Research on cross-language comparisons provides special opportunities and vantage points for a better understanding of the components of reading ability. These comparisons can approach the analysis of skills and abilities from two different perspectives — the study of reading development in bilinguals (including here the subset of individuals who are second language learners), and the comparative study of reading across language and writing systems among monolingual literacy learners. An assumption that ties these two approaches together conceptually is that the research in reading in any single language is relevant in every way to second language and bilingual literacy. The same underlying cognitive structures form the foundation for reading ability cross-linguistically. Conversely, the findings from bilingual literacy will help us better understand the components of reading ability in general, for example, in the case of monolingual speakers. For beginning second language readers, imbalances and uneven development provide opportunities to examine the relevant components and subcomponents.

The summary of the research will begin with a brief overview of theoretical approaches to the study of reading that have made reference to the concept of modularity, followed by a discussion of the current state of investigation in the field of bilingual and second language reading, giving examples of how a componential approach might be relevant to a number of ongoing research problems. Cross-language and cross-writing system comparisons will present us in Sections 4.3 and 4.4 with a complementary viewpoint on the same issues, in particular comparisons that involve non-alphabetic writing systems. Central to all of the above will be an assessment of the Universal Phonological Principle (UPP) and the related Universal Writing System Constraint (Perfetti, 2003; Perfetti and Dunlap, 2008) and how they might be understood in relation to one or another version of the modularity hypothesis. The important claim of the UPP is that the activation of phonology in (silent) reading cannot be by-passed in the use of any writing system.

The problem of determining which aspects of literacy are universal and which are specific to each writing system is still not well understood; and much work is still needed to even conceptualize all the critical research questions coherently. As we will see, the study of the Chinese writing system, how it differs from alphabetic systems, and how it does not, holds one of the most important keys to this problem. For discussion purposes, an overview of the general approach of componential analysis, associated with the notion of modularity, will be presented as one way to frame the relevant issues. The specific purpose of this overview is to set the stage for a proposal — if future research shows that the Universal Phonological Principle and the Universal Writing System Constraint are correct, this result would be consistent with a modular approach to the study of reading. On the other hand, if Perfetti's theories cannot stand up to future disconfirming evidence, this would seriously call into question central pillars of the modularity hypothesis,[1] and not just in the area of literacy. As such, the problems of bilingual literacy learning and cross-writing system comparison (in particular, the contrast between alphabetic and morphosyllabic Chinese systems) present a critical test for an important debate in cognitive science.

4.2 The componential approach

There are a number of ways in which reading ability might be analyzed componentially; and the concept of modularity has been used to frame the various problems that arise in this type of analysis. The review of research in this chapter will do the same. While certain versions of the modularity thesis remain controversial, in particular those among them that we might characterize as "strong bottom-up" versions, it is important to keep in mind that there exists a broad diversity of views among researchers who favor one or another componential/modular approach to the study of language ability. Even if historically the concept traces its roots to Universal Grammar-oriented theories, there is no reason for insisting that the general idea of modularity is incompatible in every way with other schools of cognitive science. Keeping this in mind might turn out to be especially useful in the research on a complex ability such as reading. This section will provide an overview of a modular approach to the study of reading not for the purpose of making the claim that it is the most correct or comprehensive framework for literacy research. Rather, a more narrow claim will be offered for discussion: The main idea underlying the UPP, that activation of phonology in (silent) reading cannot be by-passed, even in non-alphabetic writing systems, follows from a componential/modular perspective on both the architecture of language and literacy knowledge and the processing of written language. While Perfetti has not explicitly drawn this connection, the questions related to how linguistic knowledge structures interact in the deployment of an ability like reading are central to this claim. If his hypotheses prove to be incorrect, this would spell trouble for modularity (for strong and weak versions alike). Thus, current and future research evidence that is inconsistent with the UPP would lend support to holistic and integrativist theories of literacy (e.g., "whole language" theories).[2] Chapter 9 will revisit this topic.

Issues related to the concept of modularity come up in the discussion of a number of important questions in the research on literacy and bilingualism, for example:

1. Can a useful distinction be made between explicit knowledge and metalinguistic awareness on the one hand and implicit knowledge on the other?
2. In reading, how do the different subsystems of grammar come on-line and how do they interact with the other (non-linguistic) knowledge structures and processing mechanisms that are engaged in reading? In relation to bilingual readers, this topic is related to the question of the differentiation between first language (L1) and second language (L2) systems;
3. What are the essential points of contention in the debate opposing holistic social-constructivist ("whole-language") theories and those that emphasize the importance of mastering the sub-skills of word identification? and
4. How do we understand the concepts of pathway, circuit, and network, and might they be compatible with models that conceive of components? In this regard, what might be some points of contact between connectionist and modular approaches to the study of reading ability?

Let us take each of these points in turn, beginning with (1) above. A basic assumption underlying modular approaches is that not all knowledge of language, for example, is of the same kind. Especially when considering complex abilities, an important distinction is between metalinguistic explicit knowledge and implicit knowledge. The phonological level, being the most basic for reading, appears to reveal this distinction most clearly. Arguably, the phonological competence that young children attain in their L1 depends on no kind of deliberate attention to form, negative evidence, or application of deliberate learning strategy. From this point of view, the early spontaneous and universal emergence of phonological competence would be the hallmark of an innately pre-programmed cognitive specialization (Petitto, 2007). On the other hand, assessments of metaphonological knowledge show evidence of developmental trends that are not spontaneous and universal, correlating (as implicit phonological competence does not) with literacy learning (Castles and Coltheart, 2004; Hu, 2004; Liberman, 1999; Morais and Kolinski, 2001).

The question of how the subsystems of language are deployed and how they interact with other cognitive domains in reading (question 2) assumes that reading ability can be analyzed ("fractionated") into subsystems or autonomous components in the first place (Stanovich, 2003). To clarify terms here, "interaction" and "interactive models" imply something very different from "integration." An "integrativist" model would reject all versions of modularity, while interaction assumes connectivity and interface among components. In fact, any conception of a modular/componential architecture that omits interfaces would be impossible. Stanovich (2000), Shatil and Share (2003) and Leikin *et al.* (2005) are perhaps the most explicit proposals in the field of reading research along these lines and serve as another important starting point in our discussion. Contrary to strong constructivist and integrativist assumptions, demarcating processing at the word identification level from that at the text comprehension level is important for understanding how different networks of components come together in each case. For word recognition, encapsulated processing applies in a manner that is different from how higher-order strategies are brought to bear on the tasks of sentence and text comprehension, according to this view. Thus, reading ability is seen as internally complex, structurally diverse.

The long-standing issue of "phonological mediation" in lexical access, following Stanovich's approach, would now seem to be more tractable. Especially in regard to our topic, cross-language and cross-writing system literacy, an analytical method of studying how phonological structure interfaces with the other subcomponents of word recognition skill should uncover interesting patterns of variation from one orthography to another. At the same time, this approach should help us refine exactly what a Universal Phonological Principle (Perfetti and Liu, 2005) leads us to claim about what is invariant in how children learn to read. The specific claims about what is invariant and what isn't then could be tested in both first and second language literacy learning.

The overall idea of the UPP is that learning to read consists of learning how a writing system encodes the *language* system associated with it, as opposed to encoding meaning directly. "Word reading activates phonology at the lowest level of language allowed by the writing system." As a corollary, the "identification-with-phonology-hypothesis places phonology as a constituent of word recognition... that the identification of a word is the retrieval of its linguistic identity (phonologically specified morpheme of word)" (Perfetti and Liu, 2005: 195). Along similar lines, in their study of a dissociation between oral and written spelling, Han and Bi (2009) conclude that "phonological identities of components are part of the orthographic representation of Chinese characters" (p. 23). Thus, the study of how phonological structure interfaces with other subcomponents of word recognition should be relevant to the claims of the UPP.

For all of the above, so far, Jackendoff (2002) has offered a usable model of language processing that appears to be particularly apt for the study of complex abilities. Its main virtue for this purpose is that it embraces interactivity (recalling that this is not the same as holistic integration) in both feed-forward and feed-back. Modules each maintain their own domain-specific computational properties, specialized for phonological structure, syntactic structure, and so forth, with interface components doing the hard work of coordinating in performance the corresponding networks and connections. Performance of language tasks is effected so rapidly and automatically that complex literacy skills, for example, appear superficially to behave like modules themselves.

The problem of the role of context is related to Stanovich's (2000) discussion of degrees of autonomy and encapsulation, how the different components of reading ability comply with their specialized functions. The findings from research on the differential effects of context and background knowledge are proposed to be consistent with the general notion of domain specificity. For the efficient processing of information provided to the lower-level decoding modules, significant advantages accrue if they are insulated to a certain degree, free from having to compute inputs from all possible sources. Thus, context and background knowledge do not "pre-select" the output of word recognition, but rather intervene primarily in the subsequent stages of the reading process (Perfetti, 1992; Stanovich and Stanovich, 1999). In short, modularity in no way excludes top-down interaction; rather, what it proposes is that input computations do not have unlimited access to the higher-level domains (Coltheart, 1999).

A different dimension of componentiality poses a problem for researchers when there are two languages. Accumulating evidence now supports the hypothesis that separate linguistic subsystems, which correspond to knowledge of specific languages, begin to differentiate in bilingual children, early in development (Kovelman *et al.*, 2008). Conceivably, a similar differentiation would unfold in second language learning (Paradis, 2004; Genesee, 2002). But as an autonomous cognitive domain, separate from the grammatical components, conceptual structure (meaning) appears not to undergo this kind of division, remaining independent and "shared in common." See Francis (2008) for alternatives for modeling this relationship in bilingualism based on Jackendoff's Tripartite Parallel Architecture, and Cheung and Lin (2005) for a proposal along the same lines.

The problem is now applied to the development of literacy in two languages, or in a second language. Which aspects of reading ability turn out to be language-specific and which form part of a Common Underlying Proficiency (Cummins, 2000)? For example, phonological competence per se would differentiate between L1 and L2 (or L_a and L_b in simultaneous bilingualism); but are some aspects of phonological *processing* skill and explicit meta-level phonological knowledge "available" from a common store, so to speak, in bilingual/cross-language situations? This, by the way, is a very hard research problem about which we know very little at this point in time.

In regard to question 3, strong top-down holistic theories of reading also tend to conceptually integrate language acquisition and literacy learning, rejecting the dichotomy between speech as a product of biological evolution and literacy as a cultural innovation. Opposing views point to research findings demonstrating that key aspects of metalinguistic awareness, which correlate with literacy, do not emerge "naturally" and spontaneously, as all aspects of speech-related phonological competence, for example, do. Liberman (1999, p. 108), in arguing against the idea that learning to read should proceed just as children "learn" to understand language, made the observation that:

> *Phonemic awareness does not result from learning to speak because the primary representations of the phonetic module are already perfectly suited*

> *for the other processes of the language specialization. These primary phonetic representations do not get attention because they do not need it, and they do not need it because...they need not be converted into something other than what they already are.*

According to this view, core linguistic competence (and the ability to use language in face-to-face conversational discourse) is biologically primary, part of our "species endowment" and a constitutive primitive of human cognition. The ability to read and write is a secondary achievement, historically (the mastery of a "technology of language" to paraphrase Walter Ong, 1982). It is also a secondary achievement developmentally in children (Perfetti, 2003).

A contrasting assessment of the merits of modular and connectionist approaches (question 4) is far beyond the scope of this chapter. However, one observation needs to be made before proceeding to the next section. The research on reading development has drawn the lines of debate in a way that perhaps is surprising. For example, on the question of the role that phonology plays in word identification and the learning of grapheme-phoneme correspondences, connectionist and modularity-oriented researchers tend to come to the same conclusion — that strong top-down constructivist theories, that minimize the importance of orthography-phonology mapping, are seriously flawed (Rayner *et al.*, 2001; Seidenberg, 2005). This coincidence between seemingly very divergent paradigms should motivate reflection on which aspects of each approach lead to this kind of convergence on specific applied problems. One possibility to explore might be related to the distinction, proposed above, between *interaction* and *integration*. A number of investigators have argued that there is no compelling reason for viewing connectionist methods and modularity as counterposed in all respects (Norris, 1990; Pinker, 1999). In the basic research on word recognition, for example, it is noteworthy that despite highly divergent approaches (Plaut *et al.*, 1996; Coltheart *et al.*, 2001), conclusions and implications for literacy learning, and teaching, diverge much less than we might expect.

4.3 Linguistic and non-linguistic components in bilingual reading

In their review of the research on reading in a second language, Grabe and Stoller (2002) highlight the persistent themes around which, it appears, a measure of consensus has begun to coalesce. Pertinent to our discussion of the analysis of reading ability into its knowledge and processing components are the following:

1. the distinction between tacit knowledge of language and metalinguistic knowledge,
2. how knowledge of L1 orthography influences L2 decoding (e.g., in transfer and interference), and
3. findings related to the Language Threshold Hypothesis (LTH).

An interesting aspect of the distinction in (1) — "implicit-explicit" in the previous section — is that, on the one hand, second language readers will often have an advantage in the development of higher-order literacy-related metalinguistic knowledge, in particular older learners already literate in their L1. In contrast, they will tend to be limited, to one degree or another, in their ability to fully exploit core grammatical knowledge in reading, for which the L1 reader has tacit knowledge, available on-line rapidly and automatically (Cummins, 2000; Grabe and Stoller, 2002; Walter, 2004). Depending on the circumstances, L1 and L2 reading each might recruit resources in different proportions from the same knowledge structures.

The research on L1 writing system knowledge and L1 linguistic knowledge influences on second language reading, related to (2), has contributed to the discussion of broad theoretical problems concerning the mental architecture of bilingual competence (Wang *et al.*, 2003). How should the mutual influences between the L1 and L2 linguistic systems be modeled? This kind of interface (or interaction) would be different from the access that L2 and bilingual readers have to a common store of higher-order, metalinguistic and discourse-level knowledge structures. Included among the latter might also be the reading-specific abilities, in particular in the domain of phonological processing and phonological awareness, which research suggests are readily accessible (termed "transferable," in the current literature) in performance in either L1 or L2 reading (Bialystok *et al.*, 2005; Chen *et al.*, 2008). Interestingly, this would be the case independently of which was the language of initial literacy learning (Geva and Wang, 2001; Hu, 2003; Mumtaz and Humphreys, 2001). The same representation and access questions arise in regard to the deployment of other non-linguistic knowledge structures. For example, research on second language reading comprehension (Morrison, 2004; Walter, 2004) has largely directed its attention to what we could characterize as abilities that are clearly not language-specific, and the extent to which these abilities can be called upon in L1 and L2 (the "transfer" metaphor commonly applied to this type of interface as well). The influence of L1 orthographic knowledge on L2 reading should now be understood better — within the framework of an analysis that conceives of components of reading ability, which component structures correspond to different kinds of knowledge and processing mechanism?

The Language Threshold Hypothesis addresses the relative weight that should be assigned to L2 linguistic competence, on the one hand, and to general reading ability and general information processing skills, on the other. The latter would have been acquired previously from L1 literacy, or from some other source in the case of non-literate L2 literacy learners. Perhaps, a better way to understand the LTH is that assuming other factors (relevant text-related background knowledge, IQ, etc.) to be constant, L2 grammatical competence and L2 lexical knowledge, up to a certain threshold, represent significant factors in reading performance. Related to this idea, Verhoeven's (2000) "componential analysis" of L2 reading emphasizes the "dual-task," that places greater or lesser strains on all aspects of reading, with the possible exception of the lowest levels of decoding. Even regarding low level decoding, the critical experiments may not have yet been carried out: for example, word recognition tasks that compare the performance of native speakers with that of L2 learners below a sufficiently low "language threshold."[3]

In another componential analysis of L2 reading that sought to test the LTH, Leikin *et al.* (2005) sharpen the focus on the critical dimension of phonological processing abilities. Methodologically, the study stands out because it controlled for prior L1 literacy attainment. Investigators addressed a factor related to the idea of linguistic thresholds that might account for difficulties among unsuccessful readers: level of L2 (Hebrew) linguistic competence. Measures of linguistic competence in Hebrew correlated with L2 reading ability. Second language grammatical knowledge was predictive, in particular, of reading comprehension. In a separate analysis of the results from a series of phonological tasks, the authors underscore the important distinction, often left ambiguous in the research literature, between two separate categories of ability, what we could term "primary" and "secondary." Assessment procedures and interpretation of results must distinguish between:

1. core phonological competence and the "basic" phonological processing modules that deploy this competence in speech and auditory reception (together comprising "primary" ability), and
2. meta-level awareness of phonology and literacy-related processing skills ("secondary").

In this way the investigators emphasize the need to attend to the distinction between *linguistic* and *metalinguistic* knowledge and their respective processing mechanisms and interfaces. Before moving on to the comparison between alphabetic and non-alphabetic literacy, we could say that the emphasis in the LTH on the importance of the components of linguistic competence in reading is in line with the emphasis in the UPP on one of these components in particular, phonology.

4.4 Comparative writing system research

The second kind of cross-language comparison that was alluded to at the beginning of this chapter is the one that doesn't necessarily involve the study of bilingual readers. It is the alphabetic/non-alphabetic dimension that has attracted growing interest among researchers, for one reason because it represents the maximum possible contrast among the world's modern languages and their corresponding orthographies. For now, we will restrict the discussion to the psycholinguistics of Chinese writing and literacy development.

4.4.1 Access to phonology when phonemes are not represented in the orthography

From a number of points of view, it would seem that the literacy development of children learning the morphosyllabic Chinese writing system could be taken as the most stringent test for the Universal Phonological Principle. In fact, some support exists for the view that non-alphabetic systems implement a direct visual-to-meaning connection that circumvents phonology, the "phonology by-pass" or "direct access" hypothesis (Chen, 1996). A strong version of this proposal would be that the only necessary route from orthography (O) to semantics (S) in silent reading is the one that is not mediated by phonology (P); O → S would then be the dominant route. The strongest claim, a second position, would be that there is no O → P → S route at all. Phonology might be activated, but as a non-essential by-product, for the purpose, perhaps, of holding words in working memory while contextual information is processed. Taft and van Graan (1998) seem to apply a version of this model to reading in all writing systems. A third position, known as the "parallel-access" hypothesis, favors a two-pathway model — one route directly from orthography to semantics with the other mediated by phonology (Xu *et al.*, 1999). Simplification aside, these models, in addition to a number of subtle distinctions and inevitable qualifications, are currently being evaluated by investigators to determine what is precisely the role of phonology in reading Chinese. Componential analyses of reading ability, it will be proposed, might be especially useful in sorting out the key research questions. One possible avenue of analysis, alluded to in the previous section, could attempt to differentiate between phonological competence and the interfaces and processing mechanisms associated with all speech and auditory reception on the one hand, and meta-level knowledge and ability, on the other.

There is another way of thinking about these three hypotheses. If Chinese presents the critical test of the UPP, it also provides for a unique opportunity for garnering support for the O → S direct access hypothesis (Chen, 1996), or at least a weaker version of it — accepting (provisionally) phonological activation in alphabetic reading while positing exceptionality for the processing of Chinese characters. Assuming that this way of framing the discussion is properly conceived, what follows is a tentative proposal for why the question of phonological activation is important — Finding the direct access hypothesis to be correct and finding that all variants of the UPP to be incorrect, for Chinese, would contradict modular approaches to reading. Decisive support for the direct access hypothseis would stand as strong evidence against modularity in general, as was suggested earlier. This approach to the discussion may turn out to be unsatisfactory because research findings often place different emphases and weights on the factor of phonological activation, qualifying claims that at first seemed to represent a clear counterposition. But for now, it serves us as a way of getting one view of the bigger picture.

Beginning with the direct access hypothesis, a fundamental difference between Chinese and even the "deepest" alphabet regarding the reliability of phonological information in the orthography poses, by itself, the question of a phonology by-pass. On this point, there should be a relatively broad agreement among supporters of all positions in the discussion (for a possible dissenting view, see DeFrancis, 1989). It has been estimated that only about 23% of semantic-phonetic compounds that Chinese-speaking children are taught during initial literacy instruction are fully regular (42% are semiregular), semantic-phonetic compounds themselves counting for less than 75% of the characters that primary school age children typically learn in school (Shu *et al.*, 2002).[4] In addition, a significant number

Chinese semantic-phonographs

of integrated characters, corresponding to free morphemes, and semantic radicals of compound characters, give the reader a graphically distinctive categorical cue to meaning, some of them containing relatively transparent iconic features (e.g., the adpositions: 下 [below], 上 [above], 中 [middle/inside]). The shared semantic radical, 口 [mouth], in 吟 [chant], 吃 [eat], 吐 [vomit], and 可口 [palatable], provides the reader with semantic information, directly. The first two characters in the phonetic rendering of Coca-Cola, 可口可樂 [ke^3-kou^3-ke^3-le^4], correspond, opportunely, to "palatable." Parenthetically, second language learners of Chinese have been know to make use of these visible and explicit links to meaning in the orthography (when they can) to help bootstrap themselves into a rudimentary interlanguage grammar (De Courcy, 2002, pp. 108–113, 126–127).

Chen (1996) summarizes evidence that favors direct access — In studies of word recognition, the processing of characters and alphabetic words differs cognitively in important ways. In naming aloud and lexical decision tasks, strategies appear to differ between Chinese characters and alphabetic words. While naming is normally faster than lexical decision, and the word frequency effect is greater for lexical decision, in reading alphabetic words, the opposite result is obtained with Chinese characters — lexical decision is usually faster and frequency effects are greater in the naming task. In an experiment that required Chinese/English bilinguals and English monolinguals to identify mathematical logographs and corresponding words, logographs and characters were named equally fast by bilinguals, while word-naming was faster for the alphabetic-reading monolinguals. Interestingly, when the bilinguals attempted the task in their L2 (English), performance resembled that of the native-speaker monolinguals. Together with findings that show pre-lexical phonological activation to be weaker in Chinese than in English, and other evidence indicating a lack of homophonic effects in semantic categorization, an important contrast between alphabetic and non-alphabetic processing appears to have been demonstrated (Chen, 1996, pp. 51–56). This contrast appears to suggest that the O $\rightarrow$ S route predominates.

For some versions of the direct access hypothesis, what is called into question is not that phonological structures are automatically activated in silent reading. Even an early activation of phonology in Chinese word identification might be possible. Rather, the claim would be that mediation of phonology does not strongly constrain access to meaning. For example, studies have shown significant effects of phonology for only a minority of Chinese characters in which the pronunciation of the compound character is the same as the pronunciation of its phonetic component (Zhou and Marslen-Wilson, 1999). According to this view, the O $\rightarrow$ P $\rightarrow$ S (mediated) route: "cannot be the predominant or default mechanism for linking orthographic form to lexical semantic representation. There is little doubt that phonology is activated early and obligatorily in reading Chinese characters… [and] that under specific circumstances phonological factors can drive semantic activation for skilled readers. It is, however, much more plausible to view phonological and orthographic factors as functioning in an interactive framework… (p. 598)."

Zhou and Marslen-Wilson's position appears to be close to the two-pathway parallel-access view. According to Xu *et al.* (1999), a model in which orthography accesses phonological and semantic codes in parallel has the virtue of not assuming different processing mechanisms for Chinese and alphabetic systems. Findings that indicate a divergence between word reading processes in the two systems can be explained simply by the relative speed of the route in which phonology is more easily activated by an alphabet versus the route to meaning in Chinese. In morphosyllabic Chinese, then, the O → P → S route would end up being slower than the direct O → S pathway. Here again, the same phonology-semantics connections of speech comprehension come on-line automatically, and are not by-passed, strictly speaking. An interactive network for literacy would consist of three "nodes," one for orthography, one for phonology, and one for semantics. During reading, all three would be in continuous interaction (p. 853).

4.4.2 Lexical entries in a mental lexicon

As we can now well appreciate, adjudicating among the various hypotheses regarding the role of phonology in Chinese reading will depend on what come to be considered as the central distinguishing claims of each competing hypothesis. However, which claims are in competition is not entirely obvious either; see Guo *et al.* (2005), Tsai *et al.* (2004), Tzeng *et al.* (1995), and Zhou and Marslen-Wilson (2000) for discussion and relevant research findings. At this point, perhaps, only the confrontation between the strongest version of direct access (Taft and van Graan, 1998) and models roughly convergent with the UPP will allow for a first approximation of a definitive test. This being a good place to begin, Packard (2000) seems to dispense with the notion of "routes" (O → S, O → P → S), suggesting rather an alternative based on a model of the mental lexicon with each lexical entry composed of sub-structures. The lexical entry is a "relation" among phonology, syntactic form class and subcategory, morphology, semantics, etc., interfaced with an orthographic representation for literate speakers. In the end, these may not be the actual sub-structures; but the basic idea would be the same for explaining how Chinese characters activate phonology and meaning. From a different vantage point, that of the neuroscience of reading, Dehaene (2009) presents findings that are consistent with Packard's model.

A brief overview of Packard's proposal on how characters access the mental lexicon will help frame our concluding assessment of the Universal Phonological Principle. The proposal assumes that Chinese orthography is completely dependent upon the natural speech lexicon. The linguistic subsystems that are accessed in reading are the same ones that all speakers of the language possess, including non-literates. It would be less plausible that literacy development recreates a parallel and duplicate competence for processing written language. What literate speakers of Chinese are typically able to count on is a more advanced explicit awareness of morphemes and words that might help them with certain analytic tasks and in reading itself, especially in the case of difficult texts. But, the development of this metalinguistic knowledge remains separate from, and leaves intact, the core components of native-speaker linguistic competence, including all interface modules. For example, in bilinguals, script differences (e.g., in English-Japanese bilinguals) apparently do not block cross-language influences that are typically expected in "same-script" bilinguals (English-Spanish) (Hoshino and Kroll, 2008).

Recall the distinction made by Liberman (1999) in Section 4.2 between primary linguistic knowledge and secondary, literacy-related, meta-level knowledge. Following this logic, the grammatical subsystems of the lexical entry are tightly interlinked, input of a linguistic form (orthographic in this case) triggering the "retrieval" of its core linguistic sub-structures, rapidly and automatically in skilled reading. In speech perception, access is triggered by sound, which can only activate the sub-structures of the lexical entry by way of phonology. In reading, on the other hand, lexical entries could be activated by triggering another sub-structure "first"; and as Packard (2000) pointed out, in Chinese this might even be more likely under certain word identification task conditions. Here again, we have an indication that modular approaches (such as those of Liberman and Packard) lend support to the UPP, and are not consistent with strong versions of direct access (i.e., phonology by-pass).

Consistent with this view, studies of dyslexia, dysgraphia and aphasia have shown that the lexical sub-structures and the corresponding linguistic subsystems and interfaces with which they are linked can suffer selective impairment. In the case of dyslexia, different networks of processing mechanism can be affected yielding a diverse array of impairments, not a single undifferentiated category of reading impairment (Chung *et al.*, 2008). And as would be expected, different patterns of disability are associated with alphabetic and non-alphabetic dyslexic reading (Ho *et al.*, 2004). Studies have revealed opposite and complementary patterns of selective impairment — fluent speech accompanied by disabled oral reading (a defective orthography-phonology link) and disrupted access to meaning in speech with spared oral reading (suggesting an intact orthography-phonology pathway and a disrupted access to semantics) (Bi *et al.*, 2007; Weekes *et al.*, 2005). With phonology and semantics being dissociable, nothing in principle then should exclude the possibility of an initial activation of either one under experimental conditions of single character or single word identification.

In unimpaired readers, however, the interfaces among the linguistic subcomponents of the lexical entry must be dedicated, fast and obligatory in their activation, revealing properties of highly encapsulated modular processing. Their deployment is mandatory. These inter-connections within the natural lexical entry have evolved as part of the specialized language faculty and would be highly resistant to being reconfigured in any fundamental way. Crucially, the connection to orthography (established through learning and extended practice) is not predetermined in this way. Therefore, a "direct" initial access to a word's meaning, demonstrable in experimental tasks, cannot be effected independently of the phonological structures of spoken language in the sense of by-passing them; in this sense, "recoding" is a "virtual reflex" (Packard, 2000, pp. 304–309). In actual reading of continuous text, if any cognitive domain is susceptible to disengagement it would be a higher-order level of conceptual structure related to interpretation and sentence/text comprehension, a phenomenon that metacognitively aware readers are quite familiar with (the reverse, not coincidentally, of the well-known tip-of-the-tongue state). Under normal receptive language processing, given a fragmentary structure in a particular format, the interface modules work rapidly to construct a fully specified structure (Jackendoff, 2002, p. 198), presumably in word identification just as in syntax. The lexicon as a whole, according to this view, is a substantive part of the language processor's network of interface components:

> *A word, by virtue of having features in each of the components of grammar, serves as part of the linkage between the multiple structures... The proper way to regard [the lexical item] is as a small-scale three way interface rule. It lists a small chunk of phonology, a small chunk of syntax, and a small chunk of semantics, and it shows how to line these chunks up when they appear in parallel phonological, syntactic, and conceptual structures (p. 131).*

4.4.3 Characters and words in context

One could perhaps question experimental methods that are restricted to studying individual word (and non-word) identification on the grounds that they lack ecological validity (Goodman, 2005). However, this would be an unfair criticism that confounds important methodological considerations of data collection, and the complementary but different requirements of reliability and interpretation (validity). For example, if consistent results demonstrate significant differences between the processing of individual words in Chinese and a given alphabetic orthography, the results stand as reported, and invite theoretically grounded explanation, speculation, and methodological critique. Competing accounts of the data inform subsequent experimental and non-experimental lines of inquiry; and if one chooses to dismiss a given method of inquiry, it is necessary to explain why it cannot yield *any* interpretable finding, under any circumstance.

At the same time, studies of reading that require subjects to decode connected text should complement single-character/word-in-isolation studies in all respects. Lin and Akamatsu (1997) appeared to suggest this approach in their observations of the research on eye movement patterns and other aspects of reading continuous text; see Frenck-Mestre (2005) for related discussion. As expected, comparative eye movement studies reveal noteworthy differences between Chinese and English. In reading Chinese, in actual connected text, phonological representations are activated and play an important role, even if we assume, for argument's sake, that activation is "post-lexical." In this case, it is proposed, we should assume that the same processing mechanisms are brought on-line in Chinese and English. What appears to follow is the conclusion that text processing in all languages and across all writing systems cannot by-pass phonological recoding for the purpose of syntactic and semantic integration in linguistic working memory. However, this conclusion should not be taken as contradicting the evidence from numerous studies "that skilled readers of different orthographies [adapt] their processing strategies to meet the different cognitive demands posed by different orthographies" (Lin and Akamatsu, 1997, p. 378).

In their study of the development of early reading ability comparing performance in the Taiwanese Mandarin alphabet, *zhuyin fuhao*, and morphosyllabic Chinese, Hu and Catts (1998) comment on the role of phonological working memory. In particular, the issue comes up in decoding less familiar words in context. Since Chinese orthography does not indicate word boundaries, phonological patterns need to be maintained in working memory until word boundaries are identified. Less skilled beginning readers, it has been proposed, have difficulty in segmenting effectively between juxtaposed characters, distinguishing in on-line processing of text between free and bound characters and parsing grammatical constituents correctly that contain two-character and multi-character compound words. In this way, phonology is activated and plays an important role in decoding.

Independently of the mixed results from single-character/word-in-isolation studies on whether phonology is "prelexical" or "postlexical," in the reading of connected text, what is the effect of an ongoing and overriding engagement of phonological working memory? If the above observations are correct, can we even plausibly pose the possibility of a direct access to meaning without phonological mediation in word identification in *text processing*? These two questions are indirectly suggested in the discussion of methodological problems in single-character/word-in-isolation studies. Chen (1996) contrasts two kinds of approach — (1) tasks are presented to the subject in which a character's name is required or can be helpful, and (2) situations in which the meaning of a character is to be consulted for a correct response with phonological information unnecessary, as in the semantic-decision task. In (2), if no effect of phonological interference is in evidence then one explanation is that phonological activation does not occur routinely or necessarily as a part of character recognition (Chen, 1996, p. 53). But, in reference specifically to the second scenario, if in context the phonological component of linguistic working memory comes on-line mandatorily (even if access to phonology on the first character of a text passage could be "post-lexical") direct, unmediated, access to meaning may be impossible. Entirely speculative, this possibility may be worth exploring in future investigations. But again, in relation to (2), if significant differences between Chinese and English, for example, continue to be evidenced, this finding requires further serious discussion, even if it turns out that "no effect of phonological interference" is only found in single-character/word-in-isolation tasks.

4.4.4 Phonology as a constituent of word identification

The Universal Phonological Principle was characterized as a "constituency hypothesis" by Guo *et al.* (2005). A more complete summary of how the UPP should or might apply to Chinese now merits our attention. Perfetti (2003) began by pointing out the incomplete and thus misleading conception of the character as morphemic. Rather, "morphosyllabic" better captures its orthographic-linguistic properties: "corresponding not to an abstract formless piece of meaning, but usually to a spoken Chinese syllable that is also a morpheme" (p. 7). On this point, a morphosyllabic writing system is not entirely exceptional; it also realizes a mapping between an orthography and the linguistic patterns of language, as do all modern orthographies. Far from a quibble about terminology, this assumption about how a "true writing system" functions (DeFrancis, 1996) points us toward an important ongoing discussion in cognitive science — assuming that the semantic domains of conceptual structure (Jackendoff's term, 2002), are autonomous from the linguistic structures (morphology, syntax, phonology), how do meaning and language, now defined narrowly, interface in language use (such as in reading)? The more fundamental debate revolves around the meaning-linguistic structure differentiation and the distinction between knowledge of language and language use (Newmeyer, 2003), both of which have also been widely challenged.

Assuming for now that in silent reading the activation of phonology occurs in both alphabetic and non-alphabetic systems, it would be incorrect to claim no difference in the execution of the decoding processing mechanism. As we could see from the brief review of the research evidence in the previous section, on this point there seems to be wide agreement. As Perfetti describes it, an alphabetic system allows activation to occur sublexically based on letter recognition, building up rapidly; word identification does not have to wait for complete processing of all lower-level units. In silent reading of Chinese, in contrast, activation of phonology awaits a threshold-level of character recognition (see Note 4). Summing up, we can consider the following contrast:

- alphabetic — cascade style,
- morphosyllabic — threshold style.

Thus, the basic idea of phonology being a constituent of word identification is that the moment of orthographic recognition is the moment of access to phonology, constituting together with the lexical entry's semantic features a "three-constituent word identity" (Perfetti, 1999, p. 177). This would stand in contrast to phonology as a by-product of identification, "post-lexically." In English, the graphemes that trigger phonological processing correspond to phonemes; in Chinese they correspond to spoken syllables that happen also to be morphemes (Perfetti and Liu, 2005, p. 195).

The intention in all of the preceding discussion is not to argue that the Universal Phonological Principle has already garnered decisive support as the best theory for Chinese literacy (if we recall, this being the most demanding test), but rather that it is broadly compatible with modular approaches to the study of language ability. If it turned out to be substantively correct, then this would favor, according to the argument, at least some versions of the modularity thesis. Another way to appreciate the argument might be to ask: why, typically, do strong top-down holistic theories of reading tend to favor models in which semantic/pragmatic context and background knowledge penetrate decoding extensively; and why do they tend to minimize the importance of bottom-up mechanisms, in regard to the development of phonological/orthographic skills in particular? Also strongly anti-modular, they appear to coalesce around a kind of "direct access" model, implying a direct interface (or degrees of "directness" depending on how strongly holistic one's position is) between orthography and semantics. On the other hand, modular models of reading (antithetical to holism) that are also "subskill-oriented," pedagogically, appear to be strongly bottom-up. This is because, following the assumptions of the modularity approach, certain components of language processing in reading are engaged in a mandatory way, not subject to by-pass or deflection by "central" top-down influences.

A pivotal concept in understanding these differences is that of *mental representation*, that actual neurophysiological structures serve competencies and processors. What does it mean when we refer to cognitive components of reading, for example, in discussing the research on feedback influences (from higher levels) on lower-level representations? How is it that in some cases the "feedback loops" are effective, in some cases less so, and in others ineffective because feedforward (relatively encapsulated) processes predominate (Perfetti, 1999, p. 171)? Along with the conception of the lexicon as a mental representation of a special kind (a part of the domain of interfaces), are these components intrinsic and constitutive of a "permanent" language faculty, or should they be considered more like emergent patterns of activation (not "permanent")? The following sections on disability and on developmental aspects of Chinese literacy might provide another point of view on the role of phonology in reading.

4.5 Advances in the study of impaired literacy development

Performance on second language literacy tasks puts a strain on the internal workings of the components of reading ability. This extra challenge for the L2 reader becomes a research opportunity, for helping us better understand how these components interact, because the effect of the difficulties that L2 learners experience is not uniform across all the components. A disorder related to one or another aspect of reading ability not only puts additional pressure on overall performance but often does this in a special way. Because components and sub-components can be selectively impaired, a sharply uneven development and performance can be studied, revealing how the system as a whole may be organized along modular lines (or maybe not), according to Coltheart (2005). In their review of the research on reading disability, Catts and Hogan (2003) take a similar approach. This internal variability and irregularity is typically different in both degree and kind from the uneven development evident in (unimpaired) L2 reading. Consistent with the componential model of reading disability outlined by these authors, Share and Leikin (2004) found evidence from a large scale longitudinal study (beginning of kindergarten to the end of Grade 1) for a dissociation between deficits that affect higher-order text comprehension and deficits that affect the "characteristically modular word recognition processes."

As was suggested in the previous chapter, in comparison to other kinds of language disorder, it is more apparent that *disorders of literacy learning*, of the different sub-types, might involve the participation of different cognitive structures:

- linguistic and non-linguistic,
- domain-specific and domain-general,
- competence structures and processing/interface components.

For example, reading disability may turn out to be caused by impairment to structures that are strictly non-linguistic, with no specific competence module (e.g., phonology) having been degraded. An example would be a sub-type of dyslexia in which defective domain-general information processing structures affect efficient written language decoding, and in which all linguistic knowledge components have been spared (manifested in normal speech comprehension and production). In addition, unlike the non-learned, primary, language abilities associated with speech/sign, reading and writing are complex abilities that are secondary, learned, non-spontaneous developmentally, and attained non-universally (review this distinction, covered in Section 4.2). And again, bilingualism and exceptionality provide us with an additional window on the question of a componential architecture of language proficiency in general (now made even more complex than before). At the same time, research from normal and unimpaired bilingual literacy learning (Genesee *et al.*, 2005) should not contradict the findings from atypical literacy learning, and vice versa.

For the system that is formed in the development of literacy ability, and for the peculiar patterns of specific breakdown, where components are differentially disrupted and spared, researchers have proposed blueprints that attempt to depict it. Developed from their work on impairments in Chinese reading and writing, Law *et al.* (2005) and Weekes *et al.* (2006) sketch out a basic model that applies to all languages and writing systems. The model includes components of — semantic structure, phonological representation, and orthographic representation. For alphabetic writing systems, Coltheart (2005) adds what would be the missing piece — a mechanism for assembling phonology from orthographic input. Designed for literacy in one language, all three can easily be adapted for bilingual and biscriptual literates. For example, a defect in the phonology-from-orthography-rule-application component (sometimes called the "non-lexical route") disables decoding of unfamiliar words (and non-words in assessment). Surface dyslexia, on the other hand, associated with defective orthographic representations and a spared phoneme-grapheme rule component results in over-regularization. More unusual cases of selective impairment provide evidence for direct pathways that at first glance seem counter-intuitive (and would seem to be impossible under the assumption of strong versions of a holistic and integrative system) — for example, a by-pass of (defective) semantic structure and/or its pathways in the implementation of a direct phonology-orthography pathway. This would result in impaired word comprehension (e.g., auditory word-picture matching) but preserved oral reading of words (Weekes *et al.*, 2006; Law *et al.*, 2005). Its attestation in morphosyllabic Chinese is even more compelling, being easier to imagine, at least, with alphabetic writing systems.

Here, the unique features of Chinese writing might shed light on a universal design feature of the mental lexicon and its associated grammatical structures. Orthography calls up lexical entries during reading, the semantic or phonological subcomponent being activated "simultaneously" or "in succession." As Weekes *et al.* (2006) describe, in normal reading, errors resulting from incomplete processing typically are not observed because all subcomponents remain on-line, in close interface: "input from the non-semantic pathway [from phonology] can inhibit semantically related (although incorrect) reading and writing responses, and input from the lexical semantic pathway inhibits the production of LARC [legitimate alternative readings of components] errors" (p. 601). In contrast, when this corrective interaction is subverted in impaired reading, the subcomponent structures are more easily observed.

Thus, under the special circumstances of bilingual dyslexia, a current line of investigation has attempted to describe and explain how impairments are expressed differentially between the two languages and their orthographies. The interesting question here would be if underlying deficits result in disabilities in the manner of true double dissociations or do they follow the same pattern, "in the same direction" so to speak. For example, do shallow and highly transparent orthographies, as a rule, present less severe processing difficulties? A related problem is that of understanding which deficits are associated with language- or script-specific disorders and which affect both sets of systems more or less equally. One difficult interaction to account for in all these studies is that between degree of transparency (a script-related factor), and level of second language attainment (a linguistic factor) (Oren and Breznitz, 2005). For example, Gupta and Jamal (2007) found a relative disadvantage for child dyslexics in the less transparent English, in comparison to Hindi, due to a misapplication of decoding strategy, a failure to recognize the difference in orthographic depth between the two scripts. This finding appears to be consistent with the currently leading "orthographic consistency" hypothesis — that in relatively opaque systems, such as in English writing, the mastery of grapheme-phoneme recoding skills and phonemic awareness proceeds more slowly, a factor that is exacerbated in dyslexia (Goswami, 2002). On this point, see an interesting commentary by Raman and Weekes (2005) and their report on the case of an acquired dyslexia "in both languages" in an English-Turkish bilingual (the latter having a completely transparent orthography).

Of course, the question that is begged in relation to the factor of orthographic consistency is how it figures in the incidence of dyslexia/dysgraphia in the complex and hybrid non-alphabetic writing systems, an area of research that has seen formidable advances in recent years. Among the most suggestive and intriguing are two reports of "bilingualism with monolingual dyslexia," i.e., bilingual individuals with impaired literacy in only one of their languages. These studies differ from most other investigations of bilingual literacy disorder in two respects:

1. The differences between writing systems are contrasting to a greater degree — Chinese-English in one case, *kanji/kana*-English in the second.[5]
2. Assessment evidence indicates one completely spared system in each case, and not "in the same direction." In the former case (Chinese-English), English is spared, in the latter, kanji/kana is spared (Ho and Kong, 2005; Wydell and Kondo, 2003).

As was suggested at the beginning of this section, how dyslexia is manifested in bilingual reading presents researchers with two dimensions of asymmetry that interact: (1) imbalances in L2 development, and (2) imbalances related specifically to reading impairment. Consistent with the Language Threshold Hypothesis (that we reviewed earlier; also see Note #3 in this chapter), even among highly skilled bilinguals, decoding texts in L2 has been shown to be less efficient, to one degree or another. With this L1-L2 processing difference in mind, Oren and Breznitz (2005) studied dyslexic and unimpaired adult bilinguals (Hebrew L1, English L2). Their findings lend support to a "Central Deficit Hypothesis," a universal basis for dyslexia. As Pugh *et al.* (2005, p. 27) also conclude from their review of the literature: "Given the evidence for common circuits in different written languages, we might expect language-invariant neurobiological signatures to be associated with reading disability as well." At the same time, disabled bilingual readers "were more differentially affected by language" (Oren and Breznitz, 2005, p. 147), i.e., they were affected to a greater degree by level of L2 mastery, consistent also with the LTH, we might venture to add. A related but separate question is how dyslexia might be manifested across writing systems (Miles, 2000); it is on this point that we will conclude this section.

Again, the recent upsurge in research on Chinese literacy presents us with some of the most interesting case studies. This most summary overview of a rapidly growing sub-field in reading disability studies serves to alert us to the decisive advances in our understanding of literacy learning in general that are pending in the near future. Studies of dyslexia in Chinese, for one, have lent support to the idea that disabled reading ability is not of a single type, that the affected population is highly heterogeneous. Placing the emphasis more on investigating aspects of processing, as opposed to phonological competence, for example, we might see that in a complex literacy ability a number of different combinations of processing mechanism might suffer impairment, not just phonological processing. So perhaps because of the special demands placed on learning non-alphabetic systems, we might see a different array of impairments than in the case of dyslexic alphabetic literacy: for example, a higher incidence of what are called rapid naming and orthographic deficits (Ho *et al.*, 2004). On the other hand, since the impaired ability of interest is specific to written language, it may be difficult, in the end, to distinguish between "orthographic" deficits and literacy-related "phonological processing" deficits.

Implicit in the study of dyslexia is the recognition of a basic dissociation, one by the way that holist theories of literacy often have difficulty recognizing — between lower-level word-recognition/decoding and higher-order text comprehension processes. Then within the domain of the former (decoding), the different patterns of breakdown, revealing which skill components are spared in each type of breakdown, help us to model the intact ability of word recognition in a comprehensive way. Recent findings from the assessment of brain-damaged patients have permitted us to do just that. Descriptions provide critical data that may eventually lead to resolving some of the difficult research questions that were posed earlier, for example, whether in Chinese (or any other writing system) phonology is, or can be, by-passed in word identification.

Yin and Weekes (2003) summarize the relevant research on aphasia and dyslexia. Accepting, for argument's sake, that in normal Chinese reading decoding is always mediated by semantics, is it possible that characters can also be processed ("read") via a non-semantic pathway? The more typical cases of dyslexia accompanied by fluent speech indicate defects specific to the link between orthography and phonology, with the semantics-phonology pathway spared. On the other hand, pathways that support picture naming and oral reading, according to the authors, are dissociable. Further evidence of a double dissociation from the study of patients showing the pattern of spared oral reading accompanied by disrupted access to the meaning of words would strongly indicate that the components of word identification are in fact functionally independent. The presentation of cases, then, in which patients manifest severe semantic deficits (unable to name pictures) with normal character reading (of words that represent the same pictured objects) stand as compelling evidence for the deployment of a non-semantic pathway. Here we would have evidence for an interface linking orthography directly to phonology (Yin and Weekes, 2003).

Studies by Law and associates, replicating these findings, support a three-way model of the Chinese mental lexicon (Law *et al.*, 2005, Figure 1), three independent components, closely linked in normal reading, with bi-directional interfaces: (1) semantic representations, (2) phonological units and (3) orthographic units. The case study of YKM that the authors report on clearly shows how these components and/or interfaces can be disrupted:

- defective spoken word-picture matching, written word-picture matching and oral naming, all in contrast to
- completely intact single word recognition in reading.

Selective impairment, anomia without dyslexia and vice versa, is compatible with an "architecture of the cognitive system" for word recognition in which semantic structures are autonomous and interconnected (Law and Or, 2001; Law *et al.*, 2005). The overall idea is that, in the mental lexicon, knowledge is stored in actual cognitive structures, and interface components effect the linkages that result in skilled performance. Impaired performance results if one or more of these structures or interfaces is disabled. Certainly, reading words via a non-semantic pathway is easier to conceive of in alphabetic literacy, an interesting decoding phenomenon commonly reported among unimpaired readers. Its discovery in Chinese literacy is more difficult to explain, and at the same time pertinent to the discussion of universal principles related to the role of phonology in reading.

One final observation needs to be made regarding the different models of reading that resort to the concept of modularity, sometimes implicitly. There is a need for a point-by-point concordance and confrontation of the features of each of the different models. Then the claims that they make need to be reexamined based on this sorting out, because presently there is more divergence in conceptions and proposals than there should be. One place to start would be to critically reflect on which parts of Coltheart's (2005) Dual-route model share a common ground with other explicitly modular approaches (those of Stanovich, Shatil, Leikin, Share, and others), and then do a careful accounting of where they differ. At the same time, we could evaluate how all of the above might be consistent with proposals like the Universal Phonological Principle and the Universal Writing Systems Constraint, that are compatible with modularity in reading (as it has been argued in this chapter). It may be in reconciling findings from the work on reading disorders in particular where this kind of evaluation of theoretical models is most productive. This is the distinct impression one gets from the study of research reports from this line of work.

So it appears that a special opportunity presents itself in the cross-writing system studies on literacy disorder that involve the alphabetic/non-alphabetic contrast. Of particular interest in future investigations will be the important issues of:

- the relative weight of phonological deficit versus non-linguistic processing impairment;

- what processing mechanisms are actually deployed in decoding via an intact non-semantic pathway (by-passing semantics);
- similarly, in other kinds of selective impairment, which components and interfaces are activated, and how do dyslexic readers implement these kinds of pathway;
- the difference in error pattern between regular and irregular characters; and
- the contrasting performance in tasks of reading and writing (Chan *et al.*, 2006; Ho *et al.*, 2006; Law, 2004; Law *et al.*, 2006; Lee *et al.*, 2006).

4.6 Literacy-related skills and awareness — A proposal for reconciling divergent findings

To wrap up this chapter on bilingual reading we turn our attention to a practical issue — that of phonological *skills* (and explicit knowledge about phonology) in *learning* how to read. One could accept the phonology-as-constituent-of-word-identification hypothesis (the UPP), and be neutral regarding the role that phonological awareness plays in actual literacy learning. The componential approach that we have been considering as an overall analytic framework might help to explain why. To start with, the difference between the two questions is mainly one between a representation problem and a learnability problem. The distinction between implicit competence and explicit knowledge/metalinguistic awareness (question 1 on the list of the four modularity-related research questions from Section 4.2) also allows us to separate the two issues — meta-level abilities associated with phonology are not relevant, or not very much, in evaluating the claims of the UPP. Evidence either for or against the UPP can be drawn from the study of the activation of the encapsulated phonological module and performance on tasks in relatively "closed" subsystems. In contrast, the study of the role of phonological awareness in literacy learning focuses on the development of metalinguistic knowledge in a domain that is "open" and subject to deliberate reflection. Fortunately, unlike the contention among the different claims regarding phonological mediation in word identification, the lines are drawn much more clearly on the issue of how explicit knowledge develops. We can outline them concisely as follows.

There are different viewpoints on the importance of phonological awareness skills in literacy learning. But there is one result around which some measure of agreement exists. It appears that learners decompose compound characters, and that they make use of and are sensitive to different degrees of partial information found in the phonetic component. There may be a stage in reading development in which an analytic stance toward the phonetic component of compound characters facilitates children's mastery of the orthography (Shu, 2003; Tzeng, 2002). It has also been suggested that Chinese dyslexic readers have difficulty applying phonological processing strategies, and that direct teaching of script-sound regularities improves reading performance in these cases (Ho and

Ma, 1999). All of this might be true even if it turns out that phonological awareness and phonological processing skills, overall, play a role in Chinese literacy that is significantly different from that in alphabetic systems (Ko and Tzeng, 2000). Morphological awareness, for example, might play a much more prominent role in literacy learning (Li *et al.*, 2002; Shu *et al.*, 2006).

One interpretation of this finding is that the development of phonological awareness gets its boost mainly from literacy learning itself, or that there is a complex reciprocal relationship *subsequent* to initial experience with literacy and literacy-related language use in general. This argument has been well developed in the research literature on alphabetic literacy learning over the years; see Castles and Coltheart (2004) and Ziegler and Goswami (2005) for a comprehensive review. Long ago, Perfetti (1992) observed that: "Downgrading phonological awareness from causal status to reciprocal status does not diminish its importance for reading. Indeed, it allows it to be seen as a central component of reading instead of as a prerequisite" (p. 166).

Among researchers who question the hypothesis that phonological awareness, *per se*, predicts successful literacy learning, we might be able to discern two approaches: (1) that the hypothesis should be disfavored in general, and (2) that it can be discarded in the case of non-alphabetic literacy learning. In regard to Chinese, we could assume for now that the consideration of the factor of phonological awareness is restricted to the *syllable* level, not to phonemic awareness; for discussion and relevant findings, see Tong *et al.* (2011) and the Glossary entry for *phonological awareness*. Syllables correspond closely to morphemes, and morphological awareness, and "radical awareness," have been shown to strongly favor early development of reading ability (Shen and Ke, 2007; Wu *et al.*, 2009). For now, we will set aside the first approach and consider the possibility that in Chinese the relationship between reading development and phonological awareness is secondary or even marginal. This was the conclusion of Tan *et al.* (2005) in a study that attempted to analyze the "component skills" that are relevant to the complex ability of character recognition. Recalling that children must grapple with "system-level" complications (both linguistic and orthographic) in Chinese that make mapping between characters and linguistic and meaning structures significantly more complex than in any alphabetic system, the first assumption might be that the learning task is unlikely to be supported by phonological awareness in a major way. The authors propose that the formation of an "integrated reading circuit that links orthography, meaning and pronunciation" (Tan *et al.*, 2005, p. 8781) occurs at the visual-orthographic level facilitating children's awareness of the character's internal structure. This "orthographic awareness" appears to depend on the establishment of long-term motor memories of characters through extensive practice in copying and writing. Naming speed and measures of accuracy in copying characters were found to be strongly related to reading ability; the relationship with measures of phonological awareness (oddity test and syllable deletion) was minor. Addressing the developmental/learning issue, these findings confirm the results of a number of other studies, suggesting an important difference on this point between alphabetic and non-alphabetic literacy development (Taylor, 2002).

A number of studies make a strong case for an alternative view. Starting from the idea that children might implicitly "analyze" patterns in the internal structure of characters and make use of both the phonetic in fully regular compounds and partial information elsewhere, researchers have proposed a greater role for awareness of phonology (at the syllable-level, presumably). Evidence from studies of the regularity effect (more accuracy in reading regular characters), analysis of reading errors (overgeneralization) and pseudo-character naming (positively correlated with reading achievement) suggests the development of a "phonetic principle." This aspect of phonological awareness helps children store compound characters more systematically and facilitates the learning of new characters (Chen *et al.*, 2003), for example, by using an "analogy strategy," decoding unfamiliar characters with recourse to knowledge of the same phonetic of a familiar character (He *et al.*, 2005).

While findings on the relationship between phonological processing, phonological awareness and Chinese reading remain mixed, the number of studies that have found a positive correlation, contrary to Tan *et al.* (2005), for example, is noteworthy and future work in this important area of literacy learning will need to reconcile the differences. Memory tasks involving sets of nonwords, sound categorization (which word out of a group is different) (Hu and Catts, 1998) and syllable deletion (Chow *et al.*, 2005; McBride-Chang and Ho, 2000) have been shown to be significant predictors of reading ability in young children. Consistent with other biliteracy studies, the Chow *et al.* study found that performance on syllable detection in L1 (Cantonese) also predicted L2 reading (in English). Siok and Fletcher (2001) found that onset-rime awareness was positively related to reading ability at the higher grades (visual skills at the lower grades), but phonemic awareness, as we might predict, was not. As was noted earlier, there is a broad recognition of the reciprocity between literacy learning and phonological awareness. However, as a component of early reading development (even if it cannot be shown to be a prerequisite) the participation of phonological awareness and the importance of phonological processing are not minor or secondary for the above mentioned researchers who appear to have drawn different conclusions than the ones in the Tan *et al.* (2005) study. In other words, the importance of phonological awareness and phonological processing is not specific to alphabetic literacy learning (Chan and Siegel, 2001). Thus, at this point in the discussion of disparate findings, the most promising first step toward reconciling the different positions might be to systematically confront the opposing interpretations, starting with: (1) the importance of the role of phonological awareness (a learnability problem) among investigators who all assume (2) one version or another of the Universal Phonological Principle (mainly a representation problem).

We will be able to revisit in the next chapter a number of the themes that were important in this chapter. Also about literacy learning, the focus will now shift to writing ability. The comparison between alphabetic and morphosyllabic systems will come up again in a new proposal for future research.

Notes

1. Strong views of modularity tend to disfavor extensive inter-modular or cross-domain interaction (Fodor, 1998). Weaker versions allow for a conception of modules (knowledge structures and processing mechanisms) as "encapsulated" to a lesser extent (Francis, 2008; Marcus, 2006), and for cognitive components to show degrees of "domain-specificity" or "domain-generality." Thus for the latter, the degree of interactivity among domains is more of an open question, yet to be determined by empirical research. What weaker versions would reject is that interactivity is unconstrained and that mental architecture is entirely homogenous and holistically structured, the key distinction then being between interaction (among components/modules) and non-componential integration (no domain-specific cognitive structures). Jackendoff (2002) discusses at length the different versions of modularity in regard to these dimensions.
2. "Whole language" (also known as "literature-based" or "constructivist") approaches to literacy begin with the assumption that learning to read, overall, is a "process of natural acquisition" that is also strongly "top-down" (Hudelson, 1994, p. 132). Goodman (1997) applies this approach to reading assessment, and Krashen (2002) to a critique of "skill-building" instruction. A critical assessment by Cummins et al. (2007) of proposals for systematic phonics instruction coincides in general terms with this constructivist orientation toward literacy teaching. See Archer and Bryant (2001), Birch (2002), Dehaene (2009), Ehri (2005), Proctor *et al.* (2005) and Singleton (2005) for counter arguments supporting a more interactive model with a more prominent role assigned to bottom-up processes (applied, for example, in direct teaching of word-identification skills).
3. The Language Threshold Hypothesis (LTH) and the "dual-task of L2 literacy" concept are at odds with proposals that minimize the factor of linguistic knowledge in learning how to read in a second language. Poorly designed studies aside, it seems that much of the counter-evidence to the LTH is based on evaluations of L2 reading ability in which subjects' L2 grammatical competence has already advanced beyond the required threshold for the specific text material or assessment task under consideration. In many studies, subjects' level of L2 grammatical competence is simply left unspecified. More controlled studies, in the coming years, should begin to converge on what has been taken as a working assumption by most researchers in the field. That even though we should recognize the effects of a number of interacting external social factors, there exists for pre-literate monolingual L1-speaking child learners, in addition to pre-literate L2-beginners, a Fundamental L1-L2 Literacy Difference, a position that we have argued in favor of from our work on second language and bilingual literacy in Central and Northern Mexico (Francis and Paciotto, 2004; Francis and Navarrete Gómez, 2009; Hamel, 2010; Hamel and Francis, 2006). See the section on "Language of instruction" (D. Francis *et al.*, 2006), in the Report of the National Literacy Panel on Language-Minority Children and Youth and related sections that are consistent with the Language Threshold Hypothesis and the Fundamental L1–L2 Literacy Difference, and Guglielmi (2008) and Restrepo and Gray (2007) for findings that support the facilitative effect of L1 literacy-related proficiency on L2 literacy attainment.

4. Compound characters are composed of two subcomponents (or radicals), each one typically an independent integrated character by itself. Usually they consist of a semantic radical, that often provides a categorical clue for meaning, and a phonetic radical (or phonetic) that can give or suggest pronunciation (see examples for "chant," "eat," and "vomit" — semantic radical on the left, phonetic on the right). Phonetics can also be "bound," not appearing as independent characters. Some compound characters, on the other hand, combine two semantic components to suggest a new meaning. Integrated characters are not composed of separate phonetic and semantic components. They consist of stroke patterns that form an integrated unit that is inseparable. In the examples given, "below," "above" and "middle" are independent integrated characters. The majority of compound characters are irregular or semi-regular, one or the other or neither radical providing a completely reliable clue for meaning or pronunciation. Perhaps the feature of the Chinese writing system that distinguishes it most from alphabetic systems is that there are no component parts of a character that encode individual phonemes. Also taking into account the overall inconsistency of the phonetic radical, the correct pronunciation of characters requires identification of the entire character, unlike in alphabetic writing where a reader can reliably "sound out" unknown words and provide a more or less correct pronunciation for them. (Chen *et al.*, 2003; Perfetti *et al.*, 2005; Shen and Ke, 2007; Xu *et al.* 1999, Xue, 2011).

5. Kanji: traditional Chinese characters adopted by the Japanese writing system. Kana: the syllabic Japanese scripts, *hiragana* and *katakana*.

Chapter 5

Self-correction — Negative evidence in second language literacy learning

Chapters 5 and 6 are about learners receiving feedback on errors and about reflecting on their own performance in language learning tasks. The term *negative evidence* refers to information that learners receive about an aspect of their developing language competence or about a still incompletely mastered skill that needs improvement or correction. So despite what it sounds like, negative evidence is a very *good* thing (not to be confused with "negative feedback" — an informal, non-scientific, expression that in fact does have a negative connotation). Negative evidence is a broad category; it can be feedback provided by a more advanced learner, a teacher, or an interactive computer program, or evidence of partial or incorrect knowledge that learners discover on their own (e.g., noticing and reflecting on language patterns that contain errors). For example, teachers can design writing activities that facilitate or encourage more effective reflection and monitoring by L2 students of their own written production.

This chapter will propose an approach for studying an aspect of writing development that is especially important for academic literacy — self-correction and revision. In fact, the ability to revise and self-correct should be considered as one of the basic foundations of writing proficiency; and making it the focus of research should help us better understand all aspects of written expression. Self-correction and revision inherently involve the deployment of metalinguistic abilities, a focus of renewed interest among researchers. Thus, the study of these literacy skills in beginning writers should also help us better understand the role of metalinguistic awareness in all aspects of literacy development. In second language writing, researchers are presented with the additional opportunity to examine how metalinguistic awareness intervenes in the development of L2 learners' grammatical knowledge.

Research in this area has attracted increasing attention in recent years; but we have barely scratched the surface of the many interesting questions still to be explored. In fact, a focus on correction and self-correction offers investigators of literacy and second language learning with a number of very attractive opportunities from a methodological point of view, opportunities in assessment that we have only begun to take advantage of. As an important literacy skill in its own right, integrally tied to both writing and reading ability applied to authentic texts (i.e., reading one's own written work in a reflective manner), validity is virtually ensured. In both open-ended and closed-ended tests, reliability is highly favored because points of assessment can be designed to be as specific and well defined as is necessary.

In line with the theme introduced in the previous chapter, the categories of analysis that will be proposed, *text-level of correction attempt* and *effectivity of attempt*, could be useful in studies of literacy cross-linguistically. They might be particularly useful in comparisons between alphabetic and morphosyllabic systems. Recall that this was one of the main themes of the previous chapter. Questions to be explored include:

- which types of error are most prevalent at the earliest stages of written expression and how might these change developmentally,
- which error types are most salient and noticeable in tasks of self-correction,

- which types tend to be self-corrected spontaneously and with high levels of accuracy, and
- which may be more difficult to notice and more difficult to correct, requiring focused attention and systematic instruction?

Language teachers need to consider the usefulness of different kinds of negative evidence, as well as positive evidence. Which are actually effective for a given language or literacy learning objective, in the sense that students receive feedback on their writing that they can use? In the case of self-correction, how can learners maximize opportunities to reflect on their writing in ways that actually help them improve their language skills? Comparisons in each of the above categories across writing systems should also contribute to the ongoing discussion on which aspects of literacy learning are writing system-specific and which aspects are writing system-independent or universal. For example, is a specific literacy skill learned through practice in the L1 applicable to and accessible during literacy tasks in the student's L2 (and vice versa)?

5.1 Historical antecedents in second language writing

Among the reasons why research on second language writing is important is that historically it has always been one of the primary learning objectives of academic literacy. Today, it might be safe to say that, world-wide, most students, at all levels including primary school, are required to learn how to read and write in a second language, or soon will be. In the country where our primary research project is located, Mexico, second language writing has a long history and a growing importance today. During the first years of the colonial period in the 16th Century, the greater part of writing for academic purposes was probably not in the first language of most writers. Religious education, evangelization, and in particular the extensive publishing of Christian texts would typically be in Nahuatl. As the language of the former Aztec empire, it became the widely recognized lingua franca of the early colonial period. Newly arriving missionaries from Spain would have to demonstrate proficiency in Nahuatl, and together with Latin it was a language of higher education, scholarship and academic literacy. Native speakers of the language, mainly former Aztec nobles and their children, enrolled in large numbers in the newly established centers of advanced learning in New Spain. In fact, it was among these first layers of post-Conquest Nahuatl intellectuals that a new generation of indigenous writers emerged. For many years following the European conquest, official documents such as land titles were often written in Nahuatl. History eventually turned the tables on the major indigenous languages of the Americas, resulting over time in a near total dominance of Spanish in schools that serve communities where they are still spoken (Hidalgo, 2001). Today, English is a required subject for school children after 6th grade; and learning Spanish in school also implies L2 literacy for many indigenous language speakers.

For a longer historical period, in Europe and East Asia, great lingua francas spread far beyond their countries of origin to become the languages of learning and high culture. For centuries, in Europe, the publishing of books and the discourse of university teaching were in Arabic and Latin. Interestingly, spanning approximately the same time period, in Korea, Japan and other countries of the region, Chinese was the primary writing system used by poets and scholars in the artistic and academic disciplines. This peculiar second language literacy tradition had established such deep roots that until modern times, long after the national languages had emerged as dominant in their respective countries, much literature and scholarship was still written in Chinese. Similarly in Europe, Latin continued to be studied for this purpose long after the national/vernacular languages had become the normal and expected medium of literacy. Bilingual literacy, in its different variants, then, could be considered to be the typical or normal circumstance of reading and writing. We could also say that literacy and bilingualism have always been closely linked.

5.2 A study comparing self-correction in two alphabetic orthographies

This chapter will report on a descriptive study of second language and bilingual writing development, with an eye on the broader discussion in the field of second language learning on the role of metalinguistic awareness and negative evidence. One of the proposals that will be presented for consideration is that metalinguistic awareness in particular is a central component of advanced literacy ability; see Buckwalter and Lo (2002), Li *et al.* (2002) and Packard (2002) for discussion. A current proposal in the research on literacy learning is that shifting greater emphasis toward systematic reflection and awareness of language patterns might favor a stronger development of academic language proficiency, especially in the domain of written expression. The examination of self-correction strategies in second language (L2) writing, the subject of this study, allows for a special opportunity to explore this question.

Participants were bilingual elementary school students from Central Mexico who completed first-draft compositions based on a narrative theme, and were then asked to re-read typed transcriptions of their stories for the purpose of making corrections and revisions for a finished version of their work. Standard self-correction and revision options were demonstrated (substitution, deletion, insertion, and transposition), after which students were instructed to make all corrections and revisions that in their estimation would improve their first draft in some way. Among the 45 participants (15 second graders, 15 fourth graders and 15 sixth graders) were L2 learners of Spanish, Spanish-speaking L2 learners of Nahuatl, and balanced (early-simultaneous) bilinguals for whom both languages were primary mother tongues.

The composition and correction task was part of a larger investigation of bilingual literacy and school-related language abilities. Even though the Nahuatl language was rarely used for academic purposes in school, teachers always conferred upon it respect and recognition. This positive valorization of students' bilingualism prompted us to evaluate their academic language abilities in both languages — the official language in which literacy skills were taught and practiced and the indigenous language which children also knew. Results from tests of reading, writing and oral expression confirmed a model of bilingual proficiency that proposes common representations for concepts, knowledge structures, and processing skills that are not language-specific. These representations appear to be "shared" between L1 and L2 and therefore are independent to a large extent of linguistic competence in each language. The confirmation of this model was suggested by comparable performance in Nahuatl on literacy and literacy-related language tasks (recall that children rarely practiced the relevant skills in their indigenous language). Predictably, performance in Spanish was superior on all tasks. However, the consistent finding of significantly improving performance in Nahuatl across the grade levels through grade 6 suggested that children were able to access advanced literacy-related abilities even though these abilities were learned through the official medium of instruction — Spanish (Francis, 2012).

The examination of the correction/revision skills was the final and culminating assessment of a larger investigation. As a more advanced literacy skill, requiring children to focus close attention on language forms, it was thought that performance on this writing task in particular would reveal indices of higher-order abilities tied to metalinguistic awareness. The composition-correction task was administered, in parallel fashion, in both languages. Indices of *text-level of the correction/revision* and *effectivity of attempt at correction/revision* were calculated for each response:

- at what level of text was the correction/revision attempted (orthographic, grammar at the sentence-level, or intersentential discourse-level), and
- to what degree was each attempt effective?

5.2.1 A proposed conceptual framework

Among the important questions related to the development of metalinguistic awareness and the use of negative evidence in second language writing that future studies will be able to resolve are:

- What is the role of different kinds of feedback in L2 literacy and in L2 learning more broadly?
- What other kinds of learning task actively promote awareness of language patterns and focused reflection by L2 students?
- How should researchers distinguish between "implicit" linguistic knowledge and "explicit" knowledge associated with literacy-related language ability?
- Which aspects of writing ability, including metacognitive strategies and

metalinguistic abilities, are language-specific and which are shared across languages and writing systems?

- How should the concept of "transfer" be properly understood?

Before examining the procedures and results of our assessment of correction/revision, let us briefly survey these theoretical and practical questions. The debate on the effects of Form-focused instruction and the provision of negative evidence in L2 writing (Bitchener *et al.*, 2005; Diab, 2010; Ferris, 2010; Lee, 2004; Truscott and Hsu, 2008) is familiar to most educators in the field of second language learning. This is not the place to assess the different claims and counter claims; and the findings from the studies that I will report on do not offer direct support to any of the current hypotheses in contention. But as a way to help shed some new light on the discussion, the following proposals might be useful in helping us design future studies. For the benefit of better understanding both points of view, the first which generally favors providing systematic negative evidence and the second which does not, we could clarify or summarize the opposing claims. They could perhaps be formulated more clearly, confronting two opposing approaches to the problem:

1. One approach proposes that providing some variety of negative evidence hastens the developing mastery of grammatical features and discourse ability in L2 writing. Learning becomes more systematic and higher levels of ultimate attainment are more likely. That exclusively communicative immersion-without-grammar-teaching and (uncorrected) practice in writing result in some measurable advances in L2 writing is not denied. But position #1 argues that Form-focused instruction (FFI) and negative evidence make learning more effective and efficient. At the same time, it should be uncontroversial among educators who favor access to negative evidence and FFI that only some kinds will actually be helpful to learners.

2. The opposing view would claim that there is no measurable effect, no facilitation in the development of any aspect of L2 writing ability as a result of corrective feedback or focused attention on errors. No variety of systematic provision of negative evidence favors higher levels of achievement in writing ability.

While it appears that hypothesis #1 is formulated more defensively, this way of proceeding, I believe, should help strip away unnecessary disputes on some secondary issues.

Another way to clarify the questions in contention could be to consider all types and categories of Form-focused instruction and negative evidence in L2 learning, and then apply them, tentatively, to L2 writing. Teacher or peer corrective feedback (Miao *et al.* 2006; Min, 2006; Rollinson, 2005; Yang *et al.*, 2006) is one way that negative evidence may be provided, but there are others. For example, in the study summarized in this chapter, beginning L2 writers who have developed robust and efficient *self*-monitoring strategies would receive, and benefit from (hypothetically), negative evidence. In this case, the evidence regarding what aspects of their interlanguage knowledge are not part of the target language system is not provided by a teacher or more advanced learner, but rather from reflection and systematic focus on language patterns as an integral part of the composing process itself. The writer is "positioned as an active agent in text creation" (Kasule and Lunga, 2010, p. 108). See Ruan (2004) and Xiang (2004) for a further discussion of metacognition and self-monitoring in bilingual writers.

One thing to keep in mind is that in L2 writing, the general problems of writing development apply in addition to, or "on top of," the special circumstances of interlanguage development. For example, in the case of initial literacy learning for non-literate children who are also monolingual speakers of their L1, the circumstances are special in ways that are very different from L2 literacy scenarios involving older, L1 literate, intermediate level L2 speakers. The more advanced learner in the second case can draw on significant resources in both language and literacy skill that the beginning learner does not possess.

Returning to the question of the wide range of different kinds of negative evidence, there are two sets of considerations in the research today that are pertinent to the problem at hand:

1. The more fundamental question asks whether negative evidence in some shape or form, and some aspect of metalinguistic awareness might facilitate higher levels of ultimate attainment in L2 linguistic knowledge and discourse-level text organizing ability. The question is important and interesting because, according to some views of child language development at least, neither negative evidence nor metalinguistic awareness play any necessary role in the ultimate attainment of L1 core linguistic competence. Discourse-level text organizing ability is an entirely different matter, depending, as it does, on skills that are largely independent of language competence. Where these skills do involve grammar knowledge, specific to L1 or L2, it's likely that much of *this* knowledge of language is above and beyond "core linguistic competence." On a related note, readers should consult Doughty's (2003) discussion of the research on implicit and explicit learning that offers an interesting account of the widely observed difference between L1 acquisition and L2 learning. How do second language learners overcome, or compensate for, the effects of the "filter of the linguistic organization of their first language" (p. 290)?
2. A separate question involves the day-to-day use of different types and categories of negative evidence in actual L2 teaching situations. All variety of practical considerations and pedagogical constraints come into play that result in one or another approach to appear effective, workable, ineffective, counterproductive or neutral. Comparative studies that seek to marshal support for one or another contrasting method are invariably plagued by these external factors, often impossible to control. From this point of view, issues of learner disposition, motivation and other affective variables, limitations of time and resources, etc. are all entirely secondary. If negative evidence, in principle, can be shown to be necessary for higher levels of attainment in one or more domains of L2 learning, then strong versions of input-based language teaching that rely solely on positive evidence and uncorrected practice cannot be correct. Specific feedback paradigms, for example, will always vary widely in effectiveness from one learning context to

another — highly motivated child second language learners, adult "high-stakes" L2 learners with advanced L1 literacy skills, English for specific purposes learners with limited instrumental motivation, American college foreign language students, and so forth. It would suffice to demonstrate the effectiveness of providing negative evidence for any one of these learner populations to settle the question, in principle.

Thus, perhaps we should step back from some of the particulars of the ongoing debate, the underlying concepts then helping us to start again with more basic questions: To what domains of knowledge and processing do the different metalinguistic abilities belong? If these abilities are not deployed in any necessary way in the acquisition of core L1 grammatical competence, then it's likely that they are independent of core linguistic knowledge acquired in the L1. As such, can this type of explicit knowledge interface in any way with implicit knowledge of language? And for a specific ability, like L2 writing, might the use of metalinguistic ability favor higher levels of ultimate attainment?

5.2.2 Application of the bilingual self-correction evaluation

Two categories of analysis were of interest in the evaluation of children's writing ability. This study focused on a specific writing skill, self-correction/revision and editing: (1) along the dimensions of *text-level* and *effectivity*, how did beginning writers differ from more advanced writers, and (2) given that in school, literacy skills are normally only practiced in Spanish, the national language of instruction, what differences might be discerned in performance between Spanish and Nahuatl on the same task?

Given the descriptive and exploratory nature of the assessments, we are not able to provide confirming or disconfirming evidence for any of the proposals for further research in the previous section. Rather, the study should be taken as a kind of base-line description of tendencies and correlations — for example, what developmental trends should we expect to see across the elementary grades? As such, it might serve to help formulate testable hypotheses and experimental designs with the potential of directly addressing the central questions concerning metalinguistic awareness and negative evidence in second language learning. Thus, the following outline of the self-correction study is offered as a proposal for replication and for designing a series of more focused studies, focused on specific written language patterns. A more discrete-point type assessment could then pick up where we left off.

5.2.3 Components of writing ability — Assessment procedures

Students composed narratives based on a model that was read aloud to each class followed by a discussion and examination of visual graphics that accompanied each story. This method helps establish uniformity of conditions for what is typically a cognitively demanding literacy exercise for elementary school children. Providing a single discursive and thematic framework in a structured writing task of this type facilitates comparison as it provides all participants with access to relevant background knowledge and a purpose for writing. Completed first drafts were collected and students were asked during the following week to make corrections and revisions to typewritten transcriptions of their own stories as described earlier.

To review, analysis of the writing samples consisted of two categories of rating: (1) text-level of the correction/revision and (2) effectivity of correction/revision. Under the first category, all attempts at correction or revision (regardless of the degree of effectiveness) were coded for text-level as follows.

1. Orthographic correction:

   (i) general grapheme/phoneme correspondence

   (ii) word segmentation

   (iii) accent placement

   vus
   (i) Jue a ~~duca~~ r nu venada

   The student changes "ducar" to "vusar." The original sequence (with the reversal of "b" — should be "buscar" [to look for]) — is a non-word in Spanish. The change, although spelling is still not correct, results in a complete and comprehensible sentence [He went to look for a deer].

   ya nomas le ba a estar
   (ii) ~~llanomasle~~ ponemos la carne y en un momento ~~bastar~~ listo

   Substitution of correct segmentation in both cases, although spelling is still not completely correct [all we have to do is put (in) the meat and in a moment it will be ready].

   (iii) como pajáros

   A missing accent is inserted, however placement should be over the first syllable ("pájaros" [birds]).

2. Morphosyntactic or semantic pattern at the sentence-level:

   no lo oyo
   lo desperto so esposa pero ~~olo oyo~~ so esposa

   Corrected version: [his wife woke him up but <u>she didn't hear him</u> (instead of: "or hear him") his wife].

   Insertion of punctuation/capitalization could be considered as a combined or intermediate level requiring attention to either or both sentence-level grammar and discourse-level coherence:

su . el joven
El joven ya se iba para ~~so~~ casa se iba muy triste proque no lo mato ^ ~~El venado y~~
estaba cansado y tenia anbre

A period is inserted after "mato" presumably because "porque no lo mato El venado" [because he didn't kill it the deer] contains a redundant element; should be either "lo" [it] or "El venado" [The deer], but not both. Having eliminated the unnecessary redundancy ("El venado") the writer reiterates "el joven" [the young man] to clarify that it was he, and not the deer, that was tired and hungry, in the process omitting "y" [and].

3. Discourse-level revisions that involve a potential change of meaning across sentence boundaries or that affect discourse-level coherence in some way:

vengan aqui les volla explicar cuando se echo a correr cuando ya lo

denme
voy a dar ~~deme~~ tortilla.

The singular form "deme" is changed to "denme" (2nd person plural imperative [give me]) to mark the cohesive tie with "vengan" (2nd person plural imperative [come]) and a series of 3rd person plural verb forms in previous text to indicate that the speaker is still addressing a group of ladies, and not just one.

The following examples of substitutions of Spanish loan words and borrowings, could also be categorized as a kind of discourse-level revision. The original versions that included the borrowed Spanish word did not introduce a grammatical error, and their substitution by a Nahuatl word did not affect sentence-level meaning or grammar. As such, we could argue that such cross-linguistic revisions represent an attempt to make the text more "coherent" or more "consistent," from a pragmatic point of view:

coyotli
okalkaya itek ~~trampa~~ guan ok quirtiquen

Revised version: "he was inside a trap and they got him out" (Spanish "trampa" [trap] is changed to Nahuatl "coyotli" [hole]).

uan
guan oktaquien se tekuani guan quistuan ~~pero~~ quienen se tekuien

tatsitsiuan nanatsin
kin noxasquien nochtin y no ~~papan~~ guan ni ~~mamas~~

Revised version: "and they saw a lion and they said and how can a lion come with two children and they said to call all the fathers and mothers" (Spanish "pero" [but] changed to Nahuatl "uan" [and]; Spanish "papan" [fathers] changed to Nahuatl "tatsitsiuan" [fathers]; Spanish "mamas" [mothers] changed to Nahuatl "nanatsin" [mothers]).

Under category #2, all attempts were coded for the resulting effectiveness of the revision or correction, independently of text-level.

Two types of effective attempts:

Correct → Correct or Correct (+)

An original sequence that contains no errors is revised; the revised version contains no errors, or represents an improvement of some kind over the original.

Error → Corrected or Improved

An original sequence that contains error(s) is significantly improved in some way, sometimes resulting in a conventional form, or correct grammatical sequence.

Four types of non-effective attempts:

No Change

Original sequence is substituted by the exact same sequence of letters or words.

Correct → Correct (-)

No orthographic or grammatical errors are introduced into the revised version; however, the revised version is now unclear, results in a loss of coherence, etc.

Correct → Error

An error-free sequence is changed, the revision results in an error.

Error → Error or Error (-)

An original sequence that contains an error is changed; the resulting sequence is either equally or more difficult to understand, equally ungrammatical or ungrammatical to a greater degree, or results in an orthographic pattern that departs from the conventional form equally or to a greater degree in comparison to the original alphabetic pattern.

5.2.4 Performance in the two languages compared

1. In regard to the category *text-level of correction/revision* (#1), we noted a tendency for 4th and 6th graders to attempt more often, and to be more successful, at the higher levels. For example, while among the 15 second graders only 5 successfully

attempted a punctuation/capitalization or discourse correction/revision in Spanish and only 1 in Nahuatl, the number of students who successfully attempted at this level increases in sixth grade to 8 and 5 respectively.

2. Comparing corrections/revisions across the grades (2nd–6th), while the number of total attempts, per word, does not vary appreciably, older students' attempts are effective at a significantly higher percentage in both languages, advancing, in Spanish from 54.2% in 2nd grade to 82.6% in 6th grade, in Nahuatl, from 32.2% to 70.6%. This finding corresponds to category #2 of the analysis.

3. Related to this tendency is the number of successful attempts that involve a language switch from Spanish to Nahuatl in the Nahuatl writing task (see examples of the substitution of "Spanish borrowings" above). Only 6th graders were able to (or chose to) make this type of revision. Although few in number (only 11 revisions in all), this result coincides with other indices of metalinguistic awareness that require the respondent to attend to aspects of codeswitching, borrowing, language choice and language identification (e.g., correctly distinguishing between the languages in literacy tasks). See the discussion of the interesting related question of "language-switching" in L2 writing in Wang (2003) and Woodall (2002).

4. Despite the fact that writing skills in school are only practiced in Spanish, performance on the correction/revision task in Nahuatl also shows a statistically significant advance across the grades, indicating that the relevant literacy skills involved are accessible in performance through the medium of either language. As expected, the overall rate of effectivity is higher for Spanish, but clearly the upward tendencies in the assessments are parallel. That is, advances in this specific literacy skill across the grades were statistically significant in both languages, a result that might help us better understand what is referred to in the literature as L1–L2 "transfer."

5. Overall, the high level of task acceptance on the part of all participants and the seemingly consistent response rates suggest that the procedures described above can be useful in future investigations of cross-language and bilingual literacy, research that could go beyond the descriptive and exploratory design of the present study. The proposed categories described above appear to provide for reliable results, and could serve as a viable alternative method for studying L2 learners' writing development in a series of more controlled experiments. Even young children find learning activities focused on language patterns interesting when these activities are presented in an engaging and motivating fashion (Bouffard and Sarkar, 2008).

5.3 Possible directions for cross-language research

An interesting possibility for future research on monitoring and self-correction could utilize our two categories of *text-level* and *degree of effectivity* to explore the strategies learners deploy in contrasting writing systems. The comparison between Spanish and Nahuatl involved two shallow orthographies. Due to the historical origins of the indigenous language alphabetic script, patterned, as it was, closely on Spanish phoneme-grapheme correspondences, the two systems, in fact, are shallow to the same degree and are highly congruent. We could point to this high degree of congruence, in fact, as an interesting limitation of the study. The two scripts were simply too similar one to the other; and we could speculate that students experienced little or no difficulty in applying writing skills learned in one language (Spanish) to a test in the other language that they also speak. Students could do this successfully even though they rarely (if ever in the case of most) use the other language (Nahuatl) for literacy.

On the other hand, cross-language and cross-writing system comparisons involving sharply contrasting systems should allow us to examine the development of specific literacy skills, such as self-correction, from a broader, more general, perspective. Which aspects of skill in self-correction, for example, are more language/writing system specific? Do morphosyllabic and alphabetic systems each impose highly contrasting error patterns and self-correction strategies in all domains of written expression, or are there common underlying knowledge structures and processing mechanisms that might be revealed below the surface, so to speak? One example of a common development of processing skill might be the tendency, evidenced in both writing systems, toward feature-clustering in reading, a more direct (and more rapid) processing of characters and alphabetic words as children advance in literacy learning (Su and Samuels, 2010)

Another interesting example of a universal processing feature might be the study of Hu and Catts (1998) who made the observation from their review of the research that deficits in phonological processing might affect learning to read in Chinese. To make effective use of word constituents in decoding unfamiliar words in context, the reader needs to maintain a phonological representation in working memory until a word boundary is identified. Since Chinese does not specify word boundaries in print, it might be difficult for the beginning reader to determine whether a character stands for a word or a bound morpheme. Unskilled readers have been shown to have difficulty in segmentation. For example, which juxtaposed characters form separate words and which do not? Do young children, when learning to write, incorrectly separate the radicals of compound characters, for example?

Beginning writers in alphabetic scripts also pass through a stage in which they segment words inappropriately — e.g., by syllable, separating out bound morphemes, combining words that conventionally do not form compounds, and vice versa (Julbe-Delgado, 2010). So, an interesting comparison might be between morphosyllabic Chinese and alphabetic Spanish or English in how children develop orthographic knowledge of segmentation. Which constituents (e.g., within and across alphabetic words and within and across characters) do children perceive as bound and which are perceived to be separable or free? In a self-correction task, which errors do children notice, and successfully correct, at different stages of development? Hypothetically, we might see writing system-specific and language-specific differences in this domain of orthographic development because of the difference in the way that English and Chinese mark word boundaries. On the other hand, both kinds of segmentation error (within word/character and across word/character) might be shown to be equally prevalent at the early stages and be corrected by beginning writers on comparable developmental timetables. How might this developing ability correlate with indices of phonological processing and phonological and morphological awareness? Many of the error patterns and self-corrections will be the same for beginning child writers and beginning adult writers. Then some will be different; older students have at their disposal more advanced analytic capabilities, which can be brought to bear on complex literacy tasks.

Another potentially fruitful avenue of research could involve comparisons of error pattern between native speakers and L2 learners, in both writing and reading; see Ferguson *et al.* (2003) for a study comparing reading miscues in L1 and L2. Hatta *et al.* (1997) analyzed *kanji* error types in writing samples of L1 Japanese students and English-speaking L2 learners. Predictably, the predominate type among L2 learners was the "mis-construction of a *kanji* segment," one of the least frequent error types among L1 writers. An interesting introductory note by the authors was a reference to the perceived difficulty on the part of Japanese college students, overall, in mastering the *kanji* system, an observation that appears to have prompted interest in their project. An analogous L1-L2/cross-writing system issue was alluded to between the use of the *kanji* and *kana* systems, the latter serving, according to the authors, as a kind of alternative that writers can fall back on to compensate for gaps in *kanji* orthographic knowledge.

Second language literacy learning in Chinese was investigated by Wang *et al.* (2004), who were interested as well in an issue related to our study — the relationship between implicit learning and explicit instruction. To what extent would L2 learners (literate in an alphabetic script) acquire knowledge of the component structure of Chinese characters implicitly by exposure through reading and typical foreign language instruction? Since research has shown that native speakers of Chinese utilize, analytically, both the semantic radical and the phonetic component of characters in literacy learning (Tzeng, 2002), the authors asked whether L2 learners would develop a sensitivity to the internal orthographic structure of characters in a similar way. Results suggested that even in the absence of direct instruction and explicit attention to the structural features of characters on the part of the students' teachers, the L2 learners did in fact acquire at least partial knowledge of the structure of their L2 orthography. In their concluding discussion, a review of similar investigations plus findings from their own follow-up study led the authors to propose further work on the question of whether explicit instruction might facilitate the ability to decompose newly encountered complex characters. This approach, hypothetically, would apply to both L1 and L2 Chinese literacy learning.

The related question of the role of morphological awareness in bilingual literacy was explored in an investigation of fifth grade, Chinese-speaking, L2 learners of English — 168 students from a large elementary school in Tianjin (Zhang *et al.*, 2010). Would focused teaching on patterns of how compound words are formed in English improve awareness of compounding in Chinese, and vice versa? The positive finding in this study, *in both directions* (morphological awareness in alphabetic English writing predicts morphological awareness for characters, and vice versa) is especially noteworthy because of the contrast between the two writing systems. This result, similar to findings in Wang *et al.* (2009), then, could be taken as an example of a literacy skill that is shared, so to speak, between abilities in different writing systems. The study addressed the question of what is referred to in the research literature as "transfer" (between L1 and L2). Development of morphological awareness appears to be especially amenable to direct instruction resulting in usable skills for both L1 and L2 literacy learners (Hayashi and Murphy, 2011).

5.3.1 A proposal for evaluating writing in a morphosyllabic orthography

In a follow-up pilot test of the bilingual writing and self-correction assessment from Mexico, a similar assessment was given to a L2 learner of Chinese. The subject first read a familiar traditional story and the following day wrote as much as she could remember from the first episode (Figure 5.1). As in the Mexican bilingual writing assessment, the subject was then asked to make any necessary corrections. Figure 5.2 shows self-correction attempts and an informal analysis of the effectivity of correction. An additional measure, not contemplated in the original study, is indicated as a proposal for future investigation — a comparison between attempted corrections and missed opportunities (errors that the subject did not attempt to correct). Comparing in this way effective attempts and non-effective attempts (see Section 5.2.3), and then factoring in missed opportunities to self-correct could add an interesting dimension to the analysis.

On first impression, the scoring rubric for effectivity appears to apply satisfactorily. The interesting question concerns the distribution of errors and self-correction attempts, comparing alphabetic and morphosyllabic beginning writers. Under the sub-categories, (word/character-level) orthographic, (sentence-level) morphology, syntax or semantic, and (text-level) discourse self-corrections, which developmental tendencies might be writing system- and language-specific and which might be common? Do independent measures of metalinguistic awareness predict successful performance in this literacy skill in both cases? Potentially, results can provide useful information for educators — which components of writing ability are early-developing, responding perhaps to simple-immersion in literacy-rich learning environments, and which might require direct and focused instruction? Would these tendencies be the same for L1 writers and L2 writers?

A more discrete-point type assessment, for example, could present children or L2 learners with a series of texts containing mal-formed characters (introduced into the passage systematically to test for the ability to notice different categories of error). Then, perhaps in a separate evaluation, among the errors that learners correctly notice, how successful are they in producing the well-formed character or sequence of characters? A

Figure 5.1
Second language writing by L2 learner of Chinese
(L1-Thai, other L2-English)

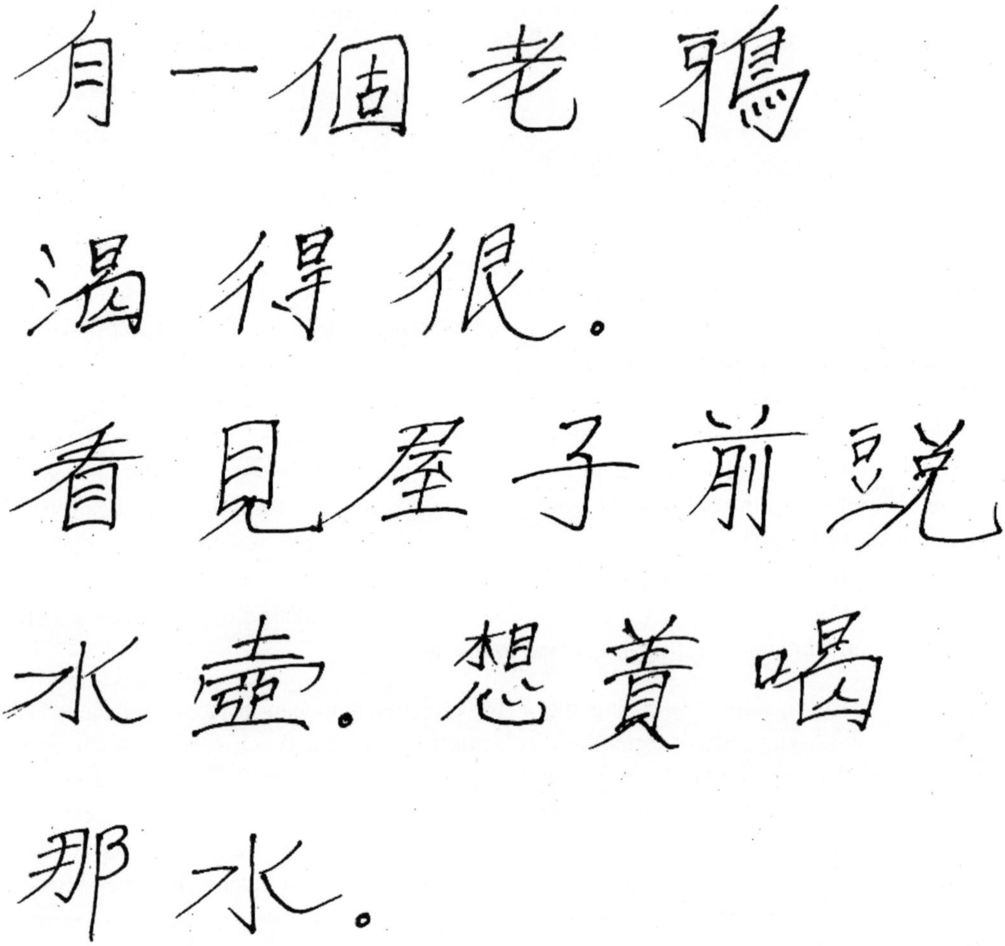

有一個老鴉
渴得很。
看見屋子前說
水壺。想著喝
那水。

Figure 5.2
Attempted self-corrections

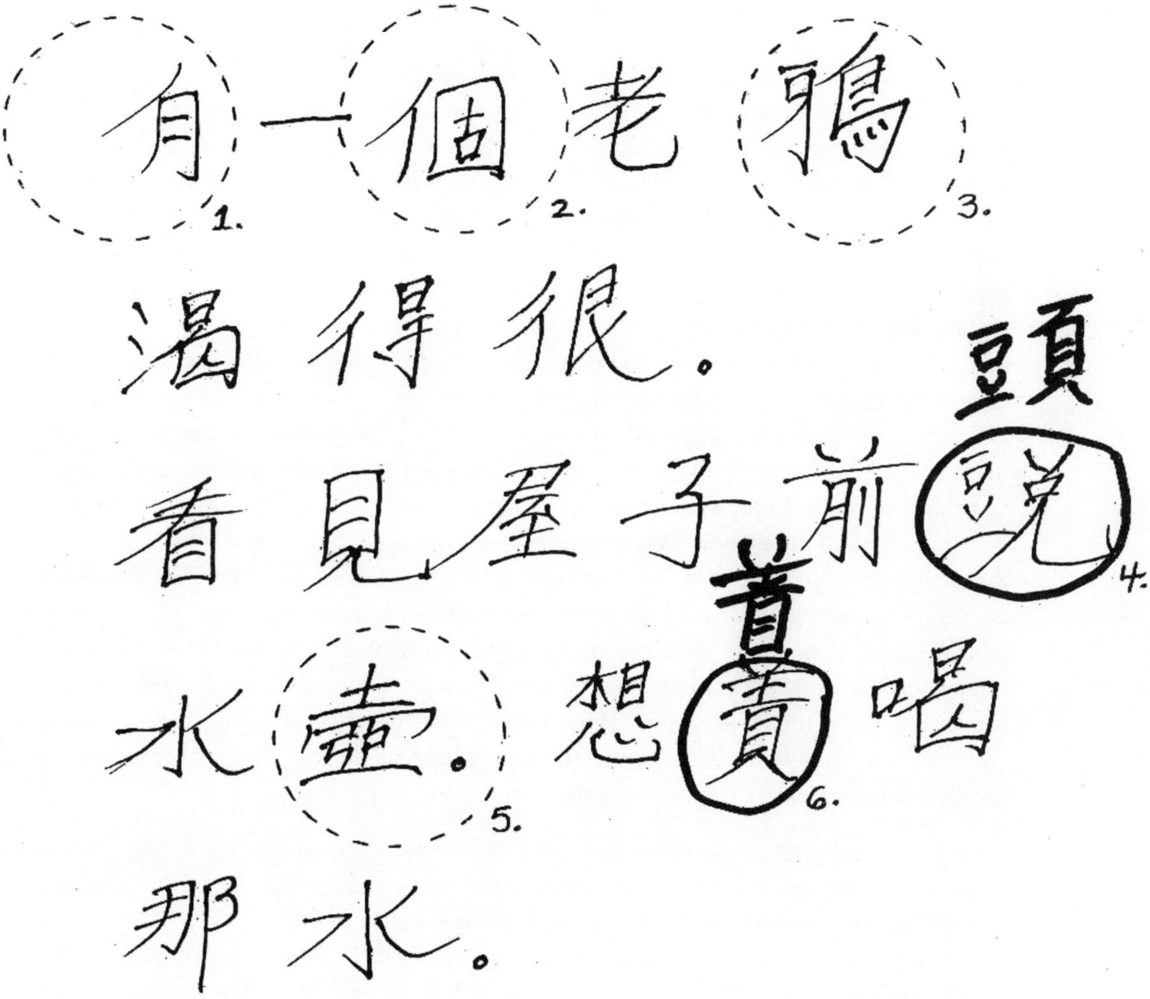

1,2,3 & 5 Missed opportunity to correct an ill-formed character
4 Effective self-correction
6 Partially effective self-correction

variant of this procedure could present learners with a multiple-choice format. For a given mal-formed character, which choice among three or four is the well-formed alternative? Distractors could systematically include incorrect components or stroke patterns hypothesized to correspond to L2 learners' or beginners' immature conceptions.

5.3.2 Other cross-language and cross-writing system comparisons

Perhaps some of the most far-reaching investigations on cross-language and cross-orthography literacy come from the study of dysgraphia. The different types of impairment to the underlying knowledge structures and information processing modules reveal how the components of a complex ability, such as writing, interact. Reich *et al.* (2003) compared the results from their assessment of a patient affected by a writing impairment with confirming findings from Law and Or (2001). In the latter case study, the patient showed more skill in writing to dictation in Chinese than written picture naming. This finding was taken as evidence that even with non-alphabetic writing systems there is a direct route between orthography and phonology; that in Chinese reading and writing there is no exclusive access to meaning that circumvents the activation of phonology. Reich and associates studied the impaired writing ability of a patient who consistently activated the orthographic form of higher-frequency homophones even when disambiguating semantic information corresponding to a lower-frequency target word was presented. That is, meaning clues compatible only with the lower-frequency target word did not prompt the patient to supplant the higher-frequency character. According to the authors, direct activation of orthographic representations by phonology in Chinese was confirmed by their findings. How might this type of writing error, related to high and low frequency homophones compare between morphosyllabic and alphabetic systems, among both impaired and non-impaired writers? What would the frequency of this error type be among child literacy learners in each system? To what extent might it be resistant to corrective feedback and how easily would it be noticed in tasks of self-correction?

Here we have an example of how evidence from a non-alphabetic writing system helps shed light on discussions in the field of literacy learning that have primarily revolved around research findings from alphabetic systems. What role does phonological processing play in all aspects of literacy development, and how might this differ from one writing system to another? The alphabetic/non-alphabetic writing system contrast is often assumed to correlate with processing differences that must be contrasting in fundamental ways (e.g., in word identification, phonologically mediated versus direct semantic access, respectively). Recent research appears to be taking a different starting point: which aspects of literacy development and literacy performance are writing system-specific and which aspects are common to all writing systems? From this point of view, the "direct access to meaning/phonology by-pass" hypothesis for Chinese would seem, tentatively, to be the least plausible. If it turns out to be incorrect for literacy in Chinese, that might settle the question for literacy in all alphabetic orthographies, "shallow" and "deep," and for writing systems universally.

Cross-language comparisons of the descriptive and naturalistic kind (as in the present study) help us get a better idea about what L2 literacy learners attend to most readily and most frequently in situations of spontaneous self-correction. Also, how these categories shift with grade level and overall proficiency can also be gauged across different writing systems, cross-linguistically, and in L1 and L2. Knowing which error patterns are more "resistant" to noticing and self-correction and which tend to be more transparent should be useful for teachers. More controlled studies could go on to evaluate responses to specific task conditions and instructions, focused on categories of error that may be important to understand, for instance, error patterns purportedly related to L1-L2 transfer.

An approach that could overcome some of the limitations of the open-ended method of studying cross-writing system comparisons presented in this chapter would be to present learners with closed-ended tasks. For example, as suggested in the previous section, selected error types can be inserted into otherwise well-formed text for identification and correction. This type of assessment has the advantage of allowing investigators to pin point specific categories of grammatical and orthographic pattern, for example in regard to the different kinds of compounding within and between characters and the different aspects of difficulty that character learning presents to young children and older second language learners — phonological regularity versus irregularity, transparency of information provided by the semantic radical, frequency, etc. In L2 English for example, closed-ended items could focus on categories of hypothesized L1 interference, phonological awareness in spelling (regular and irregular), morphological knowledge, and segmentation. Another alternative to the open-ended assessment scheme is to identify all errors of each major type committed in student writing, and then calculate the self-correction success rate for each one, as was done by Kubota (2005) in a study of *kanji* self-correction among L2 learners of Japanese.

The bigger questions regarding the precise relationship between the different aspects of metalinguistic awareness and literacy learning will also require more exacting experimental methods. But the comparative study of error patterns (e.g., which errors beginning writers notice) should help us get a better understanding of which aspects of literacy development are language and writing system-specific and which aspects could be universal. In all this we should keep in mind that there are different points of view on the efficacy of providing negative evidence in second language learning and on the role of metalinguistic awareness. To reiterate, the results of our descriptive and exploratory study of self-correction only provide suggestions for future investigation on the role of these factors. But, the development of skill in self-correction and revision in writing is an essential literacy learning objective in its own right. Few experts in writing instruction would deny that this skill is of central importance, especially for the learning objectives of formal writing in school.

This last assertion, however, might be controversial in some respects for advocates of strong versions "whole-language," who might disfavor Form-focused instruction in the teaching of writing. Actually, in the field of *second language* writing, the controversy on this point may be more interesting. Two separate, but closely related, questions need to be addressed in future research: (1) one claim by opponents of systematic Form-focused instruction (regarding the development of writing skills) might be that FFI is limited to developing explicit knowledge of the L2 grammar, not contributing to implicit linguistic competence. This implicit linguistic competence, for argument's sake, we could say is about the core linguistic competence of the second language. However, in the mastery of *writing ability*, especially *for academic purposes*, there is much more that L2 students must learn than just this core linguistic competence, starting with the conventions of orthography (from elementary stroke patterns to morphological knowledge related to formation of compound words) all the way to the grammar of discourse organization for each kind of school-related advanced literacy genre that learners need to master. (2) Would the same arguments against systematic FFI in (1) also apply to these domains of academic literacy learning? Chapter 9 will return to this question.

The next chapter examines the specific problems of corrective feedback, in particular the kind of feedback that is available to learners in Computer Assisted Language Learning. In this learning environment another kind of awareness, at a higher level than that considered so far, plays an essential role: metacognition (Ma, 2007). In particular, the kind of metacognition that is important in on-line learning is related to awareness of one's learning strategies, how to control attention, monitor understanding and misunderstanding, and how to make the most effective use of interactive learning resources.

Chapter 6

Corrective feedback in language learning

The previous chapter focused on negative evidence that learners discover for themselves in written expression. This chapter follows up with an examination of a kind of negative evidence, corrective feedback, which is provided *to* the learner. This will lead to the larger question about correction in language learning overall, not just in writing. Research in the field of instructed Second Language Acquisition has suggested that certain kinds of corrective feedback can be exploited effectively by students. If this suggestion turns out to be correct, systematic feedback on learner error could be integrated into L2 teaching practice as part of ongoing *formative assessment*. As was just mentioned, calling attention to errors can be considered as one type of negative evidence — information regarding which aspects of the developing interlanguage system do not form part of the target language (TL) system. One point of view proposes that the usefulness of corrective feedback is an empirical question to be settled on a case-by-case basis — which types might be useful to the learner and which types not. An opposing view might be that corrective feedback is not useful to the L2 learner, or that it is useful for building new language knowledge only in certain limited domains (explicit or declarative knowledge). This chapter will examine the effectiveness of corrective feedback that is provided by machine in an evaluation of one widely utilized computer program for second language learning.

One of the central issues in debate regarding corrective feedback (both by "hand and mouth" and by machine) is the reliability of feedback to the learner. If grammatically correct patterns produced by the learner are marked incorrect (for example if the instructor perceives a pragmatic difficulty that is not an error of grammar, or if the computer program cannot discriminate between a syntax error and a semantic problem) the learner receives conflicting and contradictory information about the target language grammar. This problem should be taken as a serious challenge for educators, not to be dismissed as unimportant. We will conclude with a discussion of ways in which L2 educators can improve the reliability of corrective feedback and how they can use technology more effectively in L2 teaching. Since Computer Assisted Language Learning (CALL) is an invaluable resource today for self-teaching, especially for the student without access to classes, what design features should learners look for to maximize efficiency and effectiveness?

6.1 Formative assessment for maximizing learning

Of the many kinds of assessment, corrective feedback provided to language learners can be considered as a formative type. As learners form hypotheses about the second language grammar, with feedback they receive information about which aspects of this developing system should be reconstructed or abandoned. For example, how are second language learners to know if a generalization, an application of a rule, or a reasonable attempt at transfer from their L1 is grammatically correct in the TL? Are the grammatical forms (including phonological forms) that are constructed in the process of L2 learning acceptable variants of examples noticed in the speech of native speakers, or are they errors? Some TL features, in addition, are relatively easy to notice while others are difficult. As all second language learners know, some features are completely opaque, unless someone who is familiar with the new grammar can point out what it is that we are not able to notice by ourselves.

To the extent that the relevant research questions can be formulated clearly, they will be among the most important areas of investigation for years to come, as well as ones that will continue to evoke some of the most interesting controversies in the field of language teaching. One reason why they are so important and interesting is because, unlike other questions in second language learning that primarily are either of theoretical or practical relevance, resolving the corrective feedback question is equally relevant to both theory and classroom practice.

This chapter will touch on three related topics in the next three sections:

1. In line with the theme of corrective feedback as a kind of formative assessment, there is the more general concept of negative evidence (introduced in Chapter 5),
2. The research on the effectiveness of corrective feedback in second language learning, and
3. The problems of corrective feedback by machine.

6.2 Negative evidence and positive evidence

Recall from the previous chapter that corrective feedback can be considered as belonging to the broader language input category of negative evidence, defined as all type of information available to the language learner about which patterns are not grammatical in the target language. Thus, in addition to direct and indirect feedback from "external" sources, negative evidence might also be generated from self-correction, and metalinguistic reflection, "internal" sources,[1] if we could call them that. In turn, the distinction between negative evidence and positive evidence in regard to the role that each plays in language learning is of central theoretical importance, being one of the key dimensions when considering the differences between first language development and second language learning. The complex questions of which acquisition/learning mechanisms are *shared* between L1 and L2, and in what way acquisition and learning *differ* between L1 and L2 directly inform the discussion on the role of negative evidence in L1 and L2. Recall from the study of self-correction in Chapter 5 that students generated their own negative evidence, so to speak, from a self-reflective literacy learning activity — reflection on their own texts for the purpose of making their written expression more comprehensible.

One approach to conceptualizing input and evidence for language development is to consider the learnability circumstances of both the young child and the older L2 learner

Figure 2.1
The subset-superset problem in language acquisition

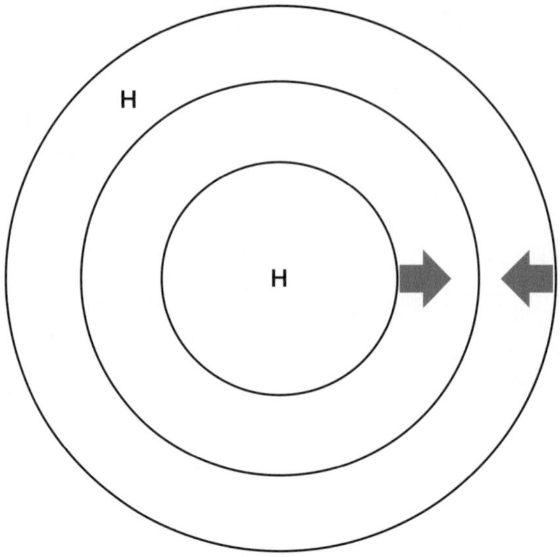

in relation to what is known as the Subset-superset problem. Referring back to Figure 2.1, reproduced above, an important aspect of the acquisition/learning task is represented graphically. The "subset-superset problem in language acquisition" figure, representing a version of Pinker's (1990) model, corresponds nicely to both L1 and L2 development. Perhaps simplifying somewhat, we can use the term "hypothesize" to refer to the process of developing a mature or more complete grammatical system, and the term "learner" to refer to both L1 and L2 subjects. Second language learners might be students; but, for good reason, we would hesitate to call the typical L1 learner (or "acquirer") a "student." In the inner most of the concentric circles the learner hypothesizes a grammar, incomplete as it always is during the early stages of development. Here the task is to build upon the incomplete grammar, indicated by the expanding arrow. At the same time, the learner forms hypotheses that are "beyond" the target language. In Figure 2.1, the TL is bounded by the intermediate circle. In other words, the learner hypothesizes a language that is also "too large" (overgeneralizations and other constructions that need to be abandoned somehow), hence the title of the figure: an acquisition problem in which the hypothesized language (H) is, at the same time, a *subset* and a *superset* of the TL. Complementary to the objective of building up subset-H (the "expanding" arrow), the learner needs to retreat from superset-H (the "contracting" arrow). The two learning objectives work hand in hand.

Assuming for a moment the application of general learning strategies for language, expanding the incomplete "hypothesis grammar" should be more or less straightforward — positive evidence should suffice. The learner expands the interlanguage system through simple-immersion — extensive exposure to correct examples. Some aspects of the grammar might require more and "richer" examples than others; but it would be positive evidence just the same. With access to the same general learning strategies, however, retreating from superset-H is not as easy with exposure to positive evidence alone; exceedingly difficult it would be in some domains according to theories based on this model. Here, negative evidence would be necessary. What facilitates first language acquisition for young children, who face the problem of a severe shortage of usable negative evidence, is access to a specialized language-specific acquisition mechanism — the Language Acquisition Device. The LAD complements, boosts, or compensates for the inadequate general learning strategies that are underdeveloped in young children, again according to the theory that we have assumed as our working hypothesis so far (Anderson and Lightfoot, 2002; Kinsella, 2009; Meisel, 2009; Pinker and Jackendoff, 2005).

For second language learning, a long-standing debate revolves around the question of whether the above scenario still applies (Clahsen and Muysken, 1996; Schachter, 1998). If it does not apply, the superfluous negative evidence of first language acquisition is no longer superfluous for learning second languages, because L2 learners no longer have free access to the same language acquisition mechanisms that children have when they are acquiring their L1. With this idea in mind, see the suggestive, in some ways provocative, case study by Ding (2007). In regard to this proposed explanation, there is an interesting potential convergence with opposing theoretical models that, for example, reject the concept of specialized language-specific acquisition mechanisms. For example, if L2 learners must rely on general learning strategies for all domains of the target language, because that's all that they have at their disposal (that's all that they had at their disposal in L1 acquisition, according to this view), positive evidence alone would still be inadequate. And finally, we should keep in mind that the Subset-superset problem should not be taken as the only framework to consider in judging the claims of one point of view or another regarding the usefulness of negative evidence in L2 learning.

Figure 6.1 presents a schema for comparing some of the proposed differences between L1 and L2. All theories accept that positive evidence is necessary for both L1 and L2 — without a rich immersion in the target language, development is severely impaired in L1, and cannot advance beyond the most rudimentary knowledge in L2. So above the dotted line, positive evidence is necessary in both columns. Now let us consider the differences between L1 and L2, starting with L1 acquisition. Cutting across theoretical lines again, most researchers would agree (for different reasons) that, for L1, negative evidence is not forthcoming in sufficient quantity and reliability; and even if it were it is doubtful that young cognitively immature children would be able to exploit it productively. Corrective feedback, in particular, may be provided to some children, but we know that it is not essential (nor useful, probably) for L1 acquisition. Continuing down the left column, we can also eliminate as necessary L1 acquisition input factors for young children the following advanced learning resources: metalinguistic awareness, direct instruction, and literacy. The reader is invited to cross off from the left hand column the "input factors" below the dotted line as "not essential."

But under the right-hand column of Figure 6.1 (L2 learning) a different picture emerges. Strong natural approach models (Krashen, 1998), which tend to draw a broad equivalence between L1 and L2 acquisition processes, generally favor the view that the

Figure 6.1
Positive evidence and negative evidence

What effect do different "input factors" have: on L1 acquisition, on L2 learning?
Which are essential?
Which contribute toward more efficient and effective mastery (e.g., in relation to required time on task and ultimate attainment)?

L1 acquisition	L2 learning
Positive evidence	Positive evidence
....	....
Negative evidence (in general)	Negative evidence (in general)
Corrective feedback (in particular)	Corrective feedback (in particular)
Metalinguistic awareness	Metalinguistic awareness
Direct instruction	Direct instruction
Literacy	Literacy

same basic acquisition mechanisms are deployed, more or less. Simplifying somewhat, for the development of *linguistic competence*, if positive evidence, along with "naturally occurring" negative evidence, is sufficient for L1, it should be sufficient for L2. This version would then maintain "negative evidence (in general)" in an intermediate category (not to be crossed off for L1 acquisition). The input factors and learning circumstances below the dotted line (or, tentatively, below "negative evidence") may contribute to conscious declarative knowledge, awareness of rules and constructions, and the ability to monitor speech and written expression, but they do not serve as input to implicit language knowledge (competence).

In contrast, approaches to second language learning that (for different reasons) conceive of it as fundamentally different from L1 development will view the "non-primary" explicit learning input factors (below the dotted line) as potentially important. They would contribute significantly to the end state mastery of the second language — not just to a peripheral declarative knowledge, but also to competence itself. From this point of view, we could propose a distinction between "secondary" and "primary" resources. The question of the role of negative evidence in L2 is part of the problem of determining the importance of "secondary" resources for L2 learning. "Secondary" here refers to the broad category of language learning resources that include: metalinguistic awareness, attention to error patterns and miscommunication, reflection on learning processes and outcomes, declarative knowledge and deliberate learning of skills (DeKeyser, 1998). These contrast to the "primary" resources that, hypothetically, suffice for the development of core linguistic competence of the mother tongue and the basic communicative abilities exemplified in face-to-face conversation.

6.3 Corrective feedback in L2 learning

First of all we should specify what the claim about corrective feedback or negative evidence in general actually should be in this discussion. It clearly is not enough to investigate whether correction or focus on form "is effective," "can facilitate," or "may play a role" in L2 learning, unless the hypothesis to reject is that corrective feedback verifiably *retards* learning, representing an inherent obstacle to learning. Some opponents of direct instruction might actually make the claim that *all* forms of CF are harmful in this way. But this extreme position would be the least plausible. Conversely, few, if any, researchers would defend the view that no demonstrable gains in L2 acquisition are possible without deliberate attention to grammatical patterns and correction; that purely naturalistic acquisition is impossible. Rather, the proposal to be tested would have to be specific (and reasonable), something along the lines of: some form of corrective feedback, or systematic negative evidence more generally, results in a *measurable difference* in overall rate of learning and ultimate attainment. In contrast, the competing hypothesis would be the following: that there will be no significant difference over exclusively input-based instruction of the simple-immersion type.

This way of framing the problem may help advance the theoretical discussion, but in practical terms, the alternatives that learners face pose new and in some ways more difficult questions. For example, which types of negative evidence should we expect to be most effective (if the general claim of a measurable difference turns out to be correct)? Self-correction and reflection might steer the learner away from incorrect hypotheses; but at present we know very little about the effect on learning of this kind of negative evidence, or about how teachers might be able to provide it in a systematic way. On the other hand, corrective feedback (directly provided by a teacher or more advanced learner) includes — recasts and modeling, request for clarification, repetition of the error, and in the more deliberate and focused category, direct correction, metalinguistic explanation, and prompt to elicit the target form. More attention in the research needs to be devoted to all these types of correction.

In regard to the direct–indirect distinction, studies have attempted to define these categories more precisely, something that has proved to be more difficult than first imagined. For example, even seemingly indirect type recasts (corrected rephrase of the learner utterance) can be formulated in a didactic manner, and be perceived by the learner as direct and focused (Ellis and Sheen, 2006). But overall, how recasts are interpreted is an issue that remains unresolved, pending the application of new methodological approaches (Carpenter *et al.*, 2006). And then there are the difficult research questions of noticing, how the learner "takes up" instances of negative evidence, and the degree to which they can be processed with the effect of advancing mastery. Again, another important topic for future research is: which aspect of mastery advances, competence or learned meta-knowledge?

With all this in mind, a specific question that has arisen in both classroom research and controlled experiments is the relative effectiveness of recasts versus prompts. On the one hand, evidence from learner "uptake" suggests that the more direct learner-generated repair in response to prompt is more effective than recast, for which the corrective function may often be ambiguous (Lyster, 2004). However, the perception of recasts by learners may depend to a large extent on the degree to which the overall instructional program is oriented toward attending to grammar patterns as opposed to exclusively communicative activities (Sheen, 2004). Other factors, such as learner disposition, aptitude, and L2 proficiency level would be relevant as well, in addition to the problem (that interacts with these factors) of noticing and perception of different kinds of corrective feedback by learners and how teachers interpret learner responses (Yoshida, 2010).

Now, if we provisionally accept as a working assumption the first hypothesis, that ultimate attainment is favored by some types of corrective feedback, a number of critiques still need to be addressed. At least until findings from comparative studies are more conclusive (Loewen and Erlam, 2006; Shehadeh, 2003), the practical objections to corrective feedback deserve our attention. For example, it has been observed that the feedback provided by language teachers can be sporadic, infrequent and inconsistent, factors that conceivably might account for conflicting and inconclusive results from one study to the other. While "noisy" and "impoverished" input (of the positive evidence type) probably does not handicap first language acquisition in any significant way, second language learners' "tolerance" for unreliable feedback, especially of the direct corrective type, may be much lower. This conjecture leads us to a series of speculations about the reliability of corrective feedback in L2 learning and a proposal for future research on this point.

The problem of consistent corrective feedback in fact is shared among all CF categories, direct and indirect — recasts, prompts and metalinguistic explanation; and it might turn out in the end to be more serious than we expect. In one sense it is less of a theoretical problem than one of implementation — how in the context of the give and take of largely uncontrolled classroom interaction does the teacher deploy corrective feedback routines that are consistently reliable, accurate, and processable by learners? For example, even highly proficient native speakers of the target language routinely fail to discriminate in their CF interventions between errors of syntax and non-native constructions that involve subtle semantic distinctions and pragmatic infelicities, the latter, despite their subtlety, often presenting themselves as more salient. Complex considerations related to the componential nature of grammar and its interface with other domains of knowledge (Coltheart, 1999; Jackendoff, 2002) are necessary to take into account sometimes in trying to disentangle which linguistic subsystems and non-linguistic knowledge components are contributing to the confusion. Not surprisingly, non-native sounding, grammatically well formed, learner speech might receive feedback that is either simply incorrect, ambiguous, incomplete or confusing. Again, neither direct nor indirect corrective feedback is immune to the reliability problem.

6.4 Electronic corrective feedback

Two reports at a conference some years ago at Tamkang University on L2 writing called our attention to the fact that the CF reliability problem is also shared by Computer Assisted Language Learning programs (Chen, 2006; Masumi, 2006). If learners are to receive feedback, it is important that it be consistent, this consistency perhaps being even more important in the CALL environment. With this idea in mind, as a part of our program at Northern Arizona University in second language teaching methods, we have critically examined the corrective feedback features of a widely used CALL software package, the *Rosetta Stone Language Library*, produced by Fairfield Language Technologies. The problems posed by the writing section are illustrative of some of the dilemmas and possibilities in machine corrective feedback.

At first glance, one might venture to describe the *Rosetta Stone* feedback options as simple and limited, restricted to a highly closed-ended type of writing task, that of dictation. First, the learner listens to an audio version of a short text, accompanied by an image that serves as context support. In a word processing window, the learner transcribes the audio version, as in traditional dictation tasks. The corrector consists of a basic spell-checker that matches the learner's typed version to a single correct model, including punctuation and capitalization. As illustrated in Figure 6.2 with hypothetical learner responses, the cursor moves along the text, highlighting each error in succession, prompting self-correction. Following along, the learner analyzes each error in turn and attempts self-correction with the help of a repetition of the audio prompt. Progressively, texts become longer and more complex, taxing both working memory and, specifically, grammatical processing ability.

We may be tempted to characterize this feedback procedure as exclusively focused on spelling patterns. While many prompts to self-correct may involve purely orthographic errors, knowledge of and reflection upon grammatical patterns greatly facilitates self-correction, as the examples in Figure 6.2 illustrate. That even in the application of a very basic text-processing and correcting program, in this case, learners are prompted to reflect on word and sentence-level grammar, and in the self-correction of punctuation more explicitly so. Pyun and Lee-Smith (2011) discuss findings of a study of corrective feedback in on-line dictation that support this observation. Admittedly, this kind of feedback feature cannot provide any information to the learner beyond what the exact words of the template provide, much less provide feedback about higher-order discourse patterns. Again, the closed-ended design appears as a limitation; but limiting the focus of attention for learners in this way may in fact work to their benefit.

All of this underscores the problem of feedback quality alluded to earlier. A predicament presents itself in a kind of "trade-off," analogous to that in language assessment in general between the considerations of validity and reliability, what Davies (1990) referred to in terms of the requirements of "being explicit" and "controlling uncertainty." In corrective feedback, discrete-point type and closed-ended tasks might be questioned regarding the restricted domain of language ability for which they provide practice to the learner. The more closed-ended, the further removed they seem to be from complex meaning, for example (the analogy to validity).

Consistency of feedback (the reliability question), however, is generally favored by narrowing the domain of ability. Conversely, the more open-ended the task, the more

Figure 6.2

Sample CALL writing activity with corrective feedback

(1) Student hears this prompt:
The woman has jumped.
Responds:
The woman as jumped.
The corrective feedback cursor highlights: as

(2) Student hears this prompt:
The horse is jumping.
Responds:
The horse is jump in.
The corrective feedback cursor highlights: in

(3) Student hears this prompt:
The child is going to jump.
Responds:
The childs going jump.
The corrective feedback cursor highlights: childs, and then jump.

(4) Student hears this prompt:
They should have studied syntax before the exam.
Responds:
They should of studied syntax before the exam.
The corrective feedback cursor highlights: of

difficult it becomes to provide learners with frequent and reliable feedback. Interestingly, this relation of "trade-off" seems to apply to both live instructor and machine correction, although it applies, and can be compensated for, in different ways in each case. So, we might also venture to say that the reliability of feedback in closed-ended prompt and correction type programs, like the one described here, is a feature that as a rule CALL should value positively, and seek to build upon. In building upon this advantageous feature, the challenge before us would then be to find ways to overcome some of the common limitations specific to closed-ended tasks.

For us, it is not a question of trying to determine which alternative is better in the abstract. Rather, in designing or selecting CALL activities, the limitations of each option should be taken into account in a deliberate way. Thus, we will be in a better position to know what to expect from different learning activities, in particular what kind of feedback is most effective for word and sentence-level skills as opposed to the discourse-level. To the more integrative abilities might correspond feedback that is more open-ended; in this case, we should remember that not all feedback needs to be corrective.

As is widely recognized, learning activities of the integrative type, requiring the application of discourse-level abilities, tend to be more intrinsically motivating for learners. A factor that educators should keep in mind, it is also one that we can set aside, for now. In fact, the degree to which learners find one or another activity enjoyable or interesting is probably not a good starting point for designing a curriculum and selecting materials. Language learning research also needs to consider what are the most effective and efficient methods for grammar and vocabulary development, for example, taking the factor of motivation as a given. The same applies to learner dispositions toward corrective feedback in particular. Again, language educators cannot be indifferent to how individual students and groups of learners (e.g., who share the same cultural background) perceive teacher correction of different types, for example of varying degrees of directness. But at the same time, it is important to determine the effect on learning of different kinds of negative evidence *in principle*, independently of contextual constraints that vary from one second language learning situation to another. In fact, computer-based corrective feedback is likely to be able to successfully cut across cultural differences regarding the constraints on attending to grammatical form during language use. Speculation aside, and taking care not to throw caution to the wind, we should acknowledge that the pragmatics of human-machine interaction is still not well understood.

This dilemma of "consistency versus open-endedness" brings us to the proposal for research alluded to earlier. If closed-ended, discrete-point CF programs have the potential of providing completely reliable feedback to the learner that is always unambiguous and accurate, this feature presents CALL researchers with an opportunity. Tentatively, or for the time being, we might set aside the issues of "validity," and "higher-order versus lower-order," not because they are unimportant, but for purely temporary methodological considerations:

1. to allow designers to push the limits, so to speak, of the closed-ended type task and determine, in practice, how complex, to what degree higher-order, and how "integrative" closed-ended CALL activities can become, without sacrificing reliability. On-line multiple-choice formats, today, offer learners opportunities that were not available just a few years ago. For example, distractor options can represent degrees of approximation to the correct form, with immediate feedback explanations (and hints, without giving away the answer) on why a response might be partially correct, totally wrong, etc. Without the ability to predict future advances in computing in the short and medium term, the question of how rich closed-ended feedback can be must be left open. Nevertheless, it should be kept in mind that one of the important features of closed-ended protocols, as in Figure 6.2, despite their inherent limitation in other respects, is that they are characteristically highly interactive, requiring the learner to be actively engaged, as opposed to simply observing, as is the case in some open-ended CALL programs.
2. If reliability of negative evidence, in fact, turns out to be a confounding variable in the CF research, then maintaining it constant should help us direct our attention better to the remaining central issues. The elimination of the CF reliability problem can be thought of as a desirable goal, even if the price to pay for it is high (temporarily), in part because the problem doesn't apply to all feedback, and for our purposes eliminating all inconsistency and ambiguity is provisional and tentative.

At the same time, as a result perhaps, we will be better able to keep an open mind on the still elusive questions, such as the relative merits of recasts and prompts and degree of explicitness. And it should go without saying that no part of this proposal should be taken as disfavoring open-ended CALL tasks. No counterposition is implied in any way. Rather, the research problems associated with closed-ended tasks appear to be somewhat more tractable at this time.

6.4.1 Computer Assisted Language Learning for learning characters

With the advent of modern input methods for character processing, a new line of research in CALL has emerged. Of far-reaching practical consequences for both native-speaker L1 literacy learners and L2 learners of Chinese, the issues raised go beyond methods and materials in literacy learning. The discussion evoked by the widespread use of personal computers for writing in Chinese (in China, and for Chinese speakers elsewhere, and for *kanji* in Japan) raises interesting questions about the new relationship between developing skill in handwriting and skill in digitized text-processing. How might advances in text-processing technology affect all literacy skills (in writing and reading) in society at large? Plausibly, the question is different for learners of the more complex morphosyllabic systems (or subsystems, as in Japan) than it is for learners of alphabetic writing. The implications of the access to new text-processing methods are also important for L2 and foreign language learners of Chinese and Japanese.

A recent investigation of college-level FL learners of Chinese compared beginners and intermediate students in their writing performance in handwriting and computer-based writing (Kang, 2011). The interesting aspect of this study was the foreign language program teaching approach that placed a relative de-emphasis on the development of writing skills in the early semesters. This program feature perhaps allowed investigators to gauge the effect of frequent access to on-line Chinese language learning materials and students' overall growth in mastery of the language, not heavily influenced by robust writing instruction. In other words, what would be the effect of exposure to and practice with character processing tools, which students used frequently, on their own and as part of classroom projects? How might error patterns differ between beginners and intermediates as a function of practice with handwriting and computer text-processing? Note that errors might be common to both modalities, or be specific to one or the other. And specifically as regards the learning situation of L2 learners' processing of characters, how might the on-line writing environment pose special circumstances for them, as opposed to native-speakers? For example, do L2 learners, because they still have not mastered the language, especially the phonological system, rely more heavily (than they should) on information provided by the semantic radical in character recognition, this problem compounded by a greater rate of error in entering *pinyin* spellings on the keyboard?

In the handwriting assessments, four error types (aside from confusion between simplified and traditional characters) were catalogued as important (Kang, 2011, pp. 114–

122):

1. homophone errors,
2. confusion of characters with similar shapes,
3. characters with omitted strokes, and
4. combining the wrong components into one character.

In computer typing, two errors types were analyzed:

5. entering an incorrect *pinyin* spelling, and
6. recognition errors.

Significant differences between beginners and intermediates were revealing. In handwriting, while the common errors among beginners were distributed among all four types, intermediates rarely made homophone errors (type 1) or combination errors (type 4) (pp. 131–132). On a separate measure of stroke sequence, while incorrect sequence correlated significantly with character error for beginners, these error patterns did not correlate for intermediates. In computer typing, intermediates outperformed beginners with their superior *pinyin* knowledge, committing few type 5 errors. Most interesting was the finding related to modality — for beginners, total errors decreased significantly from handwriting to typing conditions (total scores improving from 68.8% to 85.4%), a predicable result as the latter depends on recognition as opposed to recall/execution. But for intermediates handwriting and typing were comparable, the small difference being non-significant (96.6% and 99.1%, respectively) (pp. 106–107). Thus, the hypothesis to test in future research, based on the speculative and informal observation that we can make from the intermediates' comparable performance in both modalities, is the following — dependence on and increased use by L2 learners of computer typing using *pinyin* input does not necessarily degrade their skill in writing characters by hand. On a related note in a different study, of child "second literacy" learning, in Chinese (Singapore), Wong *et al.* (2011) recommend an early and strong introduction to *pinyin* inputting skills for the purpose of taking full advantage of computer-mediated character writing software, indispensable for complete literacy in Chinese in today's world. As the authors point out: "Writing in the 21st century" will largely be "electronic writing" (p. 234). In this instance students were speakers of Mandarin, with primary literacy in English.

One of the CALL initiatives that appears to have most successfully incorporated the central theoretical advances in language learning is the multimedia Dragonwise Project. [2] Directed at the child, native-speaking, literacy learner, it is guided by two concepts in literacy learning that we have considered in Chapters 4 and 5 — development of metalinguistic knowledge, what the authors call "structural awareness instruction," and the implementation of systematic corrective feedback as a tool of formative assessment, designed in this case especially for young children (Ki *et al.*, 2003; Lam *et al.*, 2001).

The learning of characters, according to the project investigators, cannot be simply an additive accumulation of information, even if the instructional program does not call attention to the regularities in the morphosyllabic system. But if learners are led to develop a *structural view* that stresses the combinatorial properties of characters, literacy learning could be made more productive. In the absence of this kind of direct instruction that promotes "graphic awareness," most learners, eventually, will still intuit these properties on one level or another; but learning will be less effective and less efficient. They argue that systematic reflection on orthographic patterns can be combined with a focus on meaning, contrary to popular objection that claims that this kind of focus on form obstructs comprehension (this controversy is the topic of the next chapter, by the way). The patterning of semantic and phonetic components within characters, despite considerable irregularity in the system as a whole, lends itself easily to the design of a teaching program that takes reflection on structural properties, and an emphasis on existing regularity, as a point of departure. The CALL environment capitalizes on these principles.

On-line learning environments do this by providing learners with completely reliable corrective feedback, designed at every turn to match the learner's current stage of mastery. For Ki and Lam and their associates, implicitly, the development of structural awareness (e.g., via CALL) and CF are closely interdependent, an argument that we have not yet made in this book, but that now appears intuitively self-evident. Readers are invited to engage the Dragonwise materials for themselves (see Note 2 for the URL) to see examples of this approach. In one series of activities, characters are presented in clusters in didactic (and richly meaningful) texts for the purpose of calling attention to common components (e.g., the phonic), as well as attention to how characters vary in meaning by substituting the semantic. Clustering, of course, is productive along the converse dimension: keep the semantic radical constant, vary the phonetic. In each interactive task, corrective feedback *scaffolds* learning; prompts are *hints* that lead the learner toward constructing closer and closer approximations of each target objective. Actively "[exploring] this network, students… develop a mental 'toolkit' from these properties of Chinese characters, which is helpful to them in learning other characters proficiently" (Lam *et al.*, 2001, p. 123).

6.4.2 When there is no teacher or other reliable source of language input

As was mentioned at the beginning of this chapter, computerized language learning programs are especially useful for students who do not have access to classes or proficient speakers of the target language where they live. Normally, even if it is available, television programming in the L2 cannot provide enough comprehensible input for the beginning learner. So together with extensive reading (which can be controlled to provide comprehensible input), on-line learning activities allow the student to make significant advances toward mastery in many domains of the target language. In this case, it is the provision of feedback and the interactivity of learning tasks that complements simple-immersion (reading and listening). Extensive reading by itself, for example, fails to provide interactive practice; listening, by itself, lacks feedback.

Another example of the application of CALL comes to mind that would be even more important — to a language acquisition situation of much higher stakes, that of L1 development in exceptional circumstances. As was reviewed in Chapter 3, research on deafness and sign language has shown that denial of processible input to the LAD during the Critical Period (prior to age 5 or perhaps earlier) puts deaf children at high risk of long-term language impairment, including impaired learning capacity for any subsequent L2 (Mayberry, 2007). For the majority of profoundly deaf children born to hearing parents, even early diagnosis does not ensure that correct intervention strategies are implemented. Lacking the ability or willingness on the part of caretakers to make provision for sustained contact with an adequate language acquisition model, interactive sign language software designed especially for young children could conceivably compensate for language deprivation during the narrow biological window of opportunity of the Critical Period. Even assuming the present capabilities of computational technology, engaging and linguistically rich on-line language acquisition materials can be easily designed. Of far-reaching theoretical, as well as practical implications, is the distinct possibility that such computing resources might be able to compensate for the lack of human linguistic models *completely*, at least in the domains of lexical and grammatical knowledge. "Completely" here refers strictly to sufficient language input to avert the onset of long-term language and cognitive impairment.

The question of theory that is relevant here is — what are the lower limits below which language input to the LAD can no longer ensure the development of a normal unimpaired first language grammar; and what is the minimal threshold of Primary Linguistic Data that is necessary in order to prevent damage to the language acquisition capacity? A secondary question would be — what are the optimal input conditions for language acquisition in exceptional circumstances (e.g., profound deafness for which a hearing aid is insufficient and caretakers lack ability in a sign language, or cannot learn it fast enough)? For example, what level of interactivity is necessary for ensuring normal grammatical development in a L1 — simple-immersion or immersion plus active practice including feedback on actual language production? For ethical reasons, the definitive experiments cannot be carried out, even though indirect evidence from cross-cultural studies of primary language socialization suggests that simple-immersion (assuming attention to input on the part of the child) does suffice. Nevertheless, this important theoretical question looms very large in the background in all research on L1 acquisition in exceptional circumstances.

In compensating for a significantly diminished human communication and normal language socialization, a computer clearly cannot substitute for requisite experience in all domains of language ability. An example would be ability in the pragmatic domains and the underlying knowledge structures associated with *socially appropriate and coherent language use* in context. On the other hand, sign language input that is grammatically rich enough, that is processible by infants and preschool children and engaging enough to maintain attention might be sufficient to trigger the LAD mechanisms adequately, assuring normal development in the domain of core *linguistic knowledge*. In addition, reaching this threshold of PLD might forestall for long enough the onset of a permanently impaired language acquisition and learning capacity. Hypothetically, the window of opportunity might close *early* for grammatical competence and the consolidation of an unimpaired language learning capacity, but close *later* (if at all) for pragmatic competencies and abilities.

If this line of reasoning is correct, the next important consideration is the question of feedback, mentioned earlier. In regard to the design features of a first language development program, what type of feedback is optimal and at what level? Recall from Figure 6.1 — while evidence suggests that corrective feedback facilitates L2 learning, L1 acquisition advances on the back of positive evidence alone (i.e., simple-immersion or comprehensible input). Thus, one might be tempted to conclude that a CALL program for L1 acquisition can dispense with corrective feedback, ensuring only that content is engaging, linguistically complete and age-appropriate. This hypothesis may turn out to be correct in principle, but optimal software design may nevertheless include different kinds of feedback for the purpose for maximizing interactivity and attention. We should also keep in mind that not all feedback is corrective, and creative CALL designers will incorporate the entire range of interactive tools at their disposal. Some may even be of the corrective type, which, properly configured for children, presents no impediment to language development, and probably helps them to attend more closely and extensively to learning tasks. Readers are encouraged to consult reports of pilot CALL programs for deaf students, mainly directed at older children and focused on literacy skills (Dubuisson *et al.*, 2004; Henao Alvarez *et al.*, 2004).

A consensus appears to have emerged that a bilingual approach that builds competence in sign language favors both primary linguistic development and second language literacy learning (i.e., reading and writing that corresponds to a spoken language). On this point, key aspects of CALL that have been identified as uniquely productive include: individualization of instruction and self-pacing, richness of information including hypermedia resources, and immediate and reliable feedback (corrective and non-corrective). Other investigators have piloted primary sign language development programs for young children that incorporate sophisticated feedback features (Brashear *et al.*, 2006; Henderson-Summet *et al.*, 2007).

6.5 What makes instruction and learning really interactive?

In many domains of teaching, CALL will never replace the language teacher, and at the same time the language teacher will never have the opportunity and access to resources for providing learners with the extensive practice that they need, a necessity that can be partially fulfilled by high quality interactive on-line resources.

On the research side, the investigation of the effect of different types of feedback in CALL (corrective and non-corrective) promises to put a new perspective on the continuing discussion on the role of negative evidence in L2 learning. Studies have tentatively suggested, for example, that the electronic environment may even facilitate certain kinds of reflection among learners (Sauro, 2009). Students have more time to develop and refine their observations, as in the case of requests for clarification and "negotiation moves," and more time to formulate repairs (Morris, 2005). As was mentioned earlier, in the more controlled setting of direct prompts, non-native speakers have the time and the opportunity to reflect and repair (including multiple trial-and-error attempts). The same opportunity would be difficult to have access to in real-time face-to-face feedback with an actual, live, native-speaker tutor, for example. The learner never has to be concerned with trying the patience of a software program in requesting a repetition, testing a hypothesis once too many times, or persisting in a fossilized error pattern; and the computer will provide as much corrective feedback, for as long as only *one* participant can endure, the one usually with more at stake in attaining mastery in the target language.

Precisely on the question of *prompts*, which elicit learner self-correction, versus *recasts*, in which the teacher directly provides the correct form, on-line corrective feedback may count with certain advantages. In a revealing study of classroom interaction by Yoshida (2008), even though it was apparent that both teachers and students recognized the superior merits, overall, of prompts, in actual instructional discourse, recasts predominated. Again, the minute by minute pressures of teacher-student, and student-student interchange tend to strongly disfavor the more complex, more difficult to implement and time consuming, elicitation of self-correction, negotiation of meaning, and other types of corrective feedback that require reflective attention to grammatical form and reformulation. As we saw earlier, on-line CF, even of the most primitive design, privileges prompt and self-correction over recast.

Exercises that require production can be designed to maximize attention to specific features. If the nature of the task allows for discrete-point feedback that is always reliable, followed by confirming feedback upon supplying the correct response, progressively more difficult grammatical patterns can be presented in a programmed fashion. Some evidence exists that learner uptake is highly favored by online corrective feedback of the elicitation (prompt) type (Heift, 2004). A future challenge for designers will be how to enhance and enrich feedback, as the author of this study points out.

We can now conclude this chapter with a review of the points that led to the proposal for further research. One starting point in even considering the usefulness of corrective feedback was the assumption that second language learners avail themselves, because they have to, of learning strategies that they did not need to, and were not able to, deploy in first language acquisition. Alternatively, if the above assumption can be shown to be unfounded, language learners might still find corrective feedback and other types of negative evidence useful in mastering those aspects of language ability beyond core grammatical knowledge and basic conversational skill — e.g., higher order abilities related to literacy and academic proficiency.

The current research on the effectiveness of corrective feedback in second language learning, focused on direct and indirect types and other kinds of negative evidence, is of paramount practical and theoretical importance. The question of CF reliability also needs to be investigated as it addresses an interesting and pertinent critique of corrective feedback by proponents of naturalistic approaches. CALL environments offer a special opportunity to evaluate the effect of this factor of reliability. On the practical side, educators need to develop sound criteria for critically evaluating the various on-line programs available to their second language students. These can potentially become the most important source of extra-curricular interactive practice, supplementing the comprehensible input that learners are exposed to in the electronic media. If on-line language learning resources become a major support for students outside of the traditional classroom, it is content-based language learning (immersion) that complements this support most effectively in the classroom, topic of the next chapter.

Notes

1. In a series of studies we have examined the tendencies across grade level in bilingual children's ability to deliberately attend to different grammatical and discourse-level features in their writing (Francis, 2012). In a separate investigation of self-correction in reading the same general research questions came up: (1) how is the development of metalinguistic awareness different from how other kinds of language ability develop, for example the interactive and context-embedded language abilities that are acquired spontaneously and uniformly in children's first language? (2) To what extent is the negative evidence that children provide to themselves in literacy tasks involving self-correction a necessary component of school language ability (in this case, academic literacy)? (3) If it is necessary, what kinds of instructional design promote efficient and effective self-correction strategies, as part of the broader development of advanced metalinguistic abilities? The assumption here is that without direct instruction, these strategies do not emerge spontaneously and uniformly in all children, not even among all literate children. See Bitchener *et al.* (2005), Ferris (2004) and Truscott and Hsu (2008) for research findings and discussion related to the ongoing debate on corrective feedback in L2 writing.
2. www.dragonwise.hku.hk

Chapter 7

The foundation of immersion education — integration of language and content

The concept of integrating second language learning with content learning has become one of the cornerstones of L2 pedagogy. Today, there is wide consensus regarding the basic principles of content-based language teaching among educators and SLA researchers. Interestingly, this broad agreement cuts across the different theoretical perspectives in the field.

This chapter will first trace the origins of content-based language instruction to its first large scale application in the immersion programs in North America. In particular, for school-age second language learners, content-based immersion teaching has been shown to be the most effective and efficient approach for providing high quality language instruction to L2 learners while at the same time helping students make progress in the academic content objectives. Next, we will examine the more difficult problem of how to integrate language learning objectives into the content lessons. Questions that educators and researchers are still grappling with are: (1) Is comprehensible input sufficient for mastery of the L2 or do second language learners also benefit from some form of direct instruction focused on language objectives? (2) If some form of planned and organized instruction focused on language learning objectives is recommended, what kind of focus on grammar and vocabulary is most effective? (3) How can this double task, seemingly implying a double learning burden, especially for beginners, be made feasible?

7.1 What is second language immersion?

The successful implementation of French immersion teaching in Canada, beginning in the 1960s, has generated one of the most important bodies of research on second language learning and bilingualism (Laplante, 2001; Lazaruk, 2007; Swain and Lapkin, 2005). Second language immersion techniques are all based on the basic concept of content-based language instruction (CBI) and have been incorporated into different types of program model. These techniques all apply the same underlying teaching principles. The widest application of second language immersion is to the teaching of English as a Second Language (ESL) in countries with large numbers of child L2 learners, as in the United States, and to the teaching of English as a Foreign Language (EFL), internationally. Notably, in China, Japan and other Asian countries, an important discussion has developed recently on how to most effectively implement English-medium content instruction, comparing and contrasting the different pedagogical approaches. For example, what is the best way to apply a *distribution* of L1 and L2 across the curriculum (as opposed to exclusive L2-medium instruction in all subjects), and how to strategically *combine* the key elements of both communicative and grammar-focused teaching (Rao, 2006; Wannagat, 2007; Yu, 2008)? What effect might immersion in a foreign language have on the development of academic proficiencies in the national language, and on the preservation of minority languages? Before we proceed, it needs to be made perfectly clear that while English is taken in this chapter as the typical example for the different kinds of L2 learning, the immersion approach is applicable to all second language learning situations. It applies to the learning of other languages of international communication, national languages that young people need access to in school, and indigenous and minority languages that communities have made the decision to defend and preserve.

Before discussing this research it is important to distinguish clearly between: (1) the *methodological approach* of immersion teaching and (2) some *program models* that propose the implementation of immersion teaching to the exclusion of instruction in students' first language. The methods of content-based language teaching (in this book synonymous with immersion, #1 above) can be applied to any type of program model that includes a second language component, including the various types of bilingual education. Such was, in fact, the purpose for which these methods were originally conceived. Immersion program models of the type that do not contemplate any participation of learners' primary language, #2, belong to two categories:

2a. exclusive use of the L2 for all instruction as a default option given the unavailability of resources to provide for a dual-language curriculum (e.g., the practical limitations imposed by situations of a high degree of linguistic diversity, many L1s in the same classroom, shortage of teachers who are bilingual in the target language and children's L1) and

2b. the programmatic exclusion of L2 learners' first language; in this instance, the second language is the exclusive medium of instruction for deliberate language policy reasons, sometimes ideologically motivated, as has become increasingly common in the United States. For example, Structured English Immersion (SEI) is a *program model* in the U.S. that typically implies the exclusive use of English in all instruction.

In contrast, for example in the United States, immersion *teaching methods* are utilized in both all-English programs and bilingual programs. In the latter case, the special modifications of immersion teaching (for beginners, higher levels of context support, controlled vocabulary, simplification of grammar, etc.) are applied to L2-medium content lessons, while L1-medium instruction proceeds normally. In SEI programs, the L1-medium component is eliminated, so to speak. Of course, L2-only immersion program models do not apply to elementary level EFL settings because the L1-medium component (or the national/official language-medium component, as the case may be) cannot be eliminated. In the next two sections, the interesting debate on the relative merits of the different second language and bilingual program models will be temporarily set aside, allowing us to attend to the curriculum features of content-based L2 teaching as they would appear in any second language or bilingual classroom. The question of how CBI methods are implemented in bilingual versus second language-only program models will be taken up in the concluding section.

7.2 The logic and rationale of content-based language teaching

To review the first question that was posed at the beginning of this chapter: Is comprehensible input sufficient for L2 mastery or do second language learners benefit from some form of direct instruction focused on language objectives?

Early implementations of immersion often followed different versions of the so-called communicative approach to L2 learning — subject matter classes are taught in the second language, applying the special modifications of immersion teaching to classroom discourse, necessary for L2 beginners in academic subjects. In a complementary way, classroom routines and other highly context-embedded non-academic uses of language can easily dispense with this kind of Language Learner Sensitive Discourse (LLSD). Thus, for beginners, the right combination of LLSD and enhanced context support makes L2 input comprehensible. In this fashion, extensive and intensive comprehensible input provides the positive evidence, the Primary Linguistic Data, which L2 learners need in large quantities. While for more advanced L2 learners simplification and other modifications in speech and teacher discourse become progressively unnecessary, additional context support, such as "enhancement strategies" (Lin and Chen, 2006), continue to provide scaffolding when needed. Interestingly, while there is no principled contradiction between communicative methods and grammar teaching, in some versions of the communicative approach, direct instruction of grammar and vocabulary was, and still is, viewed as potentially useful only for developing conscious declarative knowledge of the target language and related metalinguistic abilities. According to this view, language instruction that fosters the development of explicit knowledge and ability would not contribute to implicit competence. Versions of the communicative approach that rejected systematic reflection on grammar patterns and developing metalinguistic ability, in theory, would minimize direct language instruction. Instead, language learners would acquire the L2 grammar by exposure to comprehensible input and implicitly through meaningful interaction — practice speaking with native-speakers and more advanced learners, negotiation of meaning, getting naturally occurring feedback on their attempts at production in the L2, and so forth.

Independent of this de-emphasis on specific language objectives, to be clear, most of the early elementary immersion programs did include a good measure of explicit grammar instruction as part of the Language Arts and Literacy curriculum (spelling, phonics and word analysis, rules of usage such as punctuation and capitalization of complete sentences, and other grammar conventions of academic writing). In addition, for these young language learners, core L2 grammar learning objectives (verb inflection, patterns of singular-plural, concordance, etc.) could be easily incorporated into the weekly Language Arts units, most notably in writing activities. In fact, this is a potentially fortuitous coincidence for L2 immersion, that teachers can take advantage of. The elementary and secondary Literacy/Language Arts curriculum (academic language proficiency) and the basic language learning objectives that L2 learners need to master (the core grammar and vocabulary of the target language) are not the same. But in the L2 immersion classroom they can be organized and taught in a way such that the learning of academic language proficiency serves the objectives of learning the L2 core grammar and vocabulary. In a sense, the "content areas" of Reading and Writing, lend themselves to a special kind of CBI because so much of their content consists of language learning objectives already. In this way, literacy learning and the study of the conventions of academic discourse also become an opportunity for an organized and systematic learning of the basic grammar of the second language. Only those communicative-oriented immersion programs that were also strongly influenced by whole language philosophy would have suppressed the grammar learning objectives of the standard Language Arts content area.

More recent implementations of immersion teaching have extended the idea of integrating language and content beyond simply teaching content through the medium of the second language. A new version of content-based language instruction views each lesson as an opportunity for inserting a parallel grammar lesson, a language learning focus incorporated into the content learning activities of Science, Social Studies, Mathematics, and Music (Brinton *et al.*, 2003), in addition to the "special CBI" of L2 Literacy and Language Arts. The idea of a more deliberate integration of language and content was prompted in part by an interesting finding from the large-scale assessment of Canadian immersion graduates — near-grade-level abilities in academic reading and listening, but stabilized interlanguage, far from native competence, evidenced in speaking and writing. According to the new version of immersion (which includes grammar instruction), implicit and incidental language learning through rich exposure, practice and interaction does occur and should be facilitated for students. But implicit and incidental learning isn't enough for optimal progress and advanced ultimate attainment.

In CBI-plus-grammar, language learning objectives are either content-compatible, not required for full comprehension, or content-obligatory, indispensable for comprehension of the content (Gajo, 2007; Hernández, 2005). Content-obligatory language objectives would need to be pre-taught or assured by some other means prior to the lesson. In contrast, the treatment of content-compatible language objectives can be shifted toward the actual content lesson or learning activity itself, linking them to specific objectives so that they "pair naturally" with textbook passages and other materials (Snow, 2005).

In this scheme, vocabulary learning now plays a pivotal role in the linking of content learning and grammar learning. One way of conceiving of the important work of building L2 vocabulary knowledge is to start with the requisite concepts of the content lesson. In a way, learning new words is part of the content learning objectives of a unit of study. Some new words will be "obligatory," belonging to the minimum required background knowledge for new concept learning, others "compatible," lending themselves to mastery during the content lessons.

Both words for new concepts and new (L2) words for previously acquired concepts are not just conceptual entries linked to a new phonological form in the second language lexicon. The language learner also faces the task of "completing" each lexical entry with its corresponding grammatical subcomponents — each word's morphological properties and how the word combines syntactically with other words in well-formed phrases. In this way, vocabulary learning is a kind of bridge, or interface, between the content and grammar domains of CBI. Interestingly, in L2 learning in academic settings, students typically make rapid advances in the aspects of lexical knowledge, which involve a fast mapping of concept to phonological (or orthographic) form. As their overall linguistic competence advances, these early and incomplete lexical entries serve to help bootstrap the further development of grammar. A particular advantage of deliberate and systematic vocabulary learning by L2 students (aside from helping them master more rapidly the content objectives at hand) is that it lends itself ideally to explicit learning strategies that the teacher is in an especially favorable position to help facilitate and organize for them (Laufer, 2006; Read, 2004).

As should be evident, this approach to content-based language teaching has accepted the essential advances of the communicative teaching model, over traditional grammar-translation and rote memory learning approaches. Today, virtually all proponents of integrating grammar learning into the content curriculum assume a teaching model that is thoroughly communicative, providing the learner with extensive comprehensive input in all lessons and learning tasks, and rich opportunities for practice (Rothenberg and Fisher, 2007). Applications of this method of content-based language teaching, even of the structured direct instruction variety, are also fundamentally, and by their very nature, meaning-focused (for discussion, see Ellis, 2005).

From this point of view, the terminological distinctions still current in the field, opposing what are termed Focus on Meaning (FonM), Focus on Form (FonF) and Focus on Forms (FonFs) do not contribute clarity to the discussion. Research informed practice in L2 teaching, especially at the elementary level, has helped to a great degree to dissolve the demarcations among these categories, never having been very sharp to begin with. One exception is the more inclusive term, Form-focused instruction (FFI), which is the umbrella category that includes both FonF and FonFs, and as such is useful because it marks a clear opposition to all types of zero-grammar simple-immersion.

In regard to the different FFI options, the problem of selecting grammar learning objectives and balancing grammar teaching and communicative activities is solved in the new immersion approach. All instruction is meaning-based and communicative, and the principle of maximizing comprehensible input and meaningful practice applies to all domains of the curriculum, including Language Arts and Literacy. Most importantly, grammar objectives are now chosen primarily for their importance in language use for academic purposes, for the specific purposes that they serve in each subject matter content unit. In a sense, selected components of the second language grammar are prioritized based on their value or utility to language learners, as linguistic tools for the comprehension of concepts and for the solution of problems posed in each subject area. The emphasis then shifts from:

1. mastering the components of the L2 linguistic system that make the learner sound more like a native speaker to
2. attaining proficiency in literacy-related academic uses of the L2.

The latter, arguably, represents for school-age L2 learners a more critical short-term objective considering the high-stakes demands, especially for them, of academic achievement. In fact, in the medium and long term, an initial emphasis on the L2 for academic purposes may even make the mastery of the overall grammatical system more efficient and effective. From this point of view, the research in the field of English for Academic Purposes (EAP) and Content Based L2 Instruction should work toward a more complete integration, as Snow (2005) and Song (2006) have proposed. This would also allow for a more fruitful sharing of findings between investigations in the area of post-secondary L2 learning (with which EAP is often associated) and the K-12 levels.

Summing up this section — because a significant part of the elementary and secondary school teaching program is centered on attaining high levels of academic language proficiency, L2 grammar learning objectives (broadly defined) naturally find their way into the content areas. This circumstance happens to coincide with a growing consensus among SLA researchers — simple-immersion (exclusively meaning-centered L2-medium content teaching that omits grammar and other kinds of Form-focused instruction) does result in measurable gains in target language competence. But, its tendency is to be less efficient (in terms if rate of progress) and less effective (in terms of ultimate attainment) than L2-medium instruction combined with a systematic focus on grammar and vocabulary learning objectives (Ellis, 2006). In addition, for school-age L2 learners, zero-grammar pedagogical models that impose a blanket exclusion on Form-focused teaching face the serious problem of how to implement academic literacy instruction in the areas of reading and writing (Birch, 2002; Shankweiler and Fowler, 2004). This problem would be most acute for elementary grade level L2 learners who are also beginners in literacy learning.

In this comparison of the different kinds of content-based L2 instruction, the position of Krashen (2008) is interesting, as he has been closely associated with immersion teaching since the beginning. Simplifying somewhat, his *Comprehension Hypothesis* seems to be the most extreme among the input-based, reduction-of-explicit-grammar-teaching proposals. Not only does it minimize the importance of developing metalinguistic ability, learning activities focused on grammar patterns via direct instruction and systematic incorporation of language objectives in CBI (all based on the *Skill-Building Hypothesis*), but the Comprehension Hypothesis is also formulated by Krashen in direct opposition to the *Communicative Approach*. Supposedly, the flaw in communicative language teaching is that it is implicitly based on the *Comprehensible Output Hypothesis*, which places an emphasis on production, practice and interaction. No clear evidence, according to Krashen, supports this approach: "language acquisition is possible without output of any kind" (p. 182). For clarity, the proposal of this chapter is that the new immersion model should combine the Communicative Approach and the Skill-Building Hypothesis. Chapter 9 will return to this discussion.

7.3 Instructed SLA

What kind of focus on language learning objectives is most effective? First of all, it is important to emphasize that direct instruction in the L2 classroom can take many forms; a wide variety of approaches fall under this category. As a working definition, we can propose that direct instruction simply implies teaching that is planned and systematic in some way; the teacher actively engages students in learning tasks, which are organized around clearly identifiable learning objectives. For example, these might be specific aspects of the target language grammar that content learning activities and learners' current stage of mastery of the L2 show to be important. Learning activities are then designed with the purpose of having students attend to these aspects of the language system. One approach to the question of which objectives require attention would be to determine the difficulty of different grammatical patterns — patterns and constructions that pose difficulties for beginners, intermediates and advanced learners. If we recall from the previous section, the scope of this determination is narrowed by asking which aspects of the grammar are most useful for each academic purpose that presents itself to learners at each stage of their development.

Beyond describing the influence of learners' L1 (on which a relatively broad consensus has now been achieved), the question of which factors account for second language learning difficulty is still not well understood. As DeKeyser (2005) suggests in his review of the research, to the diversity of the factors that will be revealed to be important, a wide range of pedagogical implications will apply. Within some domains of the L2 grammar, development clearly unfolds spontaneously, triggered by simple comprehensible input in sufficient quantity. In contrast, mastery of other aspects of the L2 system are likely to be significantly facilitated by one kind or another of direct instruction focused on the grammar of the language.

In addition, given the results of a now substantial body of investigation on instructed SLA, we can say that it is unlikely that any single set of direct teaching methods can be held up as superior to all others across the L2 grammar and for all stages of interlanguage development. Difficulties in grammar learning are likely to vary from one domain to another, and likely, in turn, to respond differently to one treatment versus another. One hypothesis for further research, however, does appear to deserve serious attention — exclusively meaning-based simple-immersion, which rejects Form-focused instruction and corrective feedback, presents the least efficient and least effective alternative for L2 learners, children and adults alike (Doughty, 2003; Gass and Mackey, 2006; Lyster and Mori, 2006; Norris and Ortega, 2000; Williams, 2005).

Two recent discussion articles by Snow (2005) and Bigelow *et al.* (2006) serve as an important extension and elaboration on the seminal proposal for CBI offered years ago by Snow *et al.* (1989). Together, they provide much needed clarity on a number of central points in debate on how to implement language learning objectives in content-based L2 teaching. For this reason their arguments now merit our consideration in this section.

While the general concept of content-language integration is easy to understand, and has been accepted widely among educators, difficult and even controversial questions remain regarding the kind of focus on language that should be integrated into the subject areas. Bigelow *et al.* outline the problem and offer a model for conceptualizing how the different component and subcomponent parts of both content and language can come together in a given immersion lesson. Specifically, they address the issue of what we could categorize as an intermediate component — *language functions*. For teachers, planning the academic content lesson is relatively straightforward, even including the provision of additional context support required for L2 learners. But, as the authors observe, deliberate attention to grammar objectives has proven to be problematic at the actual point of instruction. Mistakenly, an emphasis on functions of language has often taken the place of a necessary attention to grammar and vocabulary, as if this emphasis could substitute for a focus on the sentence-level language objectives. As an "intermediate" category, examples of functions are:

- identification and description of concepts,
- retelling of narrative,
- explanation of processes,
- exemplification,
- analysis and synthesis,
- comparison and contrast,
- categorization,
- prediction,
- justification of a claim, and
- evaluation of knowledge.

The argument could be made that all of these functions form an integral part of standard content teaching. But as ways-of-using-language-for-academic-purposes, we can think of them as a bridge or interface with grammar (an intermediate category between content and language). Recall that we categorized vocabulary learning in a similar way. Here, in fact, a third intermediate category can be added: discourse ability — the abilities and skills required to organize and comprehend texts, patently overlapping in a major way with the above language functions. Some educators might even say (correctly) that, in practice, "functions" and "discourse abilities" are the same; that the functions are language objectives at the discourse-level.

On the other hand (in the direction of grammar), for the ability to construct and understand coherent discourses (oral and written), the language learner needs to master the use of linguistic devices that connect one proposition to another and to establish cohesive ties within and across sentences. From this point of view, second language students are faced with two aspects of grammar learning:

1. at the sentence- and word-level — the syntax and morphology of well-formed phrases and words, and
2. at the level of discourse — the grammatical constructions and operations that serve higher-order language proficiency (involving academic texts in particular); see Francis (2012), Schleppegrell et al. (2004) and Zwiers (2008) for discussion.

If we recall the rationale from the previous section for a convergence between CBI and EAP,[1] the central importance of the higher-order language *functions* and literacy-related *discourse ability* should be obvious. Part of what makes these aspects of academic language proficiency a bridge to the sentence-level grammar is that they present the learner with the need to master the complex syntactical patterns of textbooks and teachers' explanations. Fortunately for L2 learners, abilities related to working with texts and academic discourse lend themselves well to direct instruction, together with the concepts of each subject area (Snow, 2005).

Important as these functions of language use are, Bigelow *et al.* point out that it would be a mistake to limit the language learning component of CBI for L2 learners to them alone. First of all, as we just saw, any sustained treatment of the academic discourse abilities takes us into the domain of sentence-level grammar, including word analysis. For second language students, the development of basic patterns, rules and constructions still to be attained should not be neglected; and subject content and its associated language functions still happen to be the best opportunity to identify remaining difficulties and plan specific and targeted grammar instruction, for example:

- unstated arguments in the passive voice when engaging in comparison and contrast,
- nominalization in the explanation of processes,
- pronouns and the complex patterns of reference in retelling of narrative,
- patterns of derivational morphology in categorization.

Second language educators are reminded that functions can often be executed approximately (giving the appearance of being adequately expressed, especially with the help of situational context) even when the L2 learner lacks mastery of basic sentence-level grammar.

On the teacher's part, the key ingredient here is systematic monitoring and planning, keeping in mind that integration of content and language does not mean presenting the relevant learning activities to students simultaneously; "content-based" in no way necessarily implies a spontaneous, immediate and incidental focus on grammar objectives.

7.4 The problem of combining content and language objectives

How can the "double task" of content and language learning be feasible? This was our third question in this chapter. Discussion of the research on teaching methods is often confusing, a confusion that is unfortunately not ameliorated by the terms used to designate some of the major categories that the different methods fall under. To provide some clarity to the discussion, the first major distinction that is important to make is between all FFI approaches on the one hand and zero-grammar simple-immersion on the other. In the literature, the latter is often called Focus on Meaning, a particularly unhelpful term given the fact that FFI in all variants of CBI is integrated with a focus on meaning in one way or another.

A second division could be made among the different approaches that fall under the broad category of Form-focused Instruction:

1. all language-focused instruction that is an integral part, in one way or another, of a content-based methodology (by design, meaning-focused because grammar learning points are linked to concept learning points), and
2. grammar-focused methods and learning activities implemented apart from (i.e., not directly and immediately related to) the academic content objectives that students are currently working on. This category of FFI, then, is not an integral part of a content-based lesson — but we could argue that it is still useful to the L2 learner.

An example of #1 would be — as part of a literature study unit on the narrative devices that authors use to help readers shift their attention to events as they unfold in a scene (the content objective), the teacher provides instruction on past tense verb forms (the language objective). Clearly, under this definition, instruction on the language objective would not necessarily be implemented simultaneously or concurrently with instruction on the content objective; normally, in fact, it would not be. An example of #2 would be — For homework, or as a spare time activity, students work together to solve on-line grammar puzzles and exercises on the BBC language learning website, focused on constructions that still cause them difficulty in their writing, for example. So along this dimension (contrasting #1 and #2) the difference is one of how closely aligned the language objective is to the content objective, to what extent mastery of a language objective directly supports the mastery of a given content objective. In both examples the emphasis seems to be on developing explicit knowledge through direct instruction. At the same time, during teacher-led classroom lessons or student-organized activities, language objectives might be brought to learners' attention incidentally. Typically, however, this would be more likely to occur during the meaning-focused content lesson itself (in example #1 — narrative devices) or during the content-linked language lesson (in example #1 — past tense). The teacher also takes advantage of appropriate opportunities during direct instruction for negotiation of meaning and corrective feedback. Such incidental FFI may foster either implicit or explicit knowledge of the target language. In example #2, an activity on the BBC website focused on capitalization and punctuation is not tied, at that moment, to a specific content lesson; and instead of incidental, we would say that it is deliberately focused on form.

Most second language educators, it is fair to say, would consider both examples, #1 and #2, as valuable language learning activities. In fact, not all actual real-life examples, in practice, can be unambiguously divided between the two categories. Not coincidentally, to date, SLA research has not decisively singled out either one or the other as superior across the board.

In this regard, Doughty's (2003) critique of the Norris and Ortega (2000) study is premature. In her discussion of the study, the author strongly questions the finding from Norris and Ortega's meta-analysis of a general advantage for types of L2 instruction that are *planned and focused* on specific grammar objectives over types of instruction in which the focus on form is *incidental*. In addition to the overall advantage of all types of direct instruction over simple-immersion, this was, in fact, the major finding of the Norris and Ortega study. Contrary to these results, Doughty appears to be arguing that incidental attention to language forms, as they arise naturally during classroom language use, is *generally* superior for all L2 learning contexts, and that researchers have overstated the case for "explicit instruction" (p. 274). Rather, the emphasis in classroom settings should be placed on creating the conditions for implicit learning during meaning-focused activities, returning "to a discovery mode of processing" (p. 299). According to this view, metalinguistic awareness and declarative knowledge are of limited usefulness in the development of competence in L2. In the literature on instructed SLA this position is associated with the recommendations of the so-called Focus on Form approach; that instruction focused on language learning objectives should entail temporary and brief shifts of students' attention, incidentally, as problems in comprehension and expression present themselves *during* communicative tasks. For example, the teacher utilizes the corrective feedback technique of recasting, providing a correct model in response to production errors as these arise spontaneously in students' speech.

There is good reason to believe that under some conditions these kinds of incidental FonF corrective feedback (part of what is called "processing instruction") are beneficial as they promote noticing, a shift of the attentional resources toward interlanguage constructions (especially persistent error patterns) of which the learner is often unaware. Overgeneralizations, for example, are difficult to recognize without the benefit of negative evidence. Also, why do some L1 rules seem to carry over to the target language, and others do not? Some seem to correspond to their L2 counterpart "partially," causing the most difficulty for learners as they try to sort out which patterns can be "transferred" and which cannot. "To overcome the mismatch between the L1 strategy and the L2 input, processing instruction informs learners that the L1 cues are not reliable, and alerts them to cues in the L2 to which they should pay attention instead" (Doughty, 2003, p. 288).

However, as other surveys of recent research have made clear, taken together, the findings from comparative, experimental and descriptive studies do not lead us to strongly favor any one of the FFI models to the exclusion of the others. For example, a careful reading of Williams's comprehensive review of FFI suggests an important conclusion — actual implementations of one or another grammar teaching model are difficult to separate into clearly demarcated categories, purely reactive, unplanned, incidental, meaning-embedded FonF approaches versus planned, stand-alone language lessons focused on specific grammar objectives (defined in the literature as FonFs). As Ellis (2006) points out, separate grammar-focused learning activities can also form an integral part of a larger communicative CBI program. In addition, language objectives can be taught separately *and* communicatively, despite the stereotyped version of FonFs as traditional pattern drill, translation, rule explanation and rote memorization.[2]

Theoretical arguments do not conclusively tip the balance one way or the other either. For example, if we accept the (well-founded) notion that L2 learning cannot simply recapitulate L1 development, because the same internal acquisition resources are no longer accessible, there is no reason to assume a blanket advantage for incidental approaches, implemented concurrently with the content lesson, over planned grammar instruction that is provided to learners separately. Furthermore, the question of how declarative and metalinguistic knowledge is related to the development of *second* language competence is still not well understood (unlike in the case of first language competence).

For their part, practitioners have called attention to a number of practical limitations that would potentially be imposed on teachers by a narrow interpretation of incidental FonF methods that must be implemented during meaning-focused content lessons. Also, strict applications of incidental FonF are often not feasible: (1) Corrective feedback on grammatical problems would tend to be unplanned, and it is not clear how teachers might be able to attend to language objectives systematically. (2) Restricting attention only to errors that lead to a breakdown in communication may not be the best method of selecting language objectives. (3) If teachers take to heart the condition that focus on grammar should be restricted to opportunities only when learners are engaged in a meaningful content learning activity, separate skill-building, practice, and problem solving activities focused on specific grammar patterns could be potentially eliminated. (4) There would be a tendency for grammar learning activities to be occasional and sporadic. (5) It is controversial the extent to which learners are able to attend to the critical features of oral corrective feedback in the context of the dynamic give and take of classroom dialogues, especially in large groups (Sheen, 2003; Poole, 2005).

Again, incidental focus on form, skillfully executed, should form part of the overall language teaching program. But as DeKeyser suggested, learning difficulties associated with the various domains and components of the L2 grammar are not likely to all respond uniformly to a single teaching approach. From all of the above, the more important research question would seem to be: continue to draw out the distinction between FonM and FFI in general, including all its various sub-types.

In concluding this section, we return to the ideas of *combination* and *distribution* that were put forward at the beginning of this chapter as they apply to second language learning situations. The advances of research on instructed SLA to date point in a clear direction — the underlying foundation of content-based second language instruction must be the use of the target language for communication and comprehension. Even learning specific discrete points of grammar should be communicative. More research is also needed to understand how language objectives can be taught more effectively. Both investigators and educators should keep an open mind about which FFI methods are best suited for different circumstances and opportunities; and there is as yet no compelling evidence not to combine incidental and planned FFI strategies.

At the same time, the combination of content and language presents L2 learners with a "double task," one that curriculum designers need to address in a responsible fashion. The task of content learning through the medium of a language that students still have not mastered must be feasible, accessible to all learners, not just a select fraction. The distribution of L1 and L2 medium teaching is an issue that should be considered so as to maximize the efficiency of both content and second language learning. The L1-L2 distribution concept implies that total L2 immersion that excludes the L1 from the curriculum is an unnecessary restriction that potentially inhibits overall academic development, at least for many child L2 learners. Wannagat (2007) alluded to this problem in his discussion of school language policy in Hong Kong. For example, allowing L1-medium instruction for beginning L2 learners in the highly context-reduced content subjects (such as literacy and language arts) should result in a more rapid initial development in these "language-dependent" areas. This more robust early development, in turn, should provide for a stronger academic language proficiency platform from which the bilingual second language student can then leverage more efficient L2 learning strategies. Evidence suggests that even young children (pre-school age) can profit from well designed direct instruction in context-reduced literacy-related subjects; see Li and Rao (2005) for a comparison of pre-school literacy learning in Beijing, Hong Kong and Singapore. Specifically in regard to bilingual literacy and other academic objectives, Echevarría and Graves (2011, pp. 14–18) propose a L1–L2 distribution model, based on the same idea developed by Krashen and Biber (1988) many years ago.

7.5 Misconceptions about immersion and bilingualism

Research has clearly identified content-based language learning (immersion) as the most powerful methodological model, outdistancing by far traditional language-as-a-subject approaches. Immersion students' overall academic performance compares favorably (superior or equivalent) to that of non-immersion students not only in the L2 but in subjects taught in the L1 as well; see summaries and findings of pilot studies carried out in China (Chen *et al.*, 2010; Qiang *et al.*, 2011). With this in mind, misgivings and hesitations on the part of some educators should not be surprising, as the stakes in second language learning are now much higher. Immersion methods today present a radical alternative to traditional practices. For example, unlike in the past, properly implemented L2 immersion has the potential, more than ever before, of providing access to effective and efficient L2 learning to broad layers of the school-age population. Under the old regime of traditional foreign and second language teaching, high levels of attainment were generally accessible only to a relatively narrow student population (one with freer access to time and relevant material resources, such that considerations of methodological efficiency were less critical). Some educators, however, have expressed concern and even opposition to English immersion in China. In Hu's (2008) critique of Chinese-English bilingual education, L2 immersion methods in particular are singled out, the misgivings and hesitations in this case flowing from fundamental misconceptions about the essential programmatic features of content-based language learning. So, as a follow-up to the previous sections, it is important to clarify the essential conceptions of immersion methodology.

The first objection that is expressed concerns the possibility of immersion in a foreign language (English, in this case) actually resulting in the weakening of L1 (Chinese) literacy-related academic language proficiency (p. 213). As an aside we could take note of this claim as an implicit recognition of the effectiveness of immersion by exaggerating what it is capable of. Even where it has been implemented most robustly (e.g., Canada), no evidence exists even suggesting a degrading of academic language abilities in the L1 of immersion students, for example, in comparison to students in monolingual L1 programs. No study, internationally, shows a decline in L1 advanced literacy proficiencies, as a result of foreign language immersion, where students' L1 is the undisputed national language of the country in question. If such an outcome could be pointed to in China, in any population of native-speakers of Mandarin/Putonghua, it would be absolutely unprecedented in the history of foreign language learning.

In fact, because the underlying proficiencies of advanced literacy are largely language independent, their development via instruction in a L2 contributes to the development of advanced literacy skills in the L1; and of course, conversely, bilingual students have access to abilities learned via the L1 in the performance of advanced literacy tasks in the L2.[3] The measurable downgrading of L1 academic language proficiency would only follow from the, inconceivable, gradual shifting of children's dominant language from Chinese to English (the L2 actually beginning to displace Chinese as the primary language). Again, the superiority of L2 immersion, over all traditional language-as-subject approaches, is widely recognized in the field; but such a spectacular outcome has never before been contemplated. No evidence suggests that such a displacement of the native language of students is possible.

On the other hand, a different scenario might obtain for speakers of minority languages. Might content-based L2 learning of a foreign language result in a weaker acquisition of the national language on the part of young people who are L2 learners of the national language? This question takes us back to the challenge of trilingual learning, research and language policy problem introduced in Chapter 1, depicted in Figure 1.1. One proposal is that: "English medium instruction should not be offered to ethnic minority students at the expense of their acquisition of Putonghua" (Hu and Alsagoff, 2009, p. 376). No responsible language learning specialist would minimize or relativize the importance of learning the national language of the country, essential objective for full access to literacy and other academic resources in Chinese. However, a policy that differentiates between native speakers of the national language and speakers of minority languages on this point risks institutionalizing unequal access in another realm of learning.

A dilemma appears to present itself for minority language speakers: *two* second languages (of wider communication — the first one national, the second, international) compete for attention and learning resources. The problem does indeed imply an asymmetry (a kind of "unfairness"). One example among many — For the child monolingual Mandarin-speaking resident of Taipei, learning one of the minority languages of Taiwan as L2 implies different demands and consequences (e.g., if not successful) than for the monolingual speaker of Hokkien who must learn the national language, if he or she goes to school and wants to learn how to read and write. The asymmetry is more interesting in this case, similarly as in other regions of China, because Hokkien is not a minority language of Taiwan.

Strictly speaking, then, the "burden" of language learning for "minority" (now in quotes) language speakers is, in effect, greater, not just different, as I may have inadvertently suggested in Chapter 1 and Figure 1.1. The challenge is greater still if the minority language community actively seeks to preserve and strengthen its linguistic heritage, and if this (now additional) learning objective is assumed by the young language learner, by his or her family and community institutions. Importantly, in this chapter, our discussion is not about the relative weight that should be given to instruction in each of the three languages in question — how much emphasis should be given to each and the resources each deserves. And as a number of authors have pointed out, learning English may not be high on the agenda of many students. However, we could also agree that it is presumptuous to claim that for minority language students, on average, learning a LIC is a low priority. To the contrary, the learning of a LIC can even complement, in interesting ways, the work of IL revitalization (Huang, 2010). In addition, access to a LIC can provide minority language students with certain learning advantages that contribute toward "leveling the playing field," so to speak (Sunuodula and Feng, 2011). Rather, the questions at hand are:

1. the applicability of immersion methods for the purpose of addressing these language learning challenges and
2. broad access to effective bilingual education that includes all three tiers (minority/indigenous, national and international) for all learners.

With these two points in mind, it's not at all obvious that minority language students should have less access to English (under the, unproven, assumption that this will facilitate their learning of Mandarin/Putonghua), or that they should not have this access via the most effective and efficient methodology — content-based L2 learning. When motivation is adequate, trilingual development has been shown to be a realizable objective of school language policy, especially when we keep in mind that ability levels in the different domains in every language do not need to be developed equally. For example, only one language may be the one that is mastered as equivalent to a full and complete native language, and another, the LIC, may be useful, depending on the circumstances, only for reading comprehension (e.g., of academic/professional texts in one's field of work).

The second substantive critique of immersion is a warning against potentially negative cognitive and linguistic consequences of bilingualism itself. Citing studies by Bialystok (2009), summarized in the section "The bad" in a review entitled "Bilingualism: the good, the bad and the indifferent," Hu and Alsagoff (2010, p. 372), suggest that bilingualism might be linked to "language deficits" (separate and apart from reported "advantages"). In particular, the claim is made that bilingual children suffer from deficits in vocabulary, purportedly demonstrated when comparing their performance to that of monolingual children. However, to the contrary, none of the studies cited by Bialystok in the above mentioned section provide evidence to support the hypothesis that bilingualism results in or leads to inferior levels of lexical knowledge.

If the hypothesis of a diminished lexicon in bilingualism were in fact to be demonstrated, this finding would call for a major rethinking of consensus models of bilingual competence and bilingual proficiency. For example, it could resurrect the now largely discredited theory of semilingualism in non-pathological bilingual development (refer back to the discussion in Chapter 2), Today, in our understanding of the mental architecture of language knowledge, the lexicon is no longer conceived of as a simple listing of words that varies from one individual to another in unlimited and unconstrained ways. Rather, it is integrated much more closely with the components of grammatical competence, serving in turn as a complex interface among the different networks and domains of linguistic competence and conceptual knowledge (Jackendoff, 2007). Thus, the proposal of an across-the-board lexical deficiency, as a result of bilingualism, is no small matter. How might it come to be then that knowledge of two languages, all other variables held constant, leads to the development of a degraded lexicon (as compared to that of monolinguals)?

Reviewing, then, the investigations cited by Bialystok (2009) is important. We should first set aside the studies of language *processing* in bilinguals focused on lexical retrieval, interference in lexical decision, verbal fluency, and the like. The evidence for slower picture naming, more frequent cross-language interference and tip-of-the-tongue experiences in bilinguals is interesting, and the claim of a bilingual-monolingual difference on these measures entirely plausible. In language processing, from two subsystems (as opposed to just one), the additional computation required to inhibit one or the other is indeed likely to be manifested in a range of performance tasks. All bilingual speakers are familiar with the everyday parallels to the reported laboratory experiments.

It is important to emphasize that in these studies the term "deficit" is used in the narrow and technical sense to describe the peculiar processing differences in which bilinguals show evidence of "competition" and "interference." But these interesting aspects of bilingual processing are in principle independent of the actual knowledge base that resides in the dual language lexical system, what Bialystok refers to as "vocabulary size," proposing that it may be "smaller" among bilinguals (p. 4). The claim of such a "vocabulary gap," here, refers to actual lexical knowledge. On this point, the hypothesis of a bilingual "deficit" (referring now to actual knowledge as opposed to processing) is neither plausible nor is it supported in the research cited in Bialystok's (2009) review.

First of all it should come as no surprise that the measurement of vocabulary "size" of this or that group of bilingual children might suggest a knowledge deficit in this domain. Entire populations affected by this shortcoming abound in large part because most circumstances of bilingual and second language development are systematically asymmetrical to one degree or another. Truly controlled studies would need to hold constant all the variables related to learning conditions that are potentially unequal; it is generally accepted that this aspect of vocabulary knowledge is especially sensitive to these conditions. Any imbalance during development and instruction which the bilingual population in question might experience would thus undermine a valid comparison. Examples include:

1. variation in early childhood language socialization (engagement with the speech community's narrative tradition, literacy-related experience, etc.),

2. differences in quality of elementary school instruction (is instruction received in a language for which comprehensible input was not adequate, in the weaker, or attriting, language of the early bilingual or in the incipient or intermediate L2 of the second language learner?) and

3. persistent differences through middle childhood in extracurricular domains of language use (e.g., degree of comprehensible input and access to age-appropriate programming on television and radio).

These variables, of course, are difficult to control for, and it is understandably tempting on the part of investigators to lay recourse to surrogate categories or even assume equivalence. But the comparison is then simply compromised. One solution is to assure equivalence by selecting from matching populations of so-called elite bilinguals (biliterate with high levels of academic proficiency in both languages) and matching monolingual subjects with comparably rich childhood language experience, or conversely, ensuring comparably unfavorable language learning conditions between bilingual and monolingual groups. Again, the problem that is posed is the relative instability, "sensitivity" to input conditions, of vocabulary "size" (in contrast to other domains of language competence: e.g., native-speaker mastery of phonology and syntax, which are more "stable").

Another common design shortcoming in the assessment of bilinguals is the failure to specify the status of the language in which the vocabulary measure is taken. In comparison to a monolingual measure, is the vocabulary sample of the bilingual subject being taken in the dominant language, an advanced non-dominant, intermediate or beginner second language, or an attrited first language, which is no longer primary? These critical subject profile details are often missing in reports of research.

Related to the above problematic procedures is the most serious defect in this line of investigation. If in comparison to the vocabulary sample taken from the monolingual subject, word knowledge is measured by taking a sample from only *one* of the bilingual's two lexical subsystems, the assessment of the bilingual may be incomplete. This aspect of language knowledge is often distributed between the two subsystems (Oller and Eilers, 2002), the L1 and L2 lexicons complementing each other. In the cited studies (Bialystok *et al.*, 2008; Bialystok and Feng, 2009; and Mahon and Crutchley, 2006) all indications are that monolingual-bilingual comparisons were based on an estimate of only one of the lexical subsystems in the case of the bilingual subjects. From the summaries of some studies cited, it was not evident that the selected lexicon even corresponded consistently to the dominant language subsystem. Mahon and Crutchley (2006) go so far as to minimize the importance of taking a second measure in the testing of bilingual children, in this instance for purposes of assessment for special education needs, citing "several problems with this commendable sentiment" (p. 335).[4] The Oller and Eilers (2002) study is cited as providing evidence that "bilingual children control a smaller vocabulary in each language" (again predictable because of the distributed nature of lexical knowledge between L1 and L2); but in their introduction the same authors explicitly call attention to the problem of sampling vocabulary in only L1 or L2. Even in balanced bilingualism of the 2L1 type, there is no assurance that the L_a and L_b lexicons are complete sets of matching translation equivalents, requiring then, for comparison purposes, the straightforward and simple calculation of combined lexical knowledge (sum of translation equivalents and items that are specific to one lexicon and the other). In other words, researchers are not relieved of the requirement of taking a combined (L1+L2) measure of vocabulary if the bilingual subject's sample was taken from what appears to be his or her dominant/stronger language, based on the assumption that this measure corresponds to the monolingual's sample.

The interesting scientific question is not whether a "vocabulary gap" can be shown to be in evidence between selected groups of bilinguals and their monolingual peers, or even that the same discrepancy holds up for most bilinguals, or on average for bilinguals cross-culturally. For obvious reasons, some of which were mentioned above, such a statistical bilingual-monolingual "vocabulary gap" could be easily demonstrated. Rather, the important research problem consists in determining if *bilingualism*, dual-language competence itself, is causally related to a language deficit in the domain of lexical *knowledge*. In monolinguals this knowledge resides in the lexicon; in bilinguals it is distributed between *two* lexical subsystems. In addition, to reiterate, it is important not to confound the assessment of processing and the assessment of competence (knowledge of words).

The third objection to immersion teaching is one that is commonly raised in the general education field. How can students learn concepts and develop skills through instruction in a language that they still have not mastered? Doesn't content-based L2 teaching interfere with mastering the content? The first part of the solution to this problem takes us back to the introduction to this chapter — content-based instruction ideally should be integrated into a comprehensive bilingual curriculum, as one fraction of it; it is the portion that corresponds to the teaching of the second language. Of course, we are all familiar with implementations of immersion that are not an integral part of a bilingual program, in which the L2 is the exclusive medium of instruction. But this circumstance is not immediately relevant to the present discussion. No serious proposal for the teaching of a foreign language of international communication by any ministry of education excludes the national/official language of the country. On the other hand, the exclusion of indigenous or minority languages from the curriculum, where this is policy or practice, in no way follows from the principles of content-based language teaching. The inclusion of minority and indigenous languages, within the framework of a bilingual curriculum, is the preferable alternative for advancing the development of school literacy as recognized by the majority of language learning specialists today (Baker, 2011). In fact, the correct implementation of immersion methods actually facilitates this inclusion; for further discussion, see Francis (2012, chapter 2) and Francis and Navarrete Gómez (2009). Regarding another popular misconception of immersion, content-based methods do not exclude or prohibit the use of students L1. They obvious do not, by definition, exclude it from the native-language portions of the bilingual program; and do not, or rather need not, exclude it either from the L2 immersion program sections.

While not intending to do so, Hu (2008) himself provides a hint, on p. 367, to another part of the solution to the apparent paradox of integrating language and content learning. Teaching content through the medium of a second language cannot be accomplished successfully without systematic modifications on several levels. One of these modifications is the distribution of school subjects between L1 and L2 depending on the degree of extralinguistic context support naturally available in each course. So called "activity courses" (physical education, music, art, some industrial education classes) are ideally suited for early immersion for beginner L2 learners precisely because of the very high level of context support that is automatically embedded in learning activities.

"Activity courses" lend themselves perfectly to the initial second language learning experiences for *all* students, starting on the very first day of school — no "elite" selection or "gate-keeping." We can now add other school activities to this list of L2 learning opportunities — lining up in the morning, dismissal time, teachers sharing lunch with their students in the cafeteria, and so forth. Far from a "lack of confidence in the quality of their English medium programmes" (p. 367), foreign language immersion programs in China that apply this principle of language distribution for learning purposes are working squarely within a theoretically informed best practice framework. In line with the concept that context support facilitates comprehension, "electives rather than core courses," and "the sciences" (including mathematics) will be opportunities for L2 immersion before immersion in "humanities" and subjects that "require more use of language." Again, these program features are not a sign of weakness but rather flow from the findings of international SLA research. In addition to context support, an entire array of instructional material and teacher discourse modifications are applied that maximize comprehensible input for learners, adjusted systematically as students advance in their mastery of the L2 (successively reducing them, along with the strategic reduction of progressively unnecessary extra context support). Pi's (2004) case study of Shanghai immersion schools that describes this curriculum design, cited critically by Hu (2008) on p. 367, may actually be for us another valuable object lesson for how to properly implement L2 immersion.

7.6 Immersion methods at the service of additive trilingualism

Picking up on Lai's (2011) proposal for additive second language teaching from Chapter 1, it is important to conclude this chapter by reiterating a fundamental principle of immersion methodology: The application of immersion methods does not imply subtractive second language teaching or exclusionary school language policy in any necessary way. To the contrary, immersion methods are completely compatible with the goal of promoting bilingualism and multilingualism as part of a pluralistic and inclusive school language policy. Correctly implemented, these methods can also serve the objectives of indigenous or minority language revitalization/conservation at the same time as they serve the objectives of effective learning of the national language, as well as the effective learning of a language of international communication. The learning objectives of all three from Figure 1.1 (NL, IL and LIC) can be served. Recall from the previous section, immersion is not an exclusionary approach by definition. While teachers typically maintain a separation of languages, avoiding, for example, the counterproductive practice of concurrent translation, rules for exclusive L1 or L2 use do not apply in the prohibitive sense to students' expression.

A series of recent studies from Hong Kong, focused on the issue of medium of instruction (MoI) in school language policy, highlight the above-mentioned learning principles and research problems. The return of sovereignty to China in 1997 prompted a shift in MoI policy, sparking in turn a rich discussion on how to address the needs of students in a unique three-language learning situation: a new NL (Putonghua) albeit not fully implemented, a new "minority/IL" (Cantonese), and the same foreign LIC (English). It seems strange to categorize as "minority/IL" a language spoken, locally, by over 90% of the population, and worldwide, with over 70 million speakers. A written language associated with both popular and high culture, possessing a long and rich literary heritage, Cantonese in Hong Kong is not "subordinate" to a "more prestigious" NL in any important domain of language use, including higher education. But projecting incipient tendencies into the near future (Li, 2009), the new post-colonial recognition of a regionally expanding Putonghua brings the situation of multilingual Hong Kong more into line with the relationships depicted in Figure 1.1 (Access to information: A triglossic hierarchy). Prior to 1997, these relationships among NL, IL and LIC were easier to visualize in other regions of mainland China and Taiwan because of the unusual historical circumstances of British rule.

In regard to MoI in Hong Kong, for the typical school-age language learner, instruction in Cantonese is L1/mother tongue instruction, with the possibility of *two* L2 immersion scenarios — the national language of China and the primary foreign language of international communication. As was pointed out in Chapter 1, under such a complex and demanding language learning circumstance, only the most efficient and systematic application of L2 immersion methodology for the NL and the LIC is capable of implementing a coherent and equitable trilingual program. But crucially, simply making a second language the MoI for a given subject, without also applying the proper teaching modifications of Language Learner Sensitive Discourse, *does not count* as an acceptable application of immersion methodology for L2 beginners. This is precisely one of the problems pointed out by Fang (2011) and Shum *et al.* (2011) in their reports on the new challenge faced by English-speaking students who now need to improve or learn Chinese, in many cases as beginners. Again, the principles of immersion teaching apply to any second language learning situation. The authors point out that Chinese-as-subject classes, in the context of English medium instruction, is seriously inadequate, especially considering an additional obstacle that the students in question face: limited opportunities for practicing the target language after school. But at the same time, Chinese-medium instruction, without scaffolding of the LLSD kind, is not immersion, but submersion — submersion is L2-medium teaching that is not comprehensible. The proposal of Tse and Tan (2011) is an example of a solution to this problem — *differentiated instruction* that provides modified Chinese MoI, compatible with immersion methods, for beginners (in this case L2 learners of Chinese in Singapore). Of course, the same problem presents itself in English-medium instruction for L2 beginners: if classroom interaction and reading materials are not comprehensible because required modifications are not implemented, the result is not immersion.

An important concept that underlies successful LLSD-type scaffolding is the now well-understood distinction between content learning areas that are highly language-dependent and those that are language-dependent to a lesser degree, at least in some aspects (Mathematics being an example of the latter). For example, all other factors being equal, beginner L2 learners can process information in their second language in subjects such as Technical Drawing, the Lab Section of Introduction to Chemistry and Physical

Education with a lower overall level of L2 mastery than in subjects that are highly language-dependent (e.g., Literature of the Qing Dynasty). This guideline helps educators determine which subjects will require more initial scaffolding, context support and L1-medium pre-teaching than others; Li (2009) is a discussion of the different instructional models that are related to this issue. Another example that is suggested of how immersion methods are compatible with bilingual teaching models involves first language support for L2 learning. As mentioned in the previous section, techniques such as L1 pre-teaching and providing certain kinds of L1 support — as long as teachers *do not concurrently translate* instructional content from the L2 to students' L1 — are entirely compatible with immersion approaches. Recall that the defining feature of immersion is the linking of academic content learning and second language (grammar) learning. The L2 is the MoI for selected subjects, applying all required LLSD-type scaffolding commensurate with the current level of students' L2 mastery. As such, students' L1 need never be excluded from the curriculum.

The transition in language education is from the pre-1997 diglossia to a triglossia, which now includes Putonghua (Tam, 2011). Content-based second language teaching (immersion) is the instrument that will make trilingual education viable, replacing traditional rule-learning and rote methods with a fully communicative approach. This is so because *comprehensible input* is the gold standard for L2 immersion (Krashen, 1996). Furthermore, the mother-tongue (Cantonese) component in this trilingual education model should be viewed not just as a pre-teaching scaffolding and L1 support for Putonghua- and English-medium instruction, but as one of the essential and long-term resources for a truly additive trilingualism. In other words, the above-mentioned "transition" should not be conceived of as a temporary measure that phases out Cantonese as students' proficiency in the national and international languages improves.

The findings of a large-scale study of learning outcomes resulting from the different MoI scenarios in Hong Kong by Li and Majhanovich (2010) is consistent with this additive trilingual model. With the policy shift after 1997 toward greater weight given to L1 mother-tongue medium instruction, it would be interesting to chart corresponding shifts in actual learning outcomes. Predictably, the greatest improvements in academic achievement over a 10-year period were demonstrated in language-dependent subject areas taught in Cantonese; positive (but less dramatic) gains in subjects that are less language-dependent were also registered — recall this important distinction from the discussion by Li (2009). This result is consistent with a trilingual approach that reserves key academic domains for instruction in the language that students understand completely; see Krashen (1996) for a detailed explanation for why this model is effective. The significant shift away from English-medium instruction over this same period, as might be expected, would be reflected in a decline in test performance. However, the reported decline in English abilities was not consistent — for younger students (end of 5-year secondary), less exposure to L2 English, by-product of the greater emphasis on L1 teaching, did not result in a decline (rather, interestingly, resulting in a rising pass rate). In contrast, declining performance in English, over the years, was evident for older students (end of 2-year sixth-form). Clearly, more research is required to reconcile or explain the discrepancy regarding the trends in English language ability. In the end, adjustments in the distribution of L1-

medium, English-medium and Putonghua-medium instruction (the last two in the modality of L2 immersion) will need to be studied for the purpose of arriving at the optimum weight and allocation of time-on-task for each language. The framework for such a distribution, proposed in this chapter, is the strategic combination of L1-medium instruction and L2 immersion throughout the curriculum. The choice of each MoI combination, at each moment, is made based on pedagogical considerations that maximize learning potential, for academic content knowledge and language proficiency in L1 and L2. Recall the theme of this chapter: the integration of content and language learning.

This concluding section wraps up the discussion of issues related to second language teaching and learning that we started in Chapter 5. The final two chapters take us back to the leading theories in the research on bilingualism.

Notes

1. The interesting design feature of English for Academic Purposes (and all other L2 for Academic Purposes) that sets it apart is its short-term efficiency. University students and their mentors who require rapid limited mastery of a second language for the specific purpose of access to academic texts have devised highly effective language learning solutions. Since there is no conceivable developmental disadvantage to this kind of fast jumpstart in second language acquisition, there is every reason to assume that further advances in overall L2 proficiency can build upon the initial (albeit specific and limited) base of language knowledge that is attained. Consistent with the idea of integrating Content Based Instruction and English for Academic Purposes, there might be interesting applications of the academic-specific methods of EAP for younger L2 learners in CBI. Granted, EAP depends on prior attainment of advanced metalinguistic abilities and the previous consolidation of other aspects of academic language proficiency through the students' L1, factors that cannot be assumed for young child L2 learners. But keeping this (important) caveat in mind, the general conceptions of EAP may be more applicable to K-12 second language programs than we previously had considered. See Evans and Green (2007) for a discussion of key issues in EAP.
2. A procedure that has been shown to be workable and motivating in engaging bilingual language learners of Spanish in our project calls students' attention to grammar errors in their own written expression (Francis, 2012). For instructional purposes, this kind of self-correction task proceeds most effectively alternating between small group discussion of grammar problems and whole-class confirmation of the error patterns and their remediation. Each cycle of reflection and self-correction begins with the teacher keeping track of error patterns in speech and writing (which of course does not preclude incidental recasting and prompting during student-teacher exchanges). Error patterns are categorized and grouped according to frequency, salience of features, learnability considerations related to L1, relation to other problematic or facilitative linguistic features, etc. Targeted constructions embedded in series of texts are presented to students for problem

solution. Texts can be either sets of anonymous samples from actual class work, mixed in with hypothetical student texts (teacher created) with concentrated exemplars of the target error patterns, or extended excerpts from the textbook rewritten to include the error patterns that are the object of direct instruction. Key aspects of this structured whole-class self-correction are that it is student-centered and focused on actual current areas of difficulty, and is systematic and organized. As such, attention to grammar is more likely to "pair naturally" with academic content. All students are engaged and participate, as opposed to only those who happen to have been attentive during the occasional recasts or prompts that teachers direct to select individuals during class discussions. It fosters the development of metalinguistic strategies that are also central to literacy-related language proficiency and a general sensitivity toward noticing and monitoring. As a culminating activity, students return to their own text for individual editing and revision (and in pairs, if appropriate, exchanging papers). Structured self-correction of this kind that targets specific grammatical features is another example of how related objectives in CBI are combined:

(1) attention to the grammatical aspects of academic language use, the conventions of writing that require reflection on word, sentence, and text-level patterns. Being attainments that correspond to the standard Language Arts curriculum for L1 learners, they represent an additional opportunity for L2 learners who can also attend to basic linguistic patterns yet to be mastered.

(2) form-focused learning for L2 learners centered on interlanguage error patterns, and

(3) development of the language learning strategies of advanced literacy (for L1 and L2 learners) and facilitation of L2 learning in general.

3. Speculatively, the concern that Hu (2008) expresses regarding the degrading of students' Chinese literacy abilities as a result of content-based English instruction is related to the question of writing abilities, specifically the possible loss of skill in handwriting of characters, a domain of literacy learning that is truly specific to Chinese (i.e., not shared with alphabetic literacy learning). For discussion of this interesting research problem (related to the digitization of character writing in which the most popular software programs do not require the formation of characters, e.g., with a correct stroke pattern, but do require skill in *pinyin*) see the summary of the research by Kang (2011), Ki *et al.* (2003) and Wong *et al.* (2011) in Chapter 6.

4. A bilingual approach to understanding assessment of second language learners is necessary, especially when the issue is the possibility of language impairment. If impairment is confirmed, the inclusion of both languages is recommended for effective intervention (Thordardottir, 2010). In the evaluation of language abilities there is no reliable way to differentiate between errors that are evidence of impairment and errors that are evidence of typical and normal L2 development if the evaluation is conducted solely the child's second language. Logically, if an individual suffers from a true language impairment, significant difficulties will be evidenced not only in the L2 but in the L1 as well. Thus, if a second language learner is also evaluated in his or her L1, and performs normally on equivalent measures, it is unlikely, very unlikely we could say, that difficulties experienced in L2 learning are the result of a language impairment. Unless assessment for suspected

language impairment can be administered in both languages of the L2 learner, we should simply conclude that the assessment is still incomplete and that results are inconclusive. See Kohnert (2010) and Kohnert *et al.* (2009) for discussion, and the summary of de Houwer (2009) in Chapter 8.

Chapter 8

Studies of bilingualism for further study

For the serious student of bilingualism, the following works stand together as an essential course of study. This series of outlines will provide a useful guide for beginning a careful reading of the core research in the field today. Starting with the most basic (≠ easy) is the place to begin — how knowledge of two languages is structured in the brain. In the subsequent outlines the reader will recognize the four themes that we have been exploring in the last seven chapters — balanced and imbalanced bilingualism, the mental architecture of bilingual competence, first and second language literacy, and second language learning and teaching.

8.1 A neurolinguistic theory of bilingualism (Paradis, 2004)

For researchers, foundational questions are the most difficult. How knowledge and use of two languages are subserved by actual neural structures is among these questions. But students of applied linguistics and anyone interested in bilingualism and second language learning will find this non-technical state of the art survey useful as an introduction to the topic of language in the brain. In the end, regardless of which theory of bilingualism ends up holding sway in the field, we should all hope that advances in both theoretical and applied research should keep the lines of communication open with new discoveries in neurology. There really is no other place outside of the central nervous system where the core mental operations that underlie language use are materially computed. So as we all return to work in our respective disciplines it will be good to keep an eye on what's going on here in this one.

Chapter 1, "Components of verbal communication," starts off, as the title suggests, by setting out the general approach to the study to bilingualism from the perspective of neuroscience — that knowledge of language and our ability to use it can be studied analytically. Not to deny that other approaches can also provide for useful points of view, the survey of the neurological research will begin with a componential perspective. Chapter 1 sets the stage for a version of modularity informed by findings from the author's branch of this field. The first of a number of component/subsystem breakdowns that we are asked to consider is the distinction between two kinds of knowledge of language — (1) the internalized implicit system, acquired incidentally and not available to conscious awareness, and (2) explicit knowledge and metalinguistic awareness. The first is primary and domain-specific, and consists of computational procedures unavailable to introspection, for example, the mental grammar structures of morphology and syntax. The second, more widely interconnected, domain-general and "flexible," would correspond, for example, to the declarative component of vocabulary, and explicit knowledge about language patterns. This kind of knowledge we construct by recourse to cognitive-general learning. Deliberate learning implies awareness.

Chapter 2, "Implicit and explicit language processes," is where applied linguists, especially educators, will find the most interesting material to reflect upon. Picking up on the discussion from the previous chapter, Paradis offers another way to understand an ongoing debate in the area of second language learning. How learners might deliberately analyze a grammatical pattern is different from the way in which it will be "internalized," i.e., how it becomes part of implicit linguistic competence. The underlying structure of this knowledge of language is "nowhere to be noticed" (p. 37). The language learner might be able to gain awareness of *what* is produced (in the input and output of performance) but not *how*. And being a matter of two different kinds of mental representation, metaknowledge (explicit declarative) cannot be converted, strictly speaking, into implicit linguistic competence (procedural knowledge). Acquisition, then, is not a matter of "proceduralizing" explicit rules that were arrived at by means of analysis, inductive learning, memorization or reflection. Rather, what happens is a gradual shift from relying on metalinguistic knowledge to using implicit knowledge. Readers familiar with the various models of L2 learning will recognize this as coinciding, more or less, with the "non-interface" hypothesis, that draws a sharp line between "learning" and "acquisition." In its strongest version, it discards the usefulness of direct instruction, focus on grammatical form, metalinguistic strategies, corrective feedback, active monitoring and controlled practice. But Paradis leaves the door open to a number of different ways of how things might actually turn out in the "non-interface" relationship between learned declarative knowledge and underlying implicit competence. A close reading of the two final sections devoted to this topic (pp. 45–53) should make both opponents and proponents of instructed second language acquisition pause before assigning the author's modular theory to one camp or the other. For example, to say that formal instruction and deliberate learning make an indirect or secondary contribution does not forcibly imply that these general learning factors do not, or cannot, significantly facilitate *second* language development. First language acquisition, on the other hand, is a different matter.

Chapter 3, "Bilingual aphasia," makes a strong case for another dimension of neurofunctional modularity, based on a comprehensive review of the literature on impairment of language ability. Bilingualism provides for a unique and privileged vantage point when we consider recovery patterns. Recovery is not always parallel (same pattern of proficiency and dominance before and after trauma), with the various kinds of differential recovery (some of them at first seem strange and implausible) requiring a working hypothesis that assumes separate representations, of some kind, for each language subsystem. But since any explanation has to take into account both parallel recovery patterns and all variety of differential recovery, the idea of a localization of each language at a gross anatomical level would have to be set aside. (Different combinations of scratches or perforations to the hard-drive of a computer would result in all sorts of compromise to a given network of information depending on how it is fragmented, distributed, and interconnected.) The leading hypothesis, then, is that first language and second language are subserved by separate and autonomous neural circuits interwoven into the same larger language areas, and that physiological inhibition is the common mechanism that can account for all of the findings.

Chapter 4, "Cerebral lateralization and localization" follows up on Chapter 3 and gets into details that are well worthwhile ploughing through. The figure for "Schematic representation of various models of the organization of languages," lays out the logical possibilities, and Paradis's Subsystems Hypothesis.

Chapter 5, "Neurofunctional modularity," brings together the two major dimensions of how "knowledge of language" (my quotes) is componential — (1) the two different kinds of knowledge (explicit/declarative and implicit/procedural), and (2) the separation of the L1 and L2 subsystems. Along another dimension, we need to reckon with the internal diversity of language, in the bilingual mind now differentiated into (instantiated by) separate networks/circuits. For example: "the morphosyntax module contains as many subsystems as the person speaks languages" (p. 130). In the end, however the different vertical and horizontal dimensions, layers, and successive subsystems might come to be parceled out, the general idea is that knowledge components are isolable *and* richly interconnected. To what degree and how they are interconnected will be settled empirically, and not any time soon. In the meanwhile, there is plenty of room still for a number of competing and potentially compatible proposals for further research.

Chapter 6, "Neuroimaging studies of the bilingual brain," is an overview of central methodological questions and an assessment of where things stand in this brave new science, still by and large at the "poking stage" (p. 186).

Chapter 7, "An integrated neurolinguistic perspective on bilingualism," features the graphic presentation of The Three-Store Hypothesis. Two related models of the architecture of bilingual proficiency that interested readers should refer to as they study this concluding series of proposals by the author are: Paivio's (1991) Bilingual Dual Coding Model and Cummins (1991) Linguistic Interdependence Model. Despite important differences, all three try to capture key features of the two dimensions of modularity discussed so far. The objective here is to account for how some aspects of language proficiency in bilinguals appear to be distributed between separate linguistic domains (autonomous subsystems comprised of two lexicons and separate subsystems for the respective morphosyntactic and phonological structures), and other aspects of proficiency appear to be "shared" (there being access to a common non-linguistic domain). This chapter covers so much ground that it deserves two readings, touching on a range of big questions from a new way of thinking about the Sapir-Whorf hypothesis to explaining in a psycholinguistically coherent way the phenomenon of borrowing and interference in second language learning.

Looking back, what calls one's attention as an overall theme, perhaps unintended by the author, is the possibility of a more open cross-discipline discussion, even on some proposals that appear at first to be controversial. In a *Language in Society* review by Burling (2003), of Jackendoff's *Foundations of language*, the author made a similar invitation — consider new developments in cognitive science that are redrawing the old lines of debate. *Foundations of language* makes a strong case for this possibility and should be studied together, chapter by chapter, with *A neurological theory of bilingualism* with the idea of bringing linguists and psychologists back together to talk about shared research problems.

8.2 Sociolinguistic and psycholinguistic perspectives (Myers-Scotton, 2006)

This comprehensive textbook on bilingualism has been written by a leading researcher in the field. Students will find it accessible, with a prerequisite beginner course on language learning and linguistics helpful for the chapters (9, 10, and 11) that cover the grammatical and psycholinguistic aspects of bilingualism. This will serve the serious student well; together with the chapter on lexical borrowing (chapter 8), these chapters are by far the most interesting and most deserving of a careful and reflective reading.

In Chapter 1, Myers-Scotton suggests one especially informative way in which language contact phenomena can be studied — for the purpose of better understanding the nature of grammatical competence and language processing. Studying the knowledge of and the ability to use two languages provides us with special research opportunities for describing the language faculty and the human "genetic potential" for language acquisition. The inclusive definition of a bilingual speaker, one who has "acquired or learned to speak or understand...some phrases that show internal structural relations in a second language (p. 3)," sets the stage for the discussion to come. What is noteworthy about the first chapter, and the author's approach overall, is that this particular cognitive science point of view does not lead us to unnecessary quarrels with any of the current sociolinguistic perspectives. The latter field of study, about how bilinguals put their knowledge of two languages to use in communication, in fact, occupies the greater part of our attention throughout the book.

Chapters 2 through 7 survey the research on the key aspects of bilingualism in society — dialectical variation, social factors that promote bilingualism, language maintenance and language shift, ideologies and attitudes, motivational factors and intercultural communication. Here, a central theme is introduced that will figure prominently in the model of bilingual competence and ability to be presented in the subsequent chapters — language contact almost always involves one kind or another of imbalance. Research questions related to inequality in bilingual and multilingual social circumstances tie many of the above-mentioned topics together in this section. From another vantage point, the different categories of asymmetry in the way linguistic knowledge is represented mentally and processed in performance seem to manifest themselves more clearly in bilingualism. The two types of imbalance often appear to be related, the cognitive asymmetries seeming to mirror, or give expression to, the social.

Contact between standard and non-standard varieties, written/official and vernacular languages, always implies either some degree of tension or outright conflict. That there are relatively few "balanced bilinguals" appears to be related to the finding from most studies that the shift to a second language of national or majority status is difficult to resist. Maintenance of first, minority, languages in many ways is double-edged — preservation of a minority language can be the result of a resurgence of ethnolinguistic loyalty and cultural self-assertion, even of nationalism. It can also be favored by social inequality, segregation, and discrimination (posing, as it does, an interesting dilemma for pluralistic-oriented language policy). The discussion in Chapter 4 of the concept of diglossia pointedly highlights some of the key relationships and apparent contradictions. The natural instability of language "allocation," socially, may interact in interesting ways with the cognitive "economy" of bilingualism in which only one language system seems to predominate in many, if not most, contact situations.

Chapter 8 on lexical borrowing makes for a good transition to the discussion of research on the cognitive aspects of bilingualism. Again, our attention is called to a number of interesting differentiations:

- Borrowing is never equal, a reflection of social inequalities and other kinds of difference. For example, some borrowed words belong to the domain of the core vocabulary (kinship terms, discourse connectors, grammatical words and morphemes); others refer to innovations introduced from other cultures (names of new animals, e.g., "caballo" [horse – from Spanish] in the lexicon of some American indigenous languages).
- Asymmetries strictly internal to the language faculty. For example, the borrowing of words versus "taking in grammatical structures" appears to depend on different processes. Just considering the borrowing of words, there are interesting differences between phonological and morphosyntactic integration into the host language, and differences in how nouns and discourse markers are integrated as opposed to verbs.

Chapter 9 presents an outline of a theory of grammars in contact — the Matrix Language Frame (MLF) model. One question that will help the reader navigate through the rest of the book is: How does the MLF proposal fit into a broader model of bilingual competence and bilingual proficiency introduced in the next chapters on psycholinguistics and language acquisition?

What's attractive in the author's approach to explaining how bilingual speech is systematic is that it tries to help us describe the nature of *knowledge* structures (bilingual competence, the mental representation of L1 and L2) with a method that starts with bilingual *ability* (performance, the processing of L1 and L2). For example, in the discussion of how morphemes are differentially accessed in bilingual speech (pp. 267–271), the categorization of the "conceptually activated" <u>content</u> and <u>early system</u> morphemes, and the "late" <u>bridge system</u> and <u>outsider system</u> morphemes is based on a language production model. So it seems, we might suggest, that the MLF model views knowledge/competence as an integral component of a larger cognitive domain of ability/performance, and not in terms of sharp dichotomy. What this general approach should favor is the possibility of opening up new lines of dialogue and convergence among the different cognitive science disciplines.

The main idea in this chapter is that in codeswitching there is a strong tendency for there to be a "division of labor" between a Matrix Language (ML) and an Embedded Language (EL); that they do not participate equally in constructing the grammatical frame of mixed language clauses. Together with the important psychological distinction between the semantic component of content morphemes and the grammatical structures of syntax, it is this asymmetry that helps to account for why codeswitching is rule-governed from the earliest stages of bilingual development in children. A question perhaps to speculate upon might be: what areas of common ground could be explored with potentially compatible approaches, such as Muysken's (2000), for example? How might the categories:

1. insertion,
2. alternation, and
3. congruent lexicalization (from Muysken) be related to:
    i. the constraints that the ML imposes on the EL in general,
    ii. the behavior of EL-islands, and
    iii. composite codeswitching?

In Chapters 10 and 11 we have the opportunity to see how well the research on bilingual speech makes contact with recent work on language development, language processing and current theories of the nature of bilingual competence (how knowledge of two languages is "stored" and "accessed"). One way to approach all of this might be to think of the asymmetries of bilingualism as implying differentiation and diversity; in what ways is the bilingual mind internally heterogeneous? In these chapters, the different theories about the organization of the bilingual lexicon are reviewed — (1) are there two separate linguistic subsystems, two separate lexicons for the grammatical subcomponents of each language, or one integrated bilingual lexicon and grammar? (2) Is there a single, shared, conceptual structure serving both language subsystems, or two separate conceptual systems, one for each language system?

The empirical questions are still pending, and the reader should expect contradictory findings. It happens to be a very good thing that an early consensus has not hardened around any one proposal or model. The sense that one comes away with from Chapter 10 is that future approximations toward a comprehensive model of bilingual cognition will have to account for *both* sets of findings: (1) that in performance, access to L1 and L2 subsystems is non-selective (i.e., no "on-off switch"), and (2) that two linguistic subsystems maintain a clearly defined separation such that it is possible to effect degrees of inhibition/suppression. The previous review, of Paradis's book, addresses this issue.

Chapter 11 begins with a summary of recent investigations in child bilingualism. One of the most important advances in this area is the emerging consensus regarding the early differentiation of the grammatical systems of each language subsystem in early bilingual development. It's clear from the way Myers-Scotton covers the research that the evidence for the early consolidation of two autonomous linguistic systems is separate from the questions of imbalanced bilingual attainment in children and cross-linguistic influence during development. It would seem, also, that there would be no other good explanation but early separation for the findings from child codeswitching studies — that children's bilingual speech is rule-governed, as it is in adults. With a "fused system," on the contrary, we would see a protracted period of non-systematic mixing in children because there would be no reliable positive evidence (surely not enough of it) in mixed language input for the young child to be able to rapidly build up a bilingual grammar.

These considerations lead us to an interesting assessment of the Critical Age Hypothesis and the related research on the role of Universal Grammar in second language learning. In this manner, Chapter 11 wraps up a long discussion with some practical implications for language educators.

8.3 Child language development in English and Cantonese (Yip and Matthews, 2007)

Recent research on child bilingual development has called into question widely held assumptions. For a while it seemed that work on transfer/interference, unequal development, and dominant language-induced attrition had come to be disfavored, undermining an ideal standard of a completely balanced bilingual with equivalent competence in each language. In their book, Yip and Matthews' extensive report of their work addresses difficult issues that practitioners and specialists in the past have tended to shy away from.

The book addresses what is one of the central objectives of current research today on early bilingual development — the construction of a model that can account for both simultaneous balanced bilingual development (of two first languages — 2L1 development) and imbalanced bilingual development, in its different expressions and ultimate attainment outcomes, for example — delayed development of one language, first language competence plus an emerging second language-type competence, or attrition of a non-dominant former-L1. The first two chapters chart out the theoretical issues. Chapter 3 provides an overview of the methodological problems of naturalistic child language study, Chapters 4–7 report the authors' findings from their study of a group of young bilingual children, and Chapters 8 and 9 conclude with some interesting speculation about the how a Faculty of Language-internal process in children might help explain external sociolinguistic phenomena in language contact-induced change. Overall, the review of the literature and discussion of findings contributes a good measure of clarity to a number of questions related to Cross-Linguistic Influence (CLI) in child bilingualism, which are still not well understood to this day.

The Introduction and Theoretical Framework present a comprehensive research agenda that identifies some of the most important problems still pending in the field. The actual findings directly bear on only part of it, but readers get a clear view from the first two chapters of the bigger picture into which this study of asymmetry in bilingual development is inscribed. The overarching conceptual backdrop to the study is the Poverty of Stimulus (PoS) problem, specifically in how it presents itself in the acquisition of two languages. Special test cases of PoS potentially provide the strongest proofs, for example, creole emergence from Nicaraguan sign pidgin (Senghas *et al.*, 2004). Early bilingualism, while not "special" because it is so widespread, and even "typical" we could say, is another example where children overcome degraded and conflicting evidence in the available input. The authors refer to this as the Logical Problem of Bilingual Acquisition and the poverty of dual stimulus. The arguments turn out to be quite convincing (pp. 5–6, 30–33). They discuss how Primary Linguistic Data made available from two grammatical systems, instead of just one, presents children with a more formidable learnability problem, one that they nevertheless surmount without recourse to additional or special learning resources.

Following a review of the research on early separation of the linguistic systems, an apparent contradiction is posed, one that has seemingly troubled researchers for some time. If the grammars of the young preschool bilingual show a precocious differentiation into autonomous linguistic systems, how can we account for prolific cross-linguistic influence, interference/transfer, and asymmetry? As it turns out, the facts of imbalance, even massive transfer in one direction (from the dominant to the non-dominant language), do not call into question the findings of early separation and autonomy of each developing linguistic system, neither does evidence of transfer from non-dominant to dominant language (Chan, 2010). In fact, a close examination, in Chapters 4–7, of transfer and CLI between Cantonese and English showed them to be selective and systematic, and largely predictable from independent assessments of dominance. This finding provides additional evidence that disconfirms the theory of a unitary and holistic mental distribution of bilingual children's language competence. Non-random and systematic transfer indicates that the knowledge of language in bilinguals is organized into systems and subsystems. Transfer and CLI, of all types, also require a model in which these autonomous systems and subsystems are interconnected within the larger bilingual mental architecture.

The details of the evidence in Chapters 4–7 are well worth plowing through, presented, as they are, with clear examples and non-technical easy-to-follow explanations. We get the beginnings of a picture here of the complexity of the actual mechanisms of cross-language interaction. Three aspects of the early English grammar of the bilingual children affected by Cross-Linguistic Influence are presented for analysis, the emergence of: *wh*-in-situ constructions in questions, null objects, and prenominal relative clauses. What is of interest in these chapters is how the accounts of transfer from Cantonese hold up a mirror to problems of development in all child bilingualism.

For example, while English interrogatives typically involve movement of the *wh*-word, in Cantonese it remains wherever the expression replaced by the *wh*-word occurred, as in English "echo-questions" (You spent HOW MUCH at the shopping mall this morning?). The bilingual children evidently appropriated this feature far more extensively than monolinguals do and maintained it longer. For now, we can put aside the questions of to what extent the non-target *wh*-in-situ development is transfer-induced or developmental, and whether it reflects competence or performance. Rather, subject Timmy's transitional construction (at 3;02) highlights a more difficult and more interesting problem for researchers, how bilingual children process input ambiguity (1):

1. What are you cutting? You want to cut the what? (p. 100)

What's interesting here is that evidence (input that children receive) from the dominant language (Cantonese) prompts them to apply *wh*-in-situ across the board, and evidence from English is divided. The relevant distinctions are subtle, belonging to the domain of interface between syntactic structure and semantics/pragmatics. The argument could even be made that non-target *wh*-situ utterances are not mal-formed from the point of view of ("narrow") syntax, strictly speaking. As the authors point out, the learnability problem is acute. How do young bilinguals overcome the poverty of dual stimulus problem, potentially compounded by input from competing input models that don't even present a clear-cut contrast? In one sense, the problem of how children master these distinctions overshadows the discussion about how early separation of the language systems is achieved. There may actually be a "delay" in effecting complete separation (e.g., in cases of dominant/non-dominant bilingualism). But consummating separation between the language subsystems by age four or five poses the same unanswered research questions as evidence of earlier separation does because of the continued unavailability to young children of higher-order meta-level learning strategies.

A similar instance of the Logical Problem of Bilingual Acquisition is presented in Chapter 5 — the persistence of null objects. This is another syntax-semantics/pragmatics interface domain issue; the input ambiguity problem is of the same order. Cantonese permits object omission widely; in English, the question of which transitive verbs require the object to be expressed, and in which contexts, is highly complex, as in (2) (from Goldberg, 2001):

2. Pat gave and gave, but Chris just took and took.

In actual language use, one could argue that "malformed" null object constructions in English could be said to usually violate expectations of coherent discourse, being grammatical in other respects.

At this point, after studying the examples of transfer and how the bilingual children began to recover from its influence, we might want to make the following proposal regarding the bilingual input ambiguity learning problem — Part of the solution must include the early separation of grammars into autonomous representations for each language. With basically only Primary Linguistic Data to work with, preschool-age bilinguals overcome, sooner or later, ambiguous evidence spontaneously in the same measure of completeness as monolingual children. Such an automatic and untutored resolution of such intra and interlinguistic distinctions would be hard to explain unless one's working model accepts one form or another of early differentiation between language systems. This suggestion by the authors prompts us to consider an important research question: would evidence of even sharper imbalances and more prolific cross-linguistic interaction between dominant and non-dominant languages be compatible with early separation?

When considering the transfer of prenominal relative clauses to English, in Chapter 6, we might assume that the issue of input ambiguity doesn't apply. It appears to be a strictly Cantonese pattern, so the contrast between English and Cantonese in the input that children receive shouldn't be ambiguous. Utterances like (3) would seem to be rare among English-speaking children, monolingual and bilingual (in another language):

3. Where's $[_{NP}[_{S}$you buy] that one] (Timmy 2;07) (p. 164)

   meaning: "Where's that one that you bought?"

The authors, however, hold out, even here, the possibility that the contrast with Cantonese may not be as straightforward for the young child as first appears — In English, adjectives and other modifiers also precede nouns, as the relative clause in this example apparently does. In any case, an interesting research question would be to compare recovery from different sets of incorrect hypotheses that young children entertain; would they be more difficult for null objects and *wh*-in situ? In the end, all of this might turn out to be quite elusive. Researchers of child language development grapple with ambiguous examples themselves. The authors leave us with an instructive example (4):

4. Just now I smell something is not very nice. (from Alicia, at 3;09)

Should we count it as a prenominal relative [just now I smell] modifying *something*, or as something (which) *is not very nice*? (p. 172)

We can now follow the logic of Yip and Matthews's claims and apply them to scenarios in which dominance and imbalance are permanent and progressive, as in L1 attrition (an unfortunate misnomer) and early stabilization of a bilingual's "weaker" language; see Paradis (2004) for one explanation for how this is possible. It appears that the subjects in this study, three of whom are the authors' own children, did not fall into the latter category of early stabilization or attrition of English. This raises the interesting possibility of whether the "temporary" imbalances at issue could be attributed to either:

1. one, more rapidly, developing language subsystem inhibiting the other (mechanisms of performance/processing) or
2. an actual uneven development of competence.

Interested readers should consult Yukawa (1997) for a discussion of some pertinent considerations in a similar study, and Meisel (2007) on the question of distinguishing between aspects of performance and competence in these situations.

Yip and Matthews argue that the theoretically more interesting aspect of imbalanced bilingual development is underlying competence, how the actual *knowledge* structures of each language subsystem interact (scenario #2 above). Saying that, presumably, does not mean that factors strictly limited to *performance and processing* cannot also account for emerging imbalances between L_a and L_b in young children (or even that a "processing inhibition" might appear as a precursor to loss of competence). In any case, the most important part of their argument seems to be that it is a mistake to limit explanations of dominance and asymmetry to aspects of performance.

As was suggested above, all of this leads us to consider an extension of the method applied in this investigation to the field of language attrition, along the same lines that the authors favor a unification of the fields of child bilingualism and second language learning. For one, in advanced Replacing Language development (for early child bilingualism, a better term than "erosion" or "attrition"), we would hesitate to attribute the end-state properties of an "attrited" (replaced) language subsystem primarily to factors of temporary inhibition, for example.

Chapter 8 considers Thomason's (2001) idea of how early bilingualism plays a role in what is called *language contact-induced change*. Table 1.2, in the Introduction, summarizes the relationship — how Faculty of Language-internal imbalances can help explain sociolinguistic changes in a community of speakers. Again, but with a different twist, the Logical Problem of Bilingual Acquisition is part of the explanation, in this instance, for rapid language shift. Just as the (undelayed) development of grammatical knowledge in two languages is underdetermined by the input available to the child, the *delayed* development of a non-dominant language may be attributed, in part, to asymmetries in the external conditions of language use, but its course is not determined exhaustively by these conditions. That is, the delayed development of a child's "weaker" language may be related to restricted input or diminished exposure to that language, but such experiential factors do not account for or explain all cases of normal delay and attrition. In such manner, first language "attrition" (now in quotes) can be studied developmentally. An immediate practical application of this approach would be to help us understand why some accounts of contact-induced change cannot be correct, for example: that language shift is caused by a diminished or incomplete form of a socially disfavored language being "passed on" from one non-balanced bilingual generation to the next, or that codeswitching and non-reciprocal borrowing from the socially preferred/prestigious language directly contributes to degrading the subordinate language. The language acquisition mechanisms, fully accessible during early childhood, have been shown to be able to upgrade the most rudimentary pidgin system (Goldin-Meadow, 2005). So therefore, an important part of the explanation for dominant/non-dominant divergence, early stabilization, and attrition must be sought in the internal dynamics of cross-language interaction. The Cantonese-English study makes an important contribution to understanding these dynamics better.

I would like to offer one last observation. Most readers will notice that the authors frame their study with the basic assumptions of Universal Grammar in mind. But at the same time, they recognize the contributions made by usage-based and functionalist approaches to our understanding of bilingualism, and incorporate them into their analyses throughout the book. The authors don't explicitly call attention to the potential dialogue. They drop a hint, though, in the concluding chapter why it is that in the study of bilingualism such a discussion has a better chance of sprouting legs. The reason for this possibility is conjunctural, but worth pursing nonetheless: that research on bilingualism must attend to a greater diversity of Faculty of Language-internal and general cognitive domains and mechanisms than is the case in monolingual development, thus allowing for a broader space for potential common ground. This initiative on their part, from within the field of bilingualism, happens to coincide with, or rather be a part of, a wider initiative within cognitive science to open new lines of discussion between generativists and researchers working on problems in language development from other perspectives.

8.4 Bilingual first language acquisition (De Houwer, 2009)

The merit of this book by Annick De Houwer (2009) on bilingual first language development (BFLA) is the clarity with which it opens on the very first page the discussion of research on a persistent problem of assessment, then returning to this important topic in its concluding chapter. The research problem is the one that we tried to get our heads around in Chapter 2. The first chart (Box 1.1) displays in simple straightforward terms where the line can be drawn between evidence of normal child development in two languages and indications of possible language impairment. Being one of the continuing puzzles for many practitioners working in the field, due to lack of clarity on fundamental principles, the relevant criteria are explained:

1. BFLA children are exposed to two languages from the first year of life; thus, two L1s emerge. One expectation is that BFLA children will develop typical (native-like) linguistic competence in both languages. A logical and plausible expectation it is, and in fact, a balanced bilingualism of this type is an outcome that many early bilingual children evidence in their performance. Findings from surveys summarized by De Houwer suggest that such a bilingual equilibrium is observed in households in which two languages are spoken during the course of every day. However, it would be an error to consider another commonly observed dual language outcome as atypical or abnormal: that of so-called "passive bilingualism" — complete receptive and expressive abilities in one language and only receptive abilities in the other language (i.e., emergence of a "stronger" and a "weaker" language). As we saw in Chapter 2, this kind of imbalance presents itself even in BFLA scenarios in which there appear to be adequate input conditions for the complete acquisition of both languages. This asymmetrical bilingual acquisition outcome is in no way a sign of language impairment.
2. Developmental outcomes in which receptive abilities are in evidence in both languages, but expressive abilities do not emerge on schedule, in either language, are cause for serious concern; and the rare cases of neither receptive nor expressive abilities in either language, cause for very serious concern. These, of course, are the same indicators of possible impairment in the monolingual condition, children's knowledge of two languages not altering in any fundamental way how we should understand what is normal and what is abnormal. If either atypical situation, especially the latter, comes to the attention of parents and teachers a formal assessment is strongly indicated. For language and speech practitioners, when faced with evidence of significant delay or failure to make progress on school-related learning objectives in one language (in practice, usually the language of instruction), the recommendation is to always administer a complete assessment battery in both languages. The common practice of relying on performance in children's L2 is clearly insufficient; thus, failure to also take a complete language sample in the L1 renders the assessment incomplete and uninterpretable.

The normal variation in BFLA is therefore wide, from complete native-like competence in L_a and L_b (the acronyms we introduced in Chapter 2 — De Houwer refers to Language A and Language Alpha, an equivalent distinction) to complete native-like competence in one language and no expressive ability in the other. Tentatively, it can be assumed that in "passive bilingualism" of this kind competence in the weaker language cannot be native-like, unless lack of expressive ability is strictly due to processing or performance factors (in the narrow sense). Nevertheless, we are reminded that the research on the relationship between receptive and expressive performance in early child bilinguals has yet no definitive answer to this question. Overall, De Houwer estimates that: "uneven development of two languages in a BFLA child is the rule rather than the exception" (p. 48). This interesting claim contradicts popular belief about early simultaneous bilingualism, and in the absence of findings from large-scale longitudinal studies it remains an open question for investigators. However, initial findings from case studies and language surveys suggest that it is not only plausible, but that it is also a good starting point for further investigation.

In relation to this research problem the concept of Early Second Language Acquisition (ESLA) is introduced. With no consensus agreement on an age range when another significant language in the child's environment should be taken as "second," as opposed to the other L1 of BFLA, the interesting question becomes the following: considering the case of a weaker and stronger bilingual combination, what properties of the weaker language would make it resemble a L2 instead of a L1? In other words, when might an imbalanced BFLA become L1 development plus ESLA? An approximation to a solution was proposed in our earlier discussion of imbalanced bilingualism — that, at the end of the day, the difference, strictly speaking, is not about age of onset. In other words, performance in the weaker language of imbalanced BFLA may show the signs of early stabilization, precursor of long-term stabilization, far from typical native-speaker grammatical knowledge, or even L1 attrition. Recall that in the model proposed in the review of research in Chapter 2, L1 attrition always unfolds (language impairment aside) parallel to Replacing Language development.

The important topic of how L_a and L_b interact in different developmental outcomes, as in the extensive and penetrating interaction of complete RL development just mentioned, leads us to consider the Separate Development Hypothesis (SDH), a major focus of De Houwer's work over the years. Stated summarily — In the early emergence of grammar, during the second year of life, bilingual children differentiate the two linguistic subsystems, giving rise to separate mental representations for each one. The linguistic subsystems maintain their autonomy, this differentiation achieved spontaneously and without awareness or deliberative attention required on the part of the young bilingual. Importantly, evidence of cross-language influences within the larger language system is not incompatible with the idea of separation, and should be studied without committing ourselves ahead of time to either the SDH or a competing hypothesis that rejects the separation of language subsystems. The SDH and its rival hypotheses are among a small number of proposals in the field that point to the most far-reaching theoretical consequences in the cognitive sciences. The discussion evokes the ongoing debate in many sub-disciplines on questions of componentiality (modularity), in this instance with an example from bilingualism.

A corollary claim, which in some ways we could consider as a strong hypothesis (perhaps too strong), is that — "the morphosyntactic development of the one language does not have any fundamental effect on the morphological development of the other" (p. 35). One way to begin to evaluate this claim is to first separate it from the basic assumptions of the SDH. That is, the autonomy of the language subsystems does not necessarily imply the blocking of cross-language interaction (CLI). Secondly, it is important to clarify what "*fundamental* effect" includes. Well-formed language mixing, for example, must engage CLI for the bilingual to be able to incorporate constituents from one subsystem into grammatical frames of the larger "host" constituents — embedded language (EL) constituents into matrix language (ML) frames, following Myers-Scotton's (2006) terminology. Also, in the imbalanced variant of BFLA where development in the weaker L1 actually begins to stabilize (growth "stagnates," p. 290) and enters into a dynamic of attrition, CLI, from stronger to weaker subsystem, is no longer occasional. And if in ESLA, where systematic transfer, L1 to L2, is widely recognized, can we confidently exclude systematic CLI in cases of imbalanced BFLA? Matthews and Yip (2011) discuss this question, as well as the related problem, alluded to above, of distinguishing between imbalanced BFLA and ESLA.

One approach to these theoretical problems could be the following — The autonomy of L_a and L_b subsystems, assumed by the SDH, is strongly supported by the robust finding of independent and separate development of L_a and L_b in the balanced variant of BFLA, showing no "fundamental" effects of CLI. The fact that CLI is more extensive or systematic in cases of imbalanced early bilingualism cannot imply that children in the latter case have a different mental architecture in the domain of language. So the default working assumption should be separate development, not contradicted by effects of interaction between the language subsystems. In fact, the evidence from different kinds of transfer and CLI also lend strong support to the hypothesis of separation. Grammatical codeswitching and other kinds of well-formed mixing would be difficult to explain if linguistic knowledge of the two languages were not compartmentalized, i.e., each network of structures integrated into a separate subsystem within the broader Faculty of Language. In the end, the extent of CLI and how systematic it turns out to be in all the different variants of child bilingualism, some of which still not easily distinguishable one from the other, should be taken as a pending empirical question. But the basic feature of SDH, compartmentalization of the language subsystems, promises to stand up to whatever definitive findings come forth on questions of interactivity (the properties of interfaces that connect up the component structures of language).

8.4.1 Input for bilingual development

No one denies that exposure to two languages is required for bilingualism, and that there must be some threshold of sufficient input in each language; refer back to Table 2.1 (e.g., overhearing occasional conversations between parents and visiting uncles from the old country falls below the threshold). But it's also clear that there is no exact one-to-one match-up between language experience (children's "linguistic soundscape," p. 98) and the resulting dual language competence profile. Some of the apparent *mismatches*, in fact, are very interesting and hard to explain. Among the various puzzles that are presented is the one related to the SDH — in all the mixing, switching and convergence between languages, dialects, registers and different bilingual discourse styles, how do young children come to treat some of this variation as part of one linguistic subsystem (e.g., varieties of French) and other aspects of it as language data that should be divided up into separate subsystems (e.g., one corresponding to French and the other to Dutch)? The causal observer might surmise that Belgian children shouldn't have too much trouble doing this because anyone, who has never heard these languages spoken before, could probably tell the difference right away. But bilingual children in Barcelona apparently do the same with Spanish and Catalan (not as easy to tell).

The mismatch between experience and resulting competence here refers to the problem of how young children construct knowledge of two languages (the resulting competence) with language experience that appears not to provide enough information to go by. In other words, the acquisition goes beyond the data. Another example is how children exposed to second language performance of their parents, especially when this is the predominant language of socialization (common in countries with many immigrants), do not reproduce their fossilized interlanguage competence (p. 106).

This brings us to another line of work that De Houwer has focused on in her research — comparing the outcomes from different bilingual input models. For many years, and still today, a widespread assumption about the most effective and "secure" approach to bilingual socialization has been the one person, one language (1P/1L) principle (e.g., one parent speaks only L_a to children and the other only L_b). Assuming that this method would more likely assure that input is not "confusing," it would also discourage mixing, and maximize the possibility of balanced ability. Interestingly (because 1P/1L has an intuitive appeal to it), research has failed to support the logic of this kind of seemingly systematic approach to promoting bilingualism. Many children surveyed in studies that compared different input conditions (including 1P/1L) spoke only one language, and a comparison with the alternate model (both parents/both languages) actually favored greater balanced ability. Even on measures of mixing in children's speech (in popular belief, evidence of "confusion") no significant differences were found between the two competing bilingual input methods. Regarding attainment of typical language acquisition milestones, no advantage was demonstrated for either one or the other approach (pp. 107–112).

Research on L1 attrition (a misnomer because a Replacing Language of primary, L1-type, status develops in parallel, and Language, with a capital L, does not erode) is a relatively new field. Of the consensus findings is the strong tendency for younger bilinguals to undergo more rapid attrition/replacement (p. 130). The final state of L1 attrition is also highly variable, from complete replacement by the stronger language to a long-term stabilized competence showing evidence of even near-native abilities in some domains. In tracing the differentiation between a stronger L_a and weaker L_b back to early childhood (e.g., in retrospect), in fact, it would be difficult determine with any precision whether the weaker language developed as a prematurely stabilized subsystem, an attrited primary language, or an example of ESLA. Again, the simple and straightforward recommendation is that *none* of these development outcomes indicates language delay such that parents should consult a speech pathologist, even under conditions of "environmental support of bilingual acquisition" (p. 320), as long as the stronger language continues to advance within the margin of normal expectation (p. 276).

The chapter on lexical development emphasizes the variability in word knowledge in young bilinguals, the same kind of variability that is found in monolingual word knowledge. The interesting special feature of the early childhood bilingual lexicon is how it is distributed among the categories of:

- translation equivalent (TE) pairs,
- lexical entries specific to L_a or L_b and
- cognates.

This schema is important to take into account in assessment, when comparing vocabulary with monolingual speakers. The common, problematic, practice of not combining the categories will consistently underestimate bilingual children's knowledge in this domain (p. 243). An ongoing research problem, related specifically to TEs, is how to compare word learning strategies in bilinguals and monolinguals; for example, how do bilingual children apply the so called Mutual Exclusivity Bias? How should we interpret TEs in bilingual performance as compatible with the bias of young children to assume that classes of objects can only have one name (p. 205)? This problem comes up later in the discussion of whether bilinguals maintain two separate lexicons or a "global" integrated lexicon (p. 242)? On the face of it, the separate lexicons hypothesis should follow from the Separate Development Hypothesis; De Houwer leaves the theoretical connection open on this question.

The concluding chapter returns to the theme of comparing monolingual and bilingual development. While many aspects of this comparison are interesting and often necessary, it also lends itself to persistent misunderstanding. Some of the confusion stems from family members and teachers who insist on imposing expectations derived from what they understand language development should be from their model of monolingualism. Bilingual competence shares some of the same properties with knowledge of only one language; and at the same time other properties are peculiar when knowledge of language is distributed between two independent subsystems of the same kind.

8.5 A different perspective on imbalanced bilingualism

(Montrul, 2008)

Montrul's (2008) *Incomplete acquisition in bilingualism* is the ideal follow-up to the overview of work on early bilingualism by De Houwer, and the case studies of Yip and Matthews that introduced the idea of imbalanced bilingual ability in simultaneous acquisition of two languages. The related questions of age factor in L1 and L2 (but not the same questions) take center stage. As we will see, after many years of study, there are still a number of fundamental problems awaiting a clear formulation concerning maturational constraints on language acquisition. What is interesting in this book is that even though Montrul appears to take an approach that is different from the one outlined in our discussion in Chapter 2, in a number of areas, especially on points of empirical finding in the research to date, interesting convergences present themselves. Among the most important of these, again, is the importance of studying asymmetry, of different kinds, as a key feature of bilingualism. The first chapter begins with the observation of imbalance in two different situations — that many of the characteristic features of second language learning appear to be shared with incomplete or attrited development of a first language, spoken by so-called "heritage speakers." Incompleteness is not unique to second languages; and understanding how it unfolds in first languages is part of the same overall research problem. The common denominator that is proposed is the relationship between incomplete acquisition and age of acquisition. Recall from our review of De Houwer (2009) that incompleteness in a L1 only (non-pathologically) occurs in bilingual development. In monolingual development, or in both L_a and L_b, incomplete language competence is evidence of impairment, abnormal development.

Related to this last point is the clarification that the concept of fossilization (early stabilization) does not apply to the dominant language of BFLA, or other kind of primary language (e.g., monolingual). Uniformity of ultimate attainment in at least one primary language in the domain of grammar among all normally developing children is assumed as the norm. In second language learning, of the L2 grammar, fossilization does apply. The non-uniformity in ultimate attainment, even under comparable conditions of instruction and experience in the L2, stands as a stubborn fact that all theories have to try to explain. Today, transfer effects from L1 are recognized as a permanent and persistent influence on interlanguage development by most investigators (p. 5). The challenge then is to account for the strength of what in Chapter 2 we called the "L1 filter," how its strength appears to vary from one L2 learner to another (in L2 learning, the "L1 filter" is basically the same idea as L1 transfer). How is it, for example, that for near native L2 competence the filter turns out to be weak or even completely porous? For most L2 learners, on the other hand, why is a noticeable effect of the L1 filter so persistent? Or is the L2 learner's difficulty due to a "fundamental difference" (the Fundamental Difference Hypothesis), a loss or decay in language acquisition capacity itself?

As an aside, the kind of asymmetry that we are considering in the case of L1 attrition or L2 fossilization is of a completely different kind than the asymmetries that are observed in different aspects of bilingual ability involving the mastery of specific skills, such as in the academic realm. For example, the variation in higher-order language abilities tied to schooling and literacy is a separate issue. The study of how bilinguals master complex abilities, such as reading and writing for academic purposes, should be considered apart from the questions at hand in this review, i.e., the development of grammatical knowledge in the linguistic subsystems of bilingual speakers. This clarification is especially important to keep in mind when bilingual children are evaluated for possible language disability.

Here is where incompleteness in both L1 and L2 can be addressed from the same perspective of age of acquisition. Uncontroversially, age of initial contact with the L2 is related to ultimate attainment; child L2 learners are more likely, in the end, on average, to attain the most advanced levels of proficiency (the reasons why are controversial). And interestingly, albeit predictably, early stabilization/attrition of the weaker language (if there is one) in child bilingualism is also related to age of initial contact with the dominant language to be. On average, the later the contact, the more resistant a weaker language turns out to be to the effects of replacement by a stronger language subsystem (in balanced or so-called "additive" bilingualism there is no weaker language). Thus, in bilingualism, age of onset of another language (e.g., the L2 of child SLA) appears to be a determining factor according to this proposal. Recall, however, from our earlier discussion of the research that there are other factors that correlate very closely with age; and secondly, in any consideration of the effects of maturation (a critical or sensitive period), it is important to carefully separate out these effects as they impact primary language development as opposed to second language learning.

While on the surface, incomplete or eroded L1 ability and non-native L2 ability show similar patterns of error in performance, their different origins might reveal different kinds of underlying competence. The Weaker Language (WL) as L1 hypothesis (p. 7) addresses this possibility. Are there vestiges, or "signatures" of uniquely first language knowledge in the incomplete L1 competence of imbalanced bilinguals? An alternate possibility would be that the stabilized/attrited language subsystem is L2-like. This is one of the interesting proposals of the book, of theoretical importance, because it evokes the broader discussion of how L1 and L2 competence are represented mentally (what kind of knowledge does each consist of), and what participation does UG and the LAD have in the development of each?

Empirically, the challenge is the following — matching near-native L2 subjects with near-native L1 attriters (or heritage speakers), can it be shown that the former consistently fail to master clearly identified domains of grammar knowledge that the latter preserve? On the other hand, we have to recognize that among child bilinguals, early evidence of attrition is difficult to distinguish from ESLA. Comparing advanced L1 attrition in later childhood with child L2 learning during the same age range makes for a better comparison. But since the trajectories in each case are going, so to speak, in opposite directions (or one stabilized and the other advancing), individual case-study type match ups are problematic. Will a large-scale quantitative confrontation of assessment results show a significant difference (to reiterate — between domains of linguistic competence that heritage speakers consistently preserve and that L2 learners consistently fail to acquire)? If yes, this would again confirm that L1 acquisition during the critical period is special (it can only normally emerge within this developmental window of opportunity); and this special status might extend even to the weaker or attrited language subsystem of imbalanced bilingualism.

Universal Grammar and LAD are specialized for language acquisition; and inhibiting access to them in L2 development implies that cognitive general learning needs to compensate for this bottleneck. If this is correct, knowledge constructed exclusively from cognitive-general learning would, by hypothesis, present a different kind of mental representation from that of UG and LAD-guided L1 acquisition. We have to admit, however, that little is known about this hypothetical distinction. An alternative hypothesis is that UG and LAD themselves actually erode and come to be degraded after successful L1 acquisition, or simply with age; Meisel (2009, p. 7) argues that "some of the optimal phases during which grammatical properties are easily and successfully developed by mere exposure to the primary linguistic data begin to fade out as early as around age 4;0." Readers will recall that I do not favor this explanation; Montrul does not endorse it either (though a fair summary of this theory appears on pp. 20 and 43–49).

In summing up the Foundations chapter, a completeness-incompleteness "trade-off" in bilingual development is proposed. The onset of incomplete acquisition in one of the language subsystems of child bilinguals occurs when some of its domains appear "not to get a chance to reach age-appropriate levels of proficiency" under the influence of a surging L2 (p. 21), or we might add, under the influence of the stronger subsystem of the "simultaneous" bilingual pair. Turning now to childhood L2, it is certainly common, even being the most common outcome, that this L2 advances steadily, even rapidly in many cases, toward native-speaker completeness. An interesting question is then posed: how typical is it that these successful L2 learners maintain the same developmental pace in their L1, or are these bilinguals even capable of maintaining their L1? Thus, L1 incompleteness/attrition is inversely related to age of onset of bilingualism (p. 22), i.e., the earlier the onset the more likely incompleteness stabilizes. By the same token, late L2 learning is associated with greater likelihood of L1 maintenance.

Montrul takes up the different SLA theories, starting with FTFA, and the self-evident observation (it should be by now) that L1 competence guides or affects initial second language development. A central question for investigators is how persistent does this kind of cross-language influence remain? In fossilization (pp. 34–41), the Full Transfer half of the process is not only full but usually permanent. Recall what makes the concept of fossilization interesting — (1) it has no counterpart in the primary L1 (it might have in the attrited L1 of BFLA), and (2) that significant and long term effects of the L1 filter (or L1 transfer) on L2 ability persist despite what appears to be provision of adequate comprehensible input and corrective feedback — see Chapters 5 and 6.

The critical period discussion enters the picture at this point. Today, with overwhelming research evidence supporting a maturational constraint on L1 development, from studies of deafness, creole genesis (Nicaraguan Sign Language — see Chapter 3), language deprivation, etc., the general question has been resolved. Controversy still remains on what the underlying cognitive foundations are. Turning now to second languages, two alternative hypotheses present themselves:

(1) a similar or analogous critical period restricts L2 ultimate attainment, that L2 is *maturationally* constrained, Meisel's (2009) position. This would seem to imply that an irreversible decay of the LAD, at some point in development/maturation, during an identifiable age range, necessarily shifts the burden of acquisition to cognitive-general learning, thus explaining the variability of L2 final state mastery.

(2) the "full transfer" effect of the L1 filter (p. 43), persistent and extensive to varying degrees, results in observed individual differences in L2. First language subsystems that evolve toward weaker/receding language status under the

expanding encroachment of a robust Replacing Language no longer block or filter the development of a competing language subsystem (Francis, 2012).

Thus, age *per se*, according to the second view, is not the determining factor in L2 mastery, but rather the strength of the L1 filter (other factors held constant, e.g., total years of exposure from onset, intensive learning opportunities in school-type settings, etc.). It happens that the degree of this strength correlates closely with age — the later the onset of a second language the more complete, full-formed and robust will be the L1 subsystem, more encapsulated and insolated from any competing influence from a L2 (Montrul, 2008, p. 60). At the same time, the more complete and full-formed the L1, the greater will be its inhibiting effect, on average, upon the late L2. The later the onset of L2, the stronger the potential transfer effect of the L1. In contrast, the earlier the introduction of a L2 in childhood, the less likely it will be that L1 transfer effects inhibit its development. An immature or weaker L_a of child bilingualism cannot block the setting of parameters in the more rapidly developing L_b. In regard to the related age factor in attrition, in early bilingualism the weaker L_a is highly vulnerable to displacement by a rapidly developing RL. With age, if the weaker L_a continues to advance in development, even though it is weaker, it becomes less vulnerable. To be fair, it's not clear if Montrul would agree with this different focus on L2 learning and L1 attrition.

Each of the competing hypotheses takes on subtle differences of formulation; but it seems that in the contrast between (1) and (2) above a clearly marked line of opposing claims can be drawn for further research. For example, is there a sharp cut-off age range (as there is for L1) for SLA, or a continuous and gradual decline? Is the effect of "full transfer" easily overcome? Are the restrictions (the L1 filter) on "full access" strictly external to the language faculty's "innate computational system" or are they internal to the workings of the Faculty of Language (pp. 50–51)? Reader beware: what is "internal" and what is "external" here is far from an approaching consensus, especially when considering what the boundaries of the Faculty of Language (broad) might be. Lastly, how do the alternative hypotheses (1) and (2) each explain native-like L2 ability?

In the chapter on early childhood, Montrul returns to the WL as L1 hypothesis, contrasting it to Schlyter's WL as L2 — refer back to references in Chapter 2, starting with Bernardini and Schlyter (2004) and Meisel (2007). We start by revisiting the "trade-off" — early immersion in L2, over the long term, is likely to result in native-like ultimate attainment. In parallel, under the long term displacing force of a developing L2, the strong tendency is that the MT/L1 attains a level that is short of native-like ability (p. 98). Why that is, we have to admit, is still an issue for continuing investigation. For example, readers may notice a nuance of difference between Montrul's hypothesis, that appears to place more emphasis on "input factors" and the one favored in Chapter 2 and in Francis (2012). Part of the still unresolved issue is related to the debate between WL as L1 and WL as L2, at first glance seeming to be one of splitting hairs. Perhaps not of immediate practical application, the problem is important conceptually. The following is one proposal for a converging discussion. To review: "Does the weaker language have the signatures of a first language acquired in childhood or does it develop like a second language acquired in adulthood, under the influence of different learning mechanisms" (p. 122)? Now, if we adhere to a strict "fundamental difference" view that first language acquisition is guided by UG and LAD, and second languages by cognitive-general problem-solving skills, we are presented with come potentially difficult contradictions, such as one pointed out by Montrul: Is it possible, assuming "fundamental difference," to draw a line between early L1 development (UG-constrained) and early child L2 development, which may be simultaneous or overlapping with L1, that is not UG-constrained (p. 125)? In the same paragraph, a way out of the contradiction is suggested: assuming, instead, a full access to UG (compatible with FTFA) in L2 development, no fundamental distinction (in the above sense) need be sought between the developing grammars of child bilingualism.

As stronger and weaker subsystems continue to diverge, a difference does become apparent: the influence of the stronger may inhibit acquisition of grammatical structures in the weaker (in Francis, 2012, the L1 filter = the FT of FTFA). But, in the other direction (weaker to stronger) transfer effects are of the "transient," processing/performance, cross-linguistic influence kind ("dynamic interference" versus "static interference" in Paradis, 2004), or of "superficial" features that do not imply incompleteness in any real sense.

This proposal doesn't dissolve all of the differences. It's actually good that it doesn't because there are still avenues of inquiry that are important to pursue along each of the diverging viewpoints. For example, in advanced attrition of a heritage language, even if in all outward appearances it resembles a L2, do there remain vestiges of primary language acquisition that can be traced to early bilingual development? If yes, this would be important to fully understand; Au *et al.* (2008) present findings from a study that directly informs this interesting question. The concluding chapter is an excellent summary of one of the central research problems in the field today, even if one takes a different view on some of the details: how do we explain that permanent incomplete acquisition and fossilization are not just common outcomes in L2 learning but also in one of the language subsystems of early bilingual acquisition (p. 258)? This question leads to a potential solution to a long-standing debate on whether second language knowledge has the same fundamental internal structure as first language knowledge, even though it is less complete.

8.6 Bilingual competence and bilingual proficiency in child development (Francis, 2012)

My recent study of child bilingualism, *Bilingual competence and bilingual proficiency (BCBP)*, serves as background to the major framing concepts of this book. Here I will review commentary and references by other authors to earlier versions of the chapters that have helped to clarify how these concepts have been used. Focused, as it was, on the development of school-related language abilities, the book took a cognitive science approach to the special research problems that bilingualism presents to educators. The kind of bilingualism in particular that was considered involved a significant inequality of material and learning resources between the two languages children learn, when the second language, a L2 of wider communication, appeared on the scene. As we have already discussed, this kind of sociolinguistic imbalance is the most common worldwide.

8.6.1 Modularity and how it may be applied to the components of bilingual proficiency

Oller (2008) and Oller and Vila (2011) engaged this question in their reports on dual language learning in Catalonia. A starting point that we all share is the work of Vygotsky in his appreciation of how language ability is marshaled as an instrument of higher-order cognitive operations in advanced literacy and related intellectual achievements of middle childhood. The key concept here is the development of decontextualized uses of language, topic of the next section. Vygotsky had little to say about bilingualism (he was interested in the connection between knowing two languages and decontextualization); but his proposed distinctions among different kinds of language use, as they might be related to different kinds of bilingual ability, are still debated today. One important distinction was between discourse ability that benefits from, or depends on, interactive context support (as in face-to-face conversation) and discourse ability that requires independent mental organizing of texts, as in reading or listening to complex non-interactive expositions, narratives and the like (Vygotsky, 2004).

In Oller's (2008) study, an extensive discussion on the applicability of modularity to bilingual proficiency brings to the fore critical theoretical distinctions that are still controversial. The pending research tasks are — (1) How to account for both separate mental representation of cognitive components and at the same time explain how the interfaces between and among these components function so rapidly and efficiently encompassing a network of connections that must be extremely elaborate and detailed. (2) Which aspects of this mental architecture are pre-programmed and which are implemented directly in response to experience? (3) The need to distinguish between the truly primitive component modules and the larger networks that are on the scale of abilities and faculties (e.g., reading ability and "language" cannot be modules), and the need to distinguish between encapsulated domain-specific components and cognitive structures that are not domain-specific and are not encapsulated. For example, how does cognitive-general learning differ from other kinds of knowledge acquisition that are specialized? One challenge in particular is how to conceptualize the separation of language subsystems in bilingual speakers, even involving closely related languages, a differentiation that is achieved early in development by young children acquiring two languages?

To this last point Oller and Vila reference a model from *BCBP* that attempted to graphically describe the relationship between the two language subsystems of the bilingual (Figure 8.1), following Cummins's (1989) well-known double iceberg representation. Even though subsequent work forced me to abandon this model for a more precise portrayal in which the "icebergs" no longer overlap (for interested readers, these are Figures 3.2 and 5.2 in *BCBP*), the reference by Oller and Vila to the first ("overlapping" subsystems) approximation serves to highlight an interesting research problem. The

Figure 8.1

Proposed relationship between the language subsystems of a bilingual speaker

Variant-A: Between two subsystems of "closely related" languages

Variant-B: Between two subsystems of "distantly related" languages

unique multilingual contact situation of Catalonia perhaps allows investigators to think about this problem more easily — immigrant children, L2 learners of Catalan, enrolled in school, speak both "distantly related" (e.g., Arabic) and "closely related" languages (e.g., Spanish and Rumanian) to Catalan.

Assuming for now the situation of beginner L2 learners, does Variant-A in Figure 8.1 allow for a freer and more effective access to the shared Common Underlying Proficiency (CUP) (see the original model in Cummins 1989) than learners whose L2 is distantly related (Variant-B)? The CUP is shared because it is not "language bound"; i.e. metalinguistic awareness, secondary discourse ability, higher order analytical capabilities, advanced information processing skills, conceptual knowledge and the like are largely independent of the linguistic subsystems. Literate adults are familiar with one scenario that is related to the problem of access to these proficiencies when reading in a new second language. Consider first the case of a monolingual speaker of Spanish on a trip, for the first time, to Barcelona. Upon picking up the morning edition of the Catalan-language daily *El Punt Avui*, he has no trouble getting the gist of a number of front page news reports, and if he finds an article on a topic about which he possess extensive previous knowledge comprehension is surprisingly adequate. The monolingual speaker of German could not do the same.

For child L2 beginners, the situation is somewhat different, but parallel — (1) assuming literacy in the L1, performance on a L2 reading task would depend on the level of development of the above mentioned CUP abilities and skills (what abilities and skills has the child developed to access in the first place), awareness of and disposition toward the decoding of written language in an unfamiliar language, and so forth. (2) On the other hand, assuming no prior L1 literacy, access to CUP-based capabilities in performance on a L2 listening task (without the facilitating resources of visual processing of text) is an aspect of bilingual ability that researchers still know very little about. Now, as both adult and child L2 learners advance in grammatical competence and lexical knowledge, the differences in performance between the student with a closely related L1 (Variant-A) the one with a distantly related L1 (Variant-B) should begin to narrow. As our Spanish- and German-speaking visitors apply themselves to learning Catalan, the initial disadvantage of the latter when reading articles in *El Punt Avui* starts to disappear. Eventually, in theory, among intermediate and near-native speakers of the L2 there would be no difference, no advantage or disadvantage of any consequence related to their L1. Thus, the interesting aspect of the question of access is this: what effect of linguistic distance-closeness can be demonstrated among *beginner* L2 learners and *beginner* readers? Then, what medium term effects might continue to present themselves along the way as learners progress in both the L2 itself and in the general academic proficiencies tied to literacy and schooling? Here, the authors point to "two routes," following Genesee *et al.* (2005), toward the mastery of L2 literacy — one via the strong development of the target language, the L2 grammar, and the other via the development of literacy abilities through the L1, the same abilities that will be accessible in L2 reading and writing tasks. In a review of research, Delgado (2010) points out that the concept of shared competencies and skills that are independent of language is still a proposal for further investigation. Understanding better how bilinguals access them (and how sometimes they are not able to) in all the different kinds of L1–L2 interaction will make the concept of CUP more concrete and less hypothetical. Yumoto's (2008) study of heritage language learning ties the concept of CUP-based academic language proficiency to the factor of additive bilingualism, a relationship that we have not explored in our project.

Oller and Vila (2011) give partial credit to Figure 8.1 for suggesting these interactions between L1 and L2 and in turn between the bilingual language system and the CUP; but truth be told, this author had not contemplated them at the time. Admittedly, also, the model of overlapping subsystems of L1 and L2 does in fact make the research issues on this question more salient, even though, for other reasons, I came to the conclusion that a more complete separation between L1 and L2 is a preferable solution. Part of the solution is that cross-language interaction between L1 and L2 is still highly productive under the assumption of separate and autonomous linguistic subsystems. The cross-linguistic interfaces (in Figure 5.2 of *BCBP*) take the place of the overlapping sectors in Figure 8.1. The Catalan study proposes a framework for accounting for the effects of L1 closeness-or-distance in child L2 learners' academic achievement (subjects were school age L2 learners of Catalan whose L1 is Spanish, Rumanian or Arabic). These effects are related to the more general factor of children's rate of L2 mastery and how this linguistic factor affects their ability to learn the context-reduced, meta-level language proficiencies associated with advanced literacy. Recall from Chapter 7, that advanced literacy consists of higher-order abilities of reading and writing for academic purposes.

In a review of the literature on a related topic, L2 learners' access to genre knowledge in L2 writing, Gentil (2011) also finds the concept of modularity to be useful in explaining how this aspect of the metalinguistic awareness-secondary discourse ability combination is applied in performance. We could say that this combination is about awareness and higher order language ability at the discourse-level — a kind of metapragmatic knowledge plus complex skill in text construction. As in other studies of language ability whose core competencies are essentially independent of the linguistic subsystems, might there be subcomponents of genre awareness and ability to implement a genre that are language-specific (e.g., closely associated with, "bound to," the L1 through which they may have been learned)? Formulated the question in this way, a specific instance of genre knowledge could be analyzed and found to consist of two kinds (because "knowledge" under the assumptions of a modular point of view is not all of one kind) — (1) underlying competencies that are strictly non-linguistic, conceptual, not bound to either L1 or L2, and (2) competencies that are in fact closely tied to the grammar of one language subsystem or the other. This type of analysis could be usefully applied, with an open mind, even though we might concur with Gentil's bias in that the fundamental and defining properties of genre abilities are probably non-language specific and shared within the domain of the common underlying proficiencies (meaning, not "belonging to" either language subsystem, e.g., the French or English grammar subsystem in a bilingual speaker of French and English).[1]

8.6.2 Awareness of language and bilingualism

One of the themes of *BCBP* was the analysis of metalinguistic awareness (MA) in the way that it forms an integral part of academic language proficiency. The proposal for further research that emerged was that the primary attainments of language development do not depend on MA in any necessary way; in contrast, literacy-related skills and the complex language abilities of schooling in general do require the participation of MA for higher level achievement. An interesting observation of researchers of MA is that apparently it applies to all levels and domains of language knowledge and language use, from phonemic awareness to the discourse-level and to pragmatic knowledge. It seems that at each level the distinction can be drawn between primary, implicit, knowledge on the one hand and explicit meta-level knowledge on the other, the second complementing the first. Naturally, an important research question for many years has been about the relationship between MA and bilingualism. Does knowledge of two languages favor the development of MA? And "in the other direction," what aspects of bilingual development might benefit from or even require attention to learning tasks that involve explicit awareness, what researchers have termed a "focus on form"?

In a series of novel experiments, Le Pichon (2010) and Le Pichon *et al.* (2010) explore the first question at the pragmatic level, suggesting conclusions that are consistent with the proposed differentiation between — (1) primary/implicit and (2) secondary/

explicit. The latter is closely associated with MA; the former is not, according to the view presented here so far. Specifically, the investigators were interested in contrasting different acquisition and learning conditions, and in particular what *aspect* of bilingualism or second language learning may be directly related to MA, in this instance — metacognitive strategies that children make use of in problems of interpersonal communication that involve a cross language mismatch. For example, what communicative strategy might be successful in an attempt to engage another child in play who speaks a different language?

Le Pichon and her associates compared the performance of bilingual children who acquired L_a and L_b in a naturalistic setting (early simultaneous bilingualism) with children whose exposure to their second language was after age 4, in a setting that included formal instruction, dubbed the Language Learning Experience (LLE) group. Results showed a significantly superior performance of the LLE students. In a separate comparison, on the same measures of cross-language communicative strategy, between child monolingual and bilingual/multilingual speakers, response patterns where remarkably uniform, crucially, showing no advantage for either group. The conclusion offered for further study is important, because it challenges the commonly held assumption that bilingualism, *per se*, enhances metalinguistic awareness. Rather, evidence from these studies suggests that implicit knowledge of two languages, product of naturalistic acquisition, alone, is not the critical factor, but a LLE that implies:

- problem solving directed at language use,
- controlled processing,
- direct attention to cross-language contrasts, and
- deliberate and reflective application of communicative/learning strategies (cf. Vygotsky, 2004, cited in the previous section).

Again, these findings lend support to the distinction between implicit and explicit knowledge systems, in this case within a domain of language ability that involves pragmatic knowledge.

A study focused on development of L2 literacy skills by Shwartz *et al.* (2005) resulted in a similar pattern of findings — suggesting that learning advantages do not flow primarily from bilingualism *per se*. Rather, previous L1 literacy showed the strongest positive correlation, a major contributing factor being the early development of explicit knowledge of relevant language patterns (in this case phonological awareness).

8.6.3 Explicit knowledge of language in learning and teaching

The study that we just reviewed touches on a topic that was the subject of speculation in *BCBP* — what practical application in the area of language learning might a better understanding of MA and explicit knowledge suggest? In this regard, the spontaneous unfolding of the L1 grammar in early childhood may not be the right model for designing a *second* language teaching program. A commentary from the field of indigenous language (IL) education that addressed this question (Peter *et al.*, 2008) was especially welcome because the fieldwork that *BCBP* was largely based on was also located in a bilingual indigenous community.

The challenges that indigenous language revitalization programs face are described by the authors, based on their experience with the Cherokee language program in the United States. For most children enrolled in these programs the IL is not their current primary language (in some cases, it may have been in early childhood, but typically is no longer). From this premise, then, IL revitalization would be most effectively conceived of as second language learning, posing the need then to draw from the SLA research base, more advanced by far than the less developed field of bilingual education. As such, the lessons of elementary school language immersion (the most instructive being that of French immersion in Canada — refer back to Chapter 7) are directly relevant. Here the authors observe, parallel to the observations of many French immersion teachers before them, that a reliance on exclusively comprehensive input based instruction seriously limits the development of grammatical competence in the target language. Despite years of naturalistic immersion in meaning focused activities, achievement levels are disappointing (p. 170).

The strong recommendation in this report is to reorient IL school programs toward considering the integration of language (i.e., grammar) learning objectives into the content-based immersion curriculum. This inclusion of Form-focused instruction into the communicative framework of immersion also requires the implementation of a systematic assessment plan that identifies the specific language learning outcomes (in both vocabulary and grammar) that are to be tested (p. 171). Formative evaluation, in this way, guides educators by providing feedback to the instructional program and by providing targeted feedback to learners (see the discussion of the role of negative evidence in L2 learning in Chapters 5 and 6). Upon rereading this report from the field, one is struck by an implication, left unstated: the proposal for a strong infusion of language learning objectives, to be implemented by a direct instruction teaching model, represents, today in North America, a minority view within the field of bilingual education, and more broadly in what is called "curriculum studies." Such makes for interesting reading for this reason alone. The debate on the inclusion of language learning objectives is the main topic of the next, and final, chapter.

8.6.4 The relationship between L1 attrition and second language learning (a revisit)

In *BCBP*, with its focus on the situation of minority and indigenous languages, the problem of explaining language attrition came to the forefront. Fortunate it was as it became clear that this problem is closely related to the most enduring discussions in bilingualism and L2 learning — critical period effects in L1 and L2, ultimate attainment in

L2, and the nature of the difference between L1 and L2 competence. A series of proposals was offered for further study that took the following observation regarding L1 attrition as a starting point:

> *Trauma and pathology aside, erosion of a primary language is always occasioned by the concurrent development of a Replacing Language (RL) — the stronger language subsystem of BFLA or a robust and rapidly developing L2 — typically during childhood.*

Interestingly, we can draw a parallel to language erosion socially — a speech community in transition away from its heritage language never loses Language (upper–case "L") ability, only ability of expression and comprehension in a particular language (lower–case "l"). From the field of sociolinguistics, the term "language shift" captures this idea in the same way as "RL development" does for the individual speaker; in fact, the two processes of shift/replacement are related in important ways.

The working assumption that follows (also a proposal for further research) concerns the characteristics of the RL — as it develops and approaches dominant language status, the RL comes to be the new primary language and as such attains the same kind of completeness that characterizes all primary languages (the dominant L1 of second language learners and other bilinguals or the mother tongue of unilingual speakers). Otherwise, semilingualism (incomplete acquisition on each language of the bilingual — in no language does the speaker command complete expressive and receptive capabilities) would be a common and typical ultimate attainment outcome of bilingual children, adolescents and even in some cases, adults. To review the remaining tentative assumptions of the proposal — the language acquisition capacity (LAD in the Universal Grammar framework) does not deteriorate after completion of L1 mastery (if RLs attain primary language status, other L2s should also have access to LAD mechanisms). This last deduction is consistent with the FTFA hypothesis of White (2003). Readers will recall that in the above review of *Incomplete acquisition in bilingualism*, Montrul (2008) took a somewhat different approach in her emphasis on age of onset (AO) factors.

In a series of reports from their project on bilingualism, specifically on L2 ultimate attainment, Abrahamson, Bylund, Hyltenstam and associates from the University of Stockholm have also developed a strong AO hypothesis — a critical period/maturational constraint for SLA (consistent with some of Montrul's conclusions regarding AO effects, differing with others). The great merit of these reports of empirical finding, by all accounts, both interesting and of far-reaching theoretical implications, is how the authors have staked out the strongest hypothesis in the discussion of critical period effects in L2: That constrained by the maturation of neural structures, SLA can approach near-native levels of competence; but this maturational constraint places full native-like mastery out of reach to all L2 learners, including for those whose L1 has eroded significantly (Abrahamsson and Hyltenstam, 2009; Hyltenstam et al., 2009).

Contrasting their assessments to previous studies by other researchers, one account that is proposed for the differing findings is the use of undemanding test item sets in previous studies that suffer from ceiling effects, resulting in the misidentification of near-natives as native-like.

Before we proceed to consider the findings of the Stockholm group, it is important to start with the common ground that is shared — (1) a framework that looks to biological and Faculty of Language-internal factors as fundamental, as opposed to the denial of any constitutive, cognitive-developmental, factor in language acquisition. The robust and rapidly converging evidence for critical period effects in L1 makes a biologically-based explanation the most plausible. (2) In the end, only empirical evidence from experimental design and systematic observation, based on reliable performance measures will be able to adjudicate among the competing proposals. Theoreticians in SLA have nothing to fear from exacting scrutiny of language abilities in bilinguals that reveal fine differentiations; there is no way ahead of time to know which of these will come to be important and which will not. Abrahamsson and Hyltenstam (2009) respond to critiques that question the usefulness or relevance of distinguishing between full native–speaker competence and near-native L2 competence for the purpose of supporting the critical period for second language (CP/L2) hypothesis. We have everything to gain, paraphrasing the authors in their response to the criticism, from resolving the question of whether L2 learners (with a late AO) can attain the same level of linguistic knowledge as L1 speakers. Keeping an open mind on the CP/L2 hypothesis, even if presently it appears to be the least plausible (the view put forward in *BCBP*), will help us sharpen our conceptions on the problem of understanding L2 ultimate attainment in all its presentations.

In fact, applying a battery of demanding assessments and detailed analyses to different cohorts of L2 learners who had been previously selected by native speaker (Swedish) judges as native speakers themselves, very few performed within the range of native-speaker (NS) controls. For example, among childhood learners (N=31), judged to be native-speakers, only three attained scores within the target range on all 10 measures of proficiency. None of the late learners (AO of 13–19 years) did (Abrahamsson and Hyltenstam, 2009). Thus, even for child L2 learners, under detailed scrutiny, the majority evidenced, many years later as adults, a profile of language proficiency that still differed from the lowest performing native speakers. In conclusion, the results suggest that "absolute nativelikeness" by late learners is never attained (p. 294). At first glance, the finding of this discrepancy stands as counter-evidence to the RL-development hypothesis because many, probably most, of the 31 early L2 learners no longer had maintained their L1 as a primary dominant language.

A separate study that applied the same 10 assessments to the performance of four adoptees (L1 Spanish, as in the previous study) directly addresses the prediction of complete RL-development. In all these cases, the first language had undergone total attrition, so there was no question about the status of either the "former L1" or that the RL was now the dominant language. Significantly, only one of the adoptee subjects evidenced mastery within the NS range across all 10 measures. Even more striking, and in contrast to the earlier child L2 (N=31) cohort, only one adoptee was perceived as native-like by all NS judges (Hyltenstam *et al.*, 2009).

Before considering possible interpretations, a summary of the assessment instruments is in order. The evaluations covered a wide range of language skills — two voice-onset time measures (production and perception), two speech perception tests, stimulus words and sentences masked by "babble" and "white noise," two versions of grammaticality judgment (auditory and written) that included demanding syntactical patterns, and a separate reaction time was taken, a cloze test of the standard reading assessment type (labeled "grammatical, lexical and semantic inferencing"), and two tests of formulaic language — knowledge of idioms and proverbs (Abrahamsson and Hyltenstam, 2009).

In effect, it was possible to consistently differentiate between native and near-native speakers, the latter L2 learners rarely attaining "absolute" mastery on the same assessments on which NSs did indeed show superior performance. Thus, the L2 learners, as advanced as they may have been, were not "indistinguishable" from the Swedish native-speakers. Critics object to the standards of "absolute" and "identical" (the authors' terms); nevertheless, the findings themselves are of theoretical interest and require explanation. The field has been left fertile for replication and challenge.

In the meanwhile, accepting tentatively, for argument's sake, the finding of a CP/L2 related impediment for L2 learners, an alternate approach to the problem of ultimate attainment (in general) might distinguish conceptually (and in the end operationally) between:

- *absolute/identical mastery* and
- *complete competence* (as contemplated, in retrospect, in *BCBP*).

Resulting unsuccessful this attempt at distinction, the no-semilingualism condition would also be shown to be incorrect, together with the RL-development hypothesis, an outcome relevant to the situation of the majority of L2 learners for whom L1 is no longer the primary dominant language.

One starting point in making the above differentiation, if future confirming evidence requires it, would be to circumscribe completeness as comprising the core grammatical competence of the proficient native-speaker, revealed in the performance of all normal/typical expressive and receptive abilities. This competence would be able to serve all expected communicative skills and suffice completely as a tool of thought in comprehension and expression (including inner speech), capable of subserving even higher-order, academic-type, literacy-related skills. However, literacy-related abilities themselves should not form part of the definition of this core grammatical competence; neither should culture-specific knowledge of constructions, formulas, colloquial sayings, and the like, define it. The reader will take note immediately of a difficulty in setting clear criteria here — even unambiguously non-native (albeit advanced) L2 speakers are capable of using their incomplete (in my sense) L2 competence, self-evidently within the range of their NS peers, in higher-order realms of language use. This interesting second language use phenomenon is typically observed in tertiary-level academic settings. At the same time, ensuring that monolingual native-speakers (who serve as controls) show categorical mastery on experimental measures is important, a potentially problematic issue alluded to by the authors. Here, an informal observation of the pattern of results may suggest an alternative assessment design — three of the four adoptee subjects scored within the NS range on both auditory and written grammatical judgment tasks in addition to evidencing NS-level reaction times (as did the majority of the thirty-one L2 learners from the previous study). As was pointed out earlier in a commentary on apparent incomplete acquisition in both languages (see Note 3 in Chapter 2), the overall approach to assessment should not take "dictionary" and prescriptive grammar standards as cut off benchmarks for determining completeness (NB: the Stockholm investigators did not do this either, strictly speaking).

Matching populations and excluding non-relevant intervening variables in experimental comparison often presents almost insurmountable challenges for researchers. But in the end, unforeseen complications need to be factored in when drawing conclusions. For example, SLI-type language impairment results not only in "distinguishable" differences, but also in measurably incomplete grammatical competence in any and all languages of the afflicted individual. Excluding this population from experimental studies (e.g., resorting to proxy categories) is not easy; the prenatal and early childhood circumstances of international adoptees, for example, may present one such complicating factor.

While the identification of mastery short of absolute nativelikeness appears to be relatively straightforward (for this purpose, we would not object to an assessment battery of the kind described above), determining completeness is less obvious. Related to the problem of avoiding circularity in setting criteria in evaluation, there still remain basic conceptual issues to resolve. For example, the distinction between core and peripheral grammar presented here does not seem to be the same as that entertained by most linguists. The problem before us consists in: around which domains of language knowledge should we frame the construct of completeness; and which information processing skills associated with the relevant ability networks are to be included?

A necessary clarification in regard to the notion of completeness of RL-development needs to be made. Bylund *et al.* (2010) mistakenly attribute to the *BCBP* model a version of a "limited capacity" explanation, related to "an inverse relationship between L1 and L2 proficiency" (p. 447). The RL-development hypothesis is about L1 attrition — how in theory completeness should be attained in the developing dominant language as grammatical domains in the attriting language subsystem give way to strong CLI of the replacing kind. It makes no claim about "limited capacity" in bilingualism or multilingualism in general. On the other hand, both Bylund *et al.* (2010) and *BCBP* might speculate about "limits" of some kind on near-native L2 ultimate attainment — limits related to AO maturational factors in the first case, in the second, the possible filtering effect of L1 vestiges from the attrited one-time primary language subsystem (hypothetically, not affecting completeness, but perhaps resulting in distinguishing features in an assessment of absolute identical mastery). Interested readers should review the studies summarized in Pallier (2007), which address this interesting research problem.

The coming final chapter takes up important theoretical problems related to our fourth theme, the one with which we concluded the previous chapter and revisited briefly in this chapter — second language teaching and learning. The theory, this time, will be directly useful for teachers in thinking about practical applications. The points of controversy by now will be familiar as they gather the threads from what we have covered so far, making for a fitting conclusion.

Notes

1. In another study from Catalonia (Chireac, 2010), the concept of a central conceptual system, independent from the L1 and L2 linguistic subsystems, is viewed as useful in explaining different patterns of second language learning and academic achievement. On the one hand, some aspects of successful performance in the L2 can be traced to the development of abilities associated with the central conceptual system; these achievements are then accessible to the learner when performing academic tasks in either L1 or L2. Other aspects of L2 mastery may be language-specific: grammatical knowledge that would be specific only to the second language, accounting for fluency in speech, grammatically well-formed sentences in written expression, and so forth.

   However, another (much more controversial) concept that is introduced is not fully elaborated upon. The possibility of "negative cognitive effects" (p. 108) resulting from a failure to attain a hypothetical minimum competence in neither language, termed "semilingualism," is presented as a potential problem of inadequate bilingual development. Described by Siguán (1998) as a linguistic deficit in both languages, this condition would negatively affect, according to this view, academic achievement and even cognitive development to a greater or lesser degree depending on circumstances of additive or subtractive bilingualism.

   If the idea of inadequate mastery as revealed in below-expectation performance in both languages refers to complex abilities such as reading and writing, there would be little controversy. Unexceptionally, a bilingual may fail to attain even minimum levels of literacy, or literacy-related language skill (demonstrated "in both languages") in the same manner as a monolingual speaker might fail to do so, this outcome not necessarily implying any kind of impairment or inherent cognitive/linguistic deficit. In this case, the use of the term "semilingualism" is confusing because it implies a specific linguistic defect (for example, in the monolingual circumstance, we would not categorize an individual who has not learned to read or has not acquired higher order abilities associated with academic discourse as "alingual").

   Now, the condition of below-expectation performance that reflects an actual deficit in linguistic competence, consistently demonstrated in both languages of a bilingual child, is possible; but this condition is considered to be an abnormal developmental outcome, the result of trauma or other inherent impairment to the neural structures that subserve language competence. It would not be a normal or typical outcome of subtractive bilingualism, imbalanced bilingual development, L1 replacement by a dominant language subsystem (termed "attrition" — recall the discussion of Montrul and De Houwer in Chapter 8), or inadequate instruction of any kind. Sometimes, normally developing bilingual children, especially young children, might give the impression that they command less than expected knowledge of language, even in structured assessments (young children might even decline to speak at all to a non-family adult). But this impression results from defects either in the evaluation instrument itself or in the interpretation of results by an inexperienced evaluator. Normally developing bilingual children, including L2 learners, possess a complete or age-appropriate grammatical competence in: (1) both languages, (2) one of the languages of early simultaneous bilingualism, or (3) the newly dominant L2 of subtractive bilingualism that comes to replace the now weaker, former primary language.

Chapter 9

Research problems that still have not been solved — Response to The Taipei lectures

We can now step back and review how the basic research on bilingualism, second language learning and literacy (Chapters 2–4) might help language educators reflect on practical issues in teaching (topic of Chapters 5–7). Concluding chapters like this one sometimes show how the different themes of a discussion are related if they contrast approaches that have led to different conclusions. This is what I will attempt to do, outlining at the same time what seem to be important avenues for future research.

The selection of basic research started with asymmetrical bilingualism in Chapter 2 not only because it is more common than balanced bilingualism, but because asymmetry seems to be an especially useful key for revealing essential properties. The proposal for moving forward in a research program of this kind quickly gravitated in Chapter 3 toward a framework of mental architecture that emphasizes components and modules and how they are interconnected. The discussion of the different ways that this kind of modularity hypothesis might be understood in relation to the development of language abilities set the stage for questioning whole language-oriented and other holistic/integrativist models of literacy (in Chapter 4). It would seem, by most accounts, that holistic theories of literacy teaching and theories that accept modularity stand in clear opposition one to the other. According to the conventional sense of the terms holistic and modular, this seems reasonable; and in fact, it is a useful way of understanding current debates about language and language learning. Interestingly, whole-language orientations in literacy also tend to carry over to second language pedagogy — e.g., teaching applications based on the input hypothesis. The well-known proposals of Steven Krashen in both of these areas, as we have seen, are in fact consistent in this regard. The opposition between these theories then should make future head-to-head research comparisons easier to design; the opposing claims should be easier to formulate and evaluate.

What is more interesting, perhaps from a purely theoretical point of view, is the observation, not widely commented upon, nor called attention to by Krashen himself, that his input hypothesis for SLA shares a view of language ability with modularity theories. The proposed distinction between *acquisition* (associated with implicit knowledge) and *learning* (explicit) is the most illustrative example. If this observation is correct, then research comparisons may not be as clear-cut as was just suggested. The related idea of how acquisition proceeds developmentally in child first language (without awareness, deliberate attention, much less direct instruction) is also a view shared with Universal Grammar (closely associated, in turn, with the modularity perspective). Thus, our proposed "clear opposition" has become a little more complicated, at least considering the view of the most prominent defender of whole-language and the natural approach to SLA. This complication, actually, is not a bad thing because debates in science are not, or should not be, about which "side" is right (about everything) and which is all wrong.

In a series of papers, published together under the title of *Explorations in language acquisition and use: The Taipei lectures*, Krashen (2003) summarizes what we could call a natural approach theory of second language acquisition. In the review of the research on instructed SLA, he takes a strong position critical of all studies that have investigated the effects of direct instruction of language objectives. Recall that the overarching theme of Chapters 5, 6 and 7 was an examination of some key features of instructed SLA. Krashen goes so far as to imply that further research on the direct teaching of language objectives is no longer of any scientific or practical value. Indeed, he finds fault in every study of form-focused instruction cited in the *Lectures*. In turn, some of his critics take a similarly categorical stance, failing to evaluate his input hypothesis in a balanced way. Sometimes the attempt is made to discredit all of its claims. In this concluding chapter, I will avoid this error. In fact, it should be recognized that most important research questions in language acquisition and literacy learning, for both L1 and L2, remain open. This is the main reason why the discussion between proponents of the input hypothesis and instructed SLA shouldn't be as polarized as it has become. All sides on the different controversies should also step back to reflect on future directions for research based on what we know so far — and what we still don't fully understand. First, let's recapitulate the discussion of Chapters 2, 3 and 4 on basic research problems of bilingualism and literacy, and then address what appears to be the controversy about the examples of instructed SLA discussed in Chapters 5, 6 and 7.

9.1 A window into the inner workings of the bilingual mind

In his survey of the neuroscience of reading, Dehaene (2009) concluded that the "standard social science model" of learning based on a cognitive structure unhindered by specific biological constraints, infinitely adaptable, and internally homogeneous is seriously flawed. Chapters 2 and 3 on the imbalances of bilingualism and Chapter 4 on reading in Chinese came to the same conclusion. To be sure, "conclusion" here means that the idea is plausible and worthy of further study.

Recall that we looked at two kinds of imbalanced bilingualism — the typical kind and the atypical (exceptional, often associated with trauma or disability). While both kinds suggest a componential organization of language ability, the latter, exceptional bilingualism, brought forward the strongest evidence for modularity. That in addition to domain-general knowledge structures and processing mechanisms, it is hard to deny the existence of domain-specific components. When imbalances are extreme and circumscribed (highly exceptional and specific) the recurring patterns of ability and stark disability suggest that broad mental faculties (much less the mind as a whole) are not completely homogeneous.

On the other hand, the typical imbalance of Chapter 2, while it is also consistent with a modular organization of language, doesn't reveal the components as sharply, with dissociations that are as starkly contrasting. But in the differentiation between primary language (mother tongue/L1) and second languages, "secondary" in interesting ways, we have the fundamental research problem that will eventually help settle the debate between natural approach/whole-language theories and instructed SLA theories. The differences between L1 and L2 are widely recognized; in exactly how they are different is a problem that we still have to work on, along with explaining why. For now, if we recall the review of research on the L1-L2 difference, this will set the stage for better understanding the acquisition-learning distinction.

In early childhood language development, the emergence of the mother tongue/L1 relies heavily on acquisition processes that are spontaneous and implicit, not subject to awareness, independent of any kind of deliberate teaching, and not dependent on practice or negative evidence. Simple-immersion/comprehensible input is sufficient for assuring the construction of the basic core grammar. These are the language *acquisition* processes. Simplifying greatly, such is the view of language development consistent with UG theories. Importantly, to say that the child "relies heavily on" these acquisition processes does not mean that domain-general explicit *learning* plays no role in mother tongue/L1 development.

Chapter 2 proposed (for further investigation) that a shift occurs in the development of second languages. Acquisition processes are not lost to the L2 learner because the specialized Language Acquisition Device is not degraded or eroded. That's why adults, for example, can still benefit from simple-immersion in a L2. However, *access* to these language acquisition resources, now for the L2, is not the same as it was for L1 (review the explanation for this shift in Sections 2.4 – 2.6 of Chapter 2). To compensate for this inhibition of access, cognitive-general learning mechanisms, metalinguistic awareness, deliberate attention, and focused practice with feedback (resources all now more well developed in the older learner) can help to boost learning effectiveness and ultimate attainment. Note to the reader — UG-oriented researchers of L2 are not all of one mind on this proposal. In any case, one of the enduring puzzles of end-state second language competence (of the basic core grammar of the L2) that future research will have to take up is the kind of wide variation among second language speakers — not seen in unattrited L1:

1. among those who have received massive amounts of simple-immersion/ comprehensible input — only,
2. among those who have received many years of intensive form-focused instruction – predominantly, and
3. among those who have taken advantage of both simple-immersion and FFI.

All of this led in Chapter 4 to a focus not on acquiring/learning the basic grammar of a first or second language, but on literacy. The research problem of modularity was carried over from Chapter 3, as it came to be applied to a specific ability — reading. The implication here is that the concept of modularity might apply broadly across the many domains of cognition. Not surprisingly, the idea of components and modules in reading contrasts sharply with whole-language philosophy. However, as the reader will recall, the central issues at hand in the research on reading in Chinese are far from being resolved. The decisive work on how morphosyllabic writing is mastered by children and how it is processed by experienced readers is just now turning the corner. So for that reason the role of phonology in reading characters and the modular-holistic debate, as it applies to Chinese writing overall, was left on hold. But the way the discussion was framed, I think, is worth considering as a guide for designing future experiments.

Chapters 5, 6 and 7 continued the discussion of second language acquisition/learning and literacy by focusing in on some specific problems of instruction. These research problems are both widely commented upon by educators and controversial — the role of correction and self-correction, the importance of the more general ability to systematically reflect on language patterns (metalinguistic awareness), and the efficacy of direct instruction in L2 immersion. Before proceeding, two clarifications about the discussion in these chapters is necessary to make — (1) the research questions examined in each case are still unresolved; and it would be wrong to suggest that the studies cited in this book have proven that instructed SLA models, which tend to strongly favor direct instruction, promotion of metalinguistic awareness and provision of corrective feedback, are superior to all others. (2) Nevertheless, the growing research base forming around these research problems also strongly suggests that this work is not in vain and ill-considered, far from it, it seems, by all indications. As has been argued already in this chapter, the way forward in the field of language and literacy learning requires a objective assessment of the advances we have made to date and of the conceptual and theoretical challenges that remain ahead.

9.2 Ten points of agreement

With this goal in mind, a good way to begin to frame a balanced assessment of Krashen's proposals is to establish where there is a shared common ground. Especially in science (as opposed to political debate, for example), the best way to proceed in a discussion of differences is to first establish clearly on which points there might be agreement, on which points does empirical evidence converge. Readers will notice that the following conclusions and recommendations taken from the *Taipei lectures* are not incompatible with the research that has been reviewed in the previous eight chapters. The common ground is substantial, this being usually a good starting point for any discussion; sometimes it is, even, in politics.

1. Comprehensible input is necessary for language acquisition (for L2 and for L1 even though the actual acquisition processes and external conditions are not the same in every way). In fact, L2 learners require massive amounts of meaningful experience in the target language in a wide variety of presentations, preferably both oral and written. Second language immersion is the most effective and efficient teaching model that can provide this necessary experience. Content-based language instruction is a kind of immersion that lends itself ideally to L2 learning, especially for school-age learners. Input (the language) that is comprehensible and is about new concepts that are motivating (the content) is the platform from which second language acquisition advances most effectively.
2. By means of rich comprehensible input alone, what we called simple-immersion in Chapter 7 (i.e., no deliberate grammar teaching or form-focused instruction), learners can make progress in their L2 competence. Extensive comprehensible

input improves both fluency and accuracy; that is, the student acquires grammatical competence, which contributes to improved ability. This most self-evident observation of second language acquisition/learning, in children and adults across all cultures, cannot reasonably be denied.

3. The proposed distinction between acquisition and learning appears to be a fundamental concept that potentially helps explain a number of difficult problems in first and second language development. Research from different sub-fields in language learning suggests that the distinction is psychologically real in an important way. If we define acquisition as development of implicit competence, typically without awareness or direct teaching, then the contrast with deliberate learning, which leads to explicit knowledge, is one that has been widely accepted in the field of language development. In the discussion of the relative importance of implicit and explicit knowledge in SLA, sometimes the possibility of developing competence without awareness is questioned (DeKeyser, 2005b). The idea is that this possibility in L2 requires more research. But the claim that denies incidental acquisition without awareness is too strong. In L1 acquisition prior to age 5, and conceivably after as well, it is widely accepted, and is largely uncontroversial, even among researchers outside of the Universal Grammar tradition. In L2, if this kind of impercipient acquisition is categorically rejected, then the conclusion must be drawn that L2 development is fundamentally discontinuous with L1 in every way, shares none of the same acquisition processes, and that for L2 learners UG-guided acquisition mechanisms have completely eroded. Under this assumption, it would be very difficult to account for intermediate or advanced L2 mastery by the many unschooled and illiterate learners who remain bilingual — especially where this L2 has not become a Replacing Language, recall from Chapter 2.

4. The monitoring of grammatical form for correctness and accuracy is more effectively or more easily implemented in certain language performance situations than others. For example, this is clearly the case in self-correction and revision of written expression in contrast to the monitoring of speech. Some forms of corrective feedback are either not practical or may actually be counterproductive (see Chapters 5 and 6).

5. Additional context support in language teaching along with modifications of speech and written text material, what was called LLSD in Chapter 7 (also known as ESL-talk or caretaker-speech), are particularly useful for L2 beginners. From this follows an important pedagogical principle — unsystematic integration of beginner second language learners with native-speakers usually does not provide them with comprehensible input, resulting rather in what is called "submersion." In addition, what are sometimes called "authentic texts" become more readable, and comprehensible, as L2 learners' ability *improves*; and importantly, unmodified texts written for literate native-speakers of the target language do not provide comprehensible input for students who are just starting off. Baker *et al.* (2007) discuss the usefulness of so-called "graded readers" for beginners to jump-start

self-teaching through extensive reading and other kinds of L2 immersion. Along the same lines, L2-medium subject matter classes for L2 beginners involving new, context-reduced, cognitively demanding and higher-order academic material should be "sheltered." Opportunities for integrating L2 learners and native-speakers should of course be sought out wherever this is feasible, but not at the expense of making input for L2 learning incomprehensible.

6. There may be a progression of acquisition to which L2 learning is subject, a kind of "natural order" that constrains progress in mastering the second language grammar. For each language certain constructions may tend to be "early-acquired," others "late-acquired." What on the surface appears "difficult" and "less difficult" is often deceiving. And there may even be a set of more abstract universal constraints on acquisition; and these conditions and possible developmental stages may not be the same for L1 and L2 (on this last point, Krashen may not agree). However, about this we still know very little.

7. The starting point for organizing syllabi for second language classes should not be based on the chapters of a traditional grammar manual. Rather, the teaching program should be content-based, predominantly focused on meaning. If classroom discourse is communicative, this condition favors learning and acquisition. The acronym CLT (Communicative Language Teaching) should be embraced by all sides in the debate on the proper role of direct instruction.

8. Teaching language by presenting learners with rules to memorize followed by rote drill of examples and translation exercises is not the most effective method for either learning or acquisition. Today, virtually all practitioners and researchers look back to these methods as antiquated, of purely historical interest.

9. Thinking about the development of academic language proficiency in the second language is a good starting point for organizing a plan of instruction, especially for school-age students and all learners who study a L2 for academic purposes. It requires different methods from those that only promote conversational discourse ability.

10. Design flaws and inherent methodological difficulties that most research in SLA suffers from prevent us at this stage of the evolution of the field from drawing definitive conclusions. Especially in comparative studies much work remains to be done in controlling relevant factors.

9.3 Five questions that remain open

The overall tenor of the *Lectures* is strikingly categorical; and on some points the conclusions seem unmeasured. Sometimes extreme proposals, what in science are called "very strong hypotheses," turn out to point investigation in the right direction. But in the field of second language acquisition, until a broader research base and consistent evidence preponderantly in one direction have been established, it is better to not discard with such absolute assurance alternative hypotheses. The book begins and ends with a series of apparent certainties that might lead the reader to think that the major research problems in SLA have already been resolved:

- The natural order of acquisition of grammatical structures is "*immune* to deliberate teaching," and that "conscious learning has only *one* function: As a "Monitor" or editor... that conscious learning has only this function" (p. 2).
- If the input/comprehension hypothesis is correct, and students can be provided with enough comprehensible input, "it means the *end* of grammatically based language teaching" (p. 5); and
- Research on the effectiveness of grammar-focused instruction is *futile* (p. 84) [Except for the original "*only*," emphasis added to "immune," "one," "end," and "futile."].

To the contrary, far from being irremediably hopeless and fruitless, advances over the past two decades in the field of SLA on how to integrate grammar learning into second language teaching have resulted in a number of well thought out proposals that cannot be dismissed out of hand.

9.3.1 Similarities and differences between L1 and L2 development

In discussions of the input hypothesis, proponents of natural approach methods rarely make reference to how development in each case is similar and how it is different. The overall assumption appears to be that L2 can, or should, develop "naturally" in the same way that children acquire their L1/mother tongue. In the case of L1, "natural" is indeed an accurate way of describing how the core grammar unfolds effortlessly and involuntarily. In young children, acquisition is spontaneous and inevitable given exposure to normal language socialization and comprehensible input (Barry, 2008; Bernal *et al.*, 2010; Christophe, 2002; Lidz, 2010; Tager-Flusberg & Zukowski, 2009; Yang, 2006). Native speaker attainment in the L1/MT is complete without recourse to instruction, literacy, corrective feedback or metalinguistic abilities.

Second language acquisition, according to the input hypothesis, should proceed along the same lines. "We acquire language in only one way — when we understand messages... language acquisition is effortless. It involves no energy, no work. All an acquirer has to do is understand messages...language acquisition is involuntary...The acquirer has no choice (Krashen 2003: 4). However, as we saw in chapters 2 and 6, there is growing evidence that both acquisition and learning in L2 do not follow the same course as in L1. And in contrast to universal native-speaker completeness, given an equivalent level of exposure to a second language, ultimate attainment varies widely (Montrul, 2008). This is the most striking and strongly consistent observation regarding the L1–L2 difference: how L1 acquisition is in fact involuntary and that completeness is inevitable; and that in L2 it is neither.

Among researchers, accounts and explanations for the L1–L2 difference also vary. For example, one hypothesis is that critical period effects not only apply to the L1, but also to L2, albeit in a different way (Long, 2005); alternatively, the difference in mastery might be related to the circumstances of development of first language versus second language, rather than maturation or age of onset. Readers will recall from Chapters 2 and 8 that the latter hypothesis is the one favored by this author. An important ancillary issue is whether the LAD is potentially fully accessible or has undergone one or another kind of deterioration and is defective in some way after a complete L1 linguistic subsystem is attained. The former position (that UG-guided acquisition mechanisms are still intact) divides into two hypotheses — (1) UG and LAD are accessible as freely and as unfettered as they were in L1 development, (2) to a greater or lesser degree the case-hardened grammatical structures of the unattrited L1 linguistic subsystem filter or block access to UG and LAD such that access is no longer universally unrestricted. Cutler (2001) and Doughty's (2003) L1 interference effect model ("developmental sharpening" in the native language constrains/alters non-native processing) explains the fundamental difference between L1 and L2 development. Recall that this is basically the same account proposed in Chapter 2, sequel to Francis (2012, Chapter 6). Hypothesis (1), unrestricted UG/LAD access, L1=L2, would be compatible with Krashen's natural approach to L2 teaching.

Does the hypothesized L1–L2 difference also apply to child L2 learners, or is there a late age cut-off (e.g., around puberty)? As was clear in our discussion of these issues in previous chapters, after many years of work on the various related problems a consensus appears to have been reached on an early critical period for L1. But for L2, we are only beginning to appreciate how complex the relevant questions are; and it is still premature to commit ourselves to one account or another. If anything, the "no-difference" hypothesis (L1 acquisition = L2 acquisition) would seem to be the least plausible, and faces the most difficult burden in trying to explain away the accumulated research findings on L2 variability. Can all non-native attainment in the L2, by all accounts the typical outcome when the bilingual's L1 maintains its primary language status, be attributed to external circumstances (e.g., inadequate comprehensible input), even after decades of immersion in a L2 environment?

For example, the "affective filter" condition is not a sufficient explanation for non-native L2 ability or failure on the part of the L2 learner to make progress. It is claimed sometimes that affective variables (anxiety, low self-esteem, lack of social integration) block the processing of input by the LAD, even if it is comprehensible. While these kinds of social context factor probably affect acquisition and learning (e.g., via diminished motivation) the way they affect second language presents us with a puzzle. First of all, the "affective filter" does not impede access to the LAD or negatively affect development of the core grammar in *first language* development. For example, children who speak minority languages as their primary L1 that are the object of persistent and widespread discrimination do not suffer from attenuated or incomplete language development. In many situations where a socially dominant national language is spoken in the speech community, and is taught in school, the minority language may undergo attrition or displacement. But in monolingual development or where the L1 mother tongue is clearly primary and the national L2 is clearly the weaker language, grammatical development maintains its normal and typical course. Special examples include sign language acquisition by deaf children and indigenous language maintenance in adverse conditions of learning and use. In this way, the problem of accounting for affective and motivational factors highlights a more complicated situation — Why in bilingual development do some factors rise to prominence, factors that play no role in monolingual or L1 development? This was the topic of Chapter 2.

9.3.2 Components of language ability and how they might interact

Interestingly, Krashen's claim that learned explicit knowledge of language does not contribute to building implicit competence (in the literature, termed the "no-interface position") appears to assume a strong version of the modularity hypotheses associated with some UG theories of language acquisition. In this sense, we could take it as a strong hypothesis for its view of (implicit) linguistic competence as highly encapsulated. Encapsulation in this instance implies that the specialized modules of grammar, strictly and narrowly constrained by the domain-specific knowledge components of UG, are sealed off from cognitive-general learning. Even though neither UG nor modularity are concepts that Krashen makes reference to, the strong differentiation/separation between implicit and explicit knowledge, and acquisition and learning, suggests an affinity with the above-mentioned strong-hypothesis arguments, allowing us here to take the liberty of interpreting the no-interface position from the perspective of this model, for argument's sake. This approach to understanding the broader controversy is in line with the idea of establishing the broadest possible common ground.

Acquisition is guided by the LAD (acquisition mechanisms that are spontaneous and do not require awareness); learning, on the other hand, is deliberate and does imply awareness. The former results in implicit knowledge of grammar, the latter, explicit knowledge — two independent acquisition/learning mechanisms and two independent domains of knowledge. To begin, let us assume that the distinction between implicit (automatic/sub-conscious) and explicit (metalinguistic) knowledge is correct. In our review of Paradis (2004) in the previous chapter we saw that this theory of two separate networks and kinds of language knowledge is entirely plausible. A modular differentiation along these lines was taken to be correct in Chapter 3 in the discussion of exceptional bilingualism and in Chapter 4 in regard to the distinction between phonological competence, *per se*, and meta-level awareness of phonological constituents (phonemes, syllables) as these correspond to letters and characters. The former is required for speech perception; the latter helps children learn how to read.

The interface question (whether explicit knowledge interfaces directly with implicit knowledge) is probably the pivotal issue at stake in the debate on actual teaching applications. Recall that the input hypothesis does not completely dismiss metalinguistic awareness and (deliberately) learned competence. It claims that the role explicit knowledge plays in attaining final state mastery is "very limited," that it serves as a monitor of performance. In the end, how limited or how or central it turns out to be is an empirical question. But no one denies that it facilitates performance to one degree or another. According to the input hypothesis, practice, interaction (e.g., negotiation of meaning) and FFI contribute to explicit knowledge. Presumably, again, the contribution to ultimate attainment in the L2 is very limited. The claim regarding the *limited effects of practice and interaction* in particular is indicative of how strongly encapsulated the acquisition mechanisms of the LAD are considered to be in Krashen's model. Practice and interaction facilitate the receiving of comprehensible input (e.g., conversation naturally generates more input), which is the real motor of acquisition, not the cognitive operations deployed in verbal expression. An example of these cognitive operations would be deliberate metalinguistic reflection on the correct form of utterances to make them grammatical and coherent. The cognitive operations associated with reflection on language patterns contribute to explicit knowledge.

The typical examples of acquisition-rich comprehensible input are — meaningful messages in conversation, engaging and interesting reading material, and listening to extended oral discourse. However, it has never been demonstrated empirically that the LAD only accepts and makes use of (for constructing grammars) *only* one kind of discourse or text-type, "naturalistic" or otherwise. The minimum requirement, we can stipulate, would be that a mapping between units of meaning and grammatical constituents, at some level, be effected (this is the essential property, we can assume, of comprehensible input). We can assume, also, that this only applies to higher-order linguistic patterns that are potentially meaningful or that have a grammatical function — at the morpheme-level and above. Requirements for the acquisition of implicit phonological knowledge — at the syllable-level and below (not units of meaning) — we will thus set aside for now.

If the above way of defining usable input ("the minimum requirement") to the LAD is correct, then this opens the door to considering other instances aside from the typical examples that usually come to mind. In particular we have to consider examples from sources associated with FFI and metalinguistic reflection in learning contexts (where cognitive-general resources are deployed):

1. Especially in applying current methodologies of grammar teaching that embed FFI in communicative lessons, if the explanation of a rule, for example, is given in the target language and is comprehensible, why isn't this input usable for acquisition? An interesting lesson about language should qualify just as well as one in geography or algebra. If the above-mentioned meaning-grammar mapping is realized, even so-called "uninteresting" content qualifies as long as learners are attentive and engaged. Taking the liberty of paraphrasing Forest Gump, we have to recognize that this elusive quality of instruction is subject to all kind of as yet poorly understood individual variation: "boring is what boring does." True,

sometimes, despite teachers' very best effort academic content is taxing, and can even get tedious. But, for students who stay in school and work at getting a passing grade in their content-based second language learning classes, it is intrinsically motivating to pay attention to the medium of instruction. Educators' eternal challenge is to keep the fire burning so that as many as possible do stay and work hard on their lessons.

2. In traditional grammar exercises, especially self-paced learning activities popular in many self-teaching situations, now more widespread that ever before via the internet, fill-in the blank sentences, cloze paragraphs, matching activities, self-correction and all variety of like grammar puzzles contain text material that is generally comprehensible, and depending on one's level of motivation and the creativity of the web designer, engaging and even fun (depending on what you think is). These traditional learning activities have been enhanced by modern interactive digital technology to now provide learners with immediate and highly reliable feedback. Recall that we covered this topic in Chapter 6. Is there any evidence that this kind of language input that features systematic focus on sets of related grammatical patterns is not processible by the LAD? If reading in general is a good source of language input at the right level of difficulty, is its usefulness for acquisition restricted only to certain genres?

3. Practicing newly learned grammatical patterns, negotiating meaning, asking native speakers and more advanced L2 interlocutors for clarification, reflecting on similar examples given by native speakers (as positive evidence), getting explanations of why others are non-examples (in the form of negative evidence), and so forth, conceivably all contribute to explicit knowledge. But is it reasonable to claim that they do not contribute to implicit competence as well? The reader is reminded here that we still accept the distinction between the two as psychologically real. As in other kinds of learning and acquisition, peripheral input-receiving processors, both specialized and cognitive-general, distribute incoming information to the relevant modules and other kinds of computational component. But it's not clear in the input hypothesis why input coming from direct instruction and metalinguistic reflection, as it makes its way up the chain of transformations of information specific to the domain of language, cannot also come to be useful to the LAD.

These problem situations now pose the most interesting question — about interfaces. One set of assumptions and a clarification need to be considered. Assumptions first — In both so-called non-interface and interface models that accept one or another version of modularity, separate and autonomous modules are assumed to maintain independence from other cognitive components regarding the kind of knowledge representations that they are designed to "enclose" (carrying out internal computations upon). To review once more, we are assuming separate domains for implicit linguistic competence built by the domain-specific LAD and metalinguistic knowledge resulting from the application of cognitive-general learning. But the question of interactions between and among these components is an *open question* accepted by virtually all proponents of a modular architecture of language ability. Thus, the terms "interface" and "non-interface" are misnomers in characterizing proposed models that try to explain the relationship between different kinds of language knowledge. No one really denies interaction and interface. Rather, the research problem must be about degrees and kinds of interaction and degrees and kinds of encapsulation; and theorists that do not accept any version of modularity (probably the majority in SLA research today) assume even greater interaction, of a more holistic and "dispersed" kind, in their models of language ability. Implicit linguistic competence must interface with other cognitive domains, of diverse kinds, most notably with systems outside of the Faculty of Language (e.g., in reading, with the visual system). Thus, it falls to proponents of the theory of "no interaction in the direction of explicit to implicit knowledge" to explain why this pathway in particular is blocked - to be clear, Krashen does not use the term "no-interface."

The clarification — When we speak of input to the domain-specific LAD (the reader is invited to substitute an equivalent acronym — e.g., LMC for Language Making Capacity), this "data," appropriately called Primary Linguistic Data (PLD), is not the unfiltered and unprocessed audio or visual information present in naturalistic discourse "out there" that is perceived by our sense organs. As was just alluded to, a series of peripheral input-receiving processors transform this information into usable data that the actual acquisition/learning mechanisms are able to compute (Jackendoff, 2007). Thus, the PLD that is derived from naturalistic comprehensible input is data that is now internal to the cognitive workings of the Faculty of Language. Most importantly, the now disaggregated instances of it must be in different formats than when the sound or visual patterns of language were received by the sense organs. In the SLA literature this distinction is informally captured by the difference between input and *intake*. Even more importantly, cognitive scientists all agree that very little is known about the specific details of this very rough idea of how language is processed in the mind for different purposes; and even the rough idea is still controversial.

Returning to our list of possible examples of interface between implicit and explicit knowledge that need to be considered, we can now add a fourth possibility, assuming that within the broad and complex network called language ability, domain-specific components (products of acquisition) must be interconnected in some way with domain-general components (of deliberate learning):

4. We can accept that not only are the two domains independent, but also agree with the idea, which follows from the non-interface hypothesis, that explicit knowledge is not transferred directly to implicit competence domains. However, in general, what interfaces do is communicate competence components and processing mechanisms that are formatted in different ways, with different internal computational structures. Why, for example, might explicit knowledge about language, learned items, memorized collocations and longer unstructured sequences not serve as a data base for system building and the acquisition processes of the LAD? Myles (2004) provides examples and a theoretical rational for considering the possibility that such information in fact can serve as a data base for the LAD. Recall that we are in the internal realm of the Faculty of Language, with

no consensus about the properties of the various participating knowledge structures or about the constraints on how they interact. It is entirely plausible that domain-specific modules might receive language-related input from cognitive-general domains and process it (carrying out computations on it so that it can in fact be "inputted," or "intaken") as Primary Linguistic Data. Note that this hypothetical scenario is not the same as what is known as proceduralization of declarative knowledge[1] — refer back to the discussion of this topic in Chapter 3, and the proposal by Marcus (2006) for a critical assessment of the standard version of the concept of modularity, a critique that happens to be pertinent in this concluding chapter as well.

9.3.3 The limits of acquisition and learning

The strong claim is made that deliberate learning is very limited, resulting in metalinguistic knowledge that doesn't contribute to "fluency," and that accepting the comprehensible input hypothesis will lead to abandoning the teaching of grammar objectives. But this prediction is premature. Generally, both laboratory and classroom studies show gains for learners whose teaching program includes direct instruction (DeKeyser, 2005b), in short term studies usually outpacing comparison incidental and natural approach methods as was shown in the Norris and Ortega (2001) meta-analysis reviewed in Chapter 7. We will return to the methodological problem that is posed by short-term controlled studies, pointed out by DeKeyser, seeming to bias results in favor of Form-focused instruction. Long term longitudinal studies are very rare, but it must be one of the most implausible claims that sustained direct instruction will not result in continued and progressive mastery, even if it may be mainly explicit knowledge that is automatized; i.e. lacking "fluency" (i.e., not sounding like a native speaker).

DeKeyser and Juffs (2005) point out that L2 learners make use of a diversity of resources that their componential language ability makes available to them. As we assumed in the previous section, these resources are not isolated modules but in actual performance support each other, so to speak. Grammar competence transferred from the L1, access to UG principles, cross-language processing strategies, formulaic knowledge and proceduralized explicit knowledge are all called upon in different configurations depending on what the real-time demands of expression or comprehension turn out to be. Grammatical patterns that the learner practices and masters near-natively (they may not really be implicit, but serve the learner almost as well) come together with structures that are implicit and UG-governed. Especially for academic purposes, L2 performance *does not have to mimic native-speaker fluency* and spontaneous on-the-spot correctness to be useful, and can even be adequate for all practical applications for the vast majority of L2 learners.

DeKeyser (2005b) poses a difficult question for the no-interface position that favors an exclusively input-based approach to teaching — Over the long term, deliberate learning, FFI and direct instruction can establish a foundation of explicit L2 knowledge that significant practice converts into mastery based on high levels of automatized skill. Aside from automatized explicit knowledge being difficult to distinguish from implicit competence, in the end, after extensive practice and proficient use, how can the two kinds of knowledge be kept completely separate, one not effecting any changes in the other? Clearly, L2 speakers use explicit knowledge for more than just monitoring expression when they are focused on form (Ellis, 2006). Even in L1 language use it's not obvious that all competence that speakers access is tacit and subconscious from domain-specific grammar modules. A good part of knowledge of language, in L1, is probably cognitive-general. If this is correct, in L2 an even greater part must be cognitive-general. In both cases, this knowledge is put to use in proficient, and even fluent, expression (and similarly in skilled comprehension). In a scenario like this, learned metalinguistic knowledge can be of great value to beginner students who are motivated and know how to bootstrap what they have practiced in self-teaching and self-organized immersion/acquisition activities such as reading and watching L2 TV.

Far from a hopelessly useless labor in vain, current research on different aspects of Form-focused instruction has become one of the most dynamic areas of scientific work in SLA. A major theme is the question: how can learners attend to meaning and form in teaching situations where classroom activity is centered on a content lesson? Can attention even be "shared" between content and language learning objectives at the same time? Different types of FFI (and in particular different types of corrective feedback), thus, are compared with this research problem in mind. For example, recasts (teacher providing the correct form) may be viewed as less "intrusive" than say prompts/elicitation (suggesting to the student to self-correct). At the same time, the question at hand in this comparison asks: which is more effective in reorganizing the learner's interlanguage grammar, considering the possibility that recasts might be ambiguous as to their CF intent (their greater perceived "indirectness" being perhaps viewed positively among educators concerned with the effect of CF that is overly "direct")? Findings have also suggested that the factor of proficiency level may affect effectiveness, lower levels profiting to a great extent from prompts (Ammar and Spada, 2006). Other types of CF that have been studied are clarification request and providing metalinguistic clues. How are these CF types noticed and perceived, then interpreted by learners, and how do they, and in what ways are they able to, respond? Important here are: the feedback dimension of oral-written, the situational context of the feedback, and different kinds of discourse constraint specific to classroom interaction (Pica, 2008; Russell and Spada, 2006; Yang and Lyster, 2010).

This line of research was prompted by the interesting finding from evaluations of second language immersion of a significant plateau effect in grammatical development. That despite years of comprehensible input in the L2-medium-of-instruction, throughout all of the elementary and middle school years, levels of mastery in the domain of morphology and syntax (revealed in expressive tasks) turned out to be surprisingly deficient. The focus of investigators has come to rest on the distinction between indirect/incidental approaches to mastering the language objectives and models of direct instruction. For example, is the well-known technique of negotiation of meaning (systematic clarification request) and other methods associated with the so-called "interaction hypothesis" sufficient to advance L2 learning? Lyster (2004), for example, is a proponent of studying the cognitive properties and effects of noticing, awareness and controlled practice that includes CF types that prompt self-correction. Within the framework of a communicative approach to L2 teaching, what, more precisely, makes grammatical features salient and maximizes metalinguistic awareness of the relevant grammatical patterns? What kinds of practice are workable and efficacious, e.g., in creating obligatory contexts of use for the target features in content-based L2 teaching?

The last question goes to the heart of new applications of immersion teaching (integration of grammar and content objectives; review Chapter 7). How can attention be directed most effectively to grammatical features that are not normally noticed? With focus on meaning as a starting point (the consensus today among educators interested in optimizing L2 grammar development), how are form-meaning mappings established consistently? Batstone and Ellis (2009) and Ellis *et al.* (2006) review the above-mentioned research problems in the previous paragraphs from the point of view of a Focus on Meaning framework (a term in the professional literature often, and unfortunately, associated with zero-grammar, simple-immersion, approaches). Today, in contrast to traditional grammar teaching of the past, FFI in language teaching assumes a Focus on Meaning (Dutro and Moran, 2003). This is a point of discussion around which there should no longer be any debate.

9.3.4 Language awareness in literacy-related academic abilities

The *Lectures* make passing mention of the development of language abilities for academic purposes. In a short section entitled "Acquisition without output," de-emphasizing practice and the importance of metalinguistic awareness is suggested again, but now extending this natural approach acquisition model beyond SLA proper. What by all estimates must count as a very strong claim, the "competence from input alone" hypothesis (p. 62) is applied to a literacy skill — spelling. If research is beginning to suggest that casting a broad equivalence between primary language development and L2 acquisition/learning is not correct, extending this input-alone hypothesis to another, even more unambiguously, secondary domain (literacy) now raises the theoretical stakes another notch. Elsewhere, in fact, Krashen (2004) makes this extension explicit.

Before proceeding, it's important, especially here, to reemphasize that what educators are most interested in is not what is possible (theoretically, or to an approximate and mediocre level of mastery), but rather the most effective and efficient instructional model for students — it's about rate of mastery and ultimate attainment, of *advanced* ability. As was mentioned in the introduction to this chapter, few researchers deny that input-alone immersion (e.g., extensive reading for developing skill in spelling) results in progress toward increased ability. But in second language learning, and now L2 literacy, educators and investigators have a more difficult problem to attend to — that of maximizing achievement, for instance, in the case of vulnerable populations and less privileged students for whom working against the clock is not just a saying. Most bilingual and second language learners are not at liberty to view the considerations of efficiency and ultimate attainment as optional; and for teachers what is "interesting" and "fun" in the abstract, is not the best starting point for designing a second language and literacy-learning program. Returning to the "competence from input-alone" proposal for the mastery of the sub-skills of writing, the overarching motivation for this most implausible hypothesis appears to be the endorsement of a strong version of whole-language philosophy (Krashen, 2002, 2004). For example, the attempt is made to discredit the growing consensus on the importance of phonics and related word identification skills, including the development of phonemic awareness and other kinds of metalinguistic knowledge associated with literacy learning. For alphabetic writing, see de Graaff *et al.* (2009), Dehaene (2009), Ehri (2005, 2009), Perfetti (2010), Shankweiler and Fowler (2004). For morphosyllabic writing, a somewhat different but converging discussion on the importance of metalinguistic awareness in relation to the processing of characters has taken on central importance among researchers (Chung *et al.*, 2011; Lei *et al.*, 2011; Liu and McBride-Chang, 2010; Mori *et al.*, 2007, to mention just a few). Review the background to this discussion in Chapter 4.

To recap, young children's acquisition of their L1/MT can indeed be described as naturalistic (in the truly biological sense), unfolding in response to adequate input-alone conditions of comprehensible language experience, the simple positive evidence of Primary Linguistic Data, without practice or corrective feedback, precisely because it is a universal *primary* human attainment. The achievement of literacy ability is a secondary attainment, in human evolution and historically, cross-culturally and socially, developmentally in children, and within each culture subject to interesting and as yet incompletely understood wide individual variation. More interesting in some ways is a hypothetical parallel — second language acquisition/learning appear to share some of these secondary properties. From this point of view, upholding the opposite parallel — that neither L2 acquisition/learning nor literacy are secondary, in the sense that they are characterized in this chapter — is a mark of consistency, but one that becomes harder to justify when we cross the line into academic literacy learning. In contrast, one can maintain the primary characterization of L2 development — that L1 and L2 are epistemologically equivalent (Schwartz's, 1998, formulation) in every way — while not extending it to literacy learning. Krashen applies a version of this equivalence across the board, a kind of whole language theory for all: reading, writing and second language. The approach to L2 writing instruction that rejects corrective feedback, for example (Truscott, 2010), would be consistent with this view.

In response to the popularity for many years of holistic models that tended to relegate the role of the teacher as instructional leader and organizer to the background, new approaches to immersion teaching have emphasized the idea of an active and systematic integration of language learning objectives in content-based teaching (and away from the view of simply working on content in the target language). This reconceptualization of content-based L2 teaching that takes such an integration seriously recognizes the important connection, especially for L2 learners, between the special demands of academic language proficiency and mastery of the grammar objectives of the second language program. In this approach, direct engagement with students starts with a focus on purposeful learning activities with special attention to prerequisite language objectives for understanding academic content. Ongoing *formative evaluation of learner achievement* points to other language objectives that emerge from the analysis of specific functions served by grammatical forms (during the content lesson). Compilation of interlanguage errors from student performance is an ideal source of new material to cover and old material to review. Prior teaching and post re-teaching is thus systematic. Selection of language objectives begins with grammar that is specifically useful for academic tasks:

- comprehension of complex patterns of expository textbook discourse,
- comprehension of similar expository discourse that L2 learners must process in classroom explanations, demonstrations, and laboratory reports,
- coherent formulation of complex clarifying questions and expositions, and
- mastery of academic writing abilities.

Dutro and Moran (2003) elaborate on all the above with special clarity; readers should take it as a follow-up to the discussion in Chapter 7 of the new approach to immersion: Bigelow et al. (2006), Schleppegrell et al. (2004) and Snow (2005).

9.3.5 Evidence from empirical studies

Almost everyone agrees that findings from research on SLA are uneven; that interpretations of results usually have to be heavily qualified and that controlling relevant factors in the study of language learning has been difficult, especially in head-to-head comparisons between incidental/whole language and direct instruction/FFI. In the comparison between the precision of experimental studies and the potentially more favorable validity of harder to control classroom studies, the advantages and limitations of each kind of approach are often hard to integrate into a single and unified analysis. As DeKeyser (2005b) and Pica (2008) point out, laboratory studies tend to show an advantage for direct instruction and FFI; but because they are uniformly of short duration, this condition appears to bias them against incidental and input-only methods. It can also be argued that the preference for discrete-point measures, over open-ended and holistic performance assessments favors access to explicit knowledge. Open-ended and spontaneous communicative tasks require, presumably, higher levels of tacit competence. However, if incidental/whole language methods benefit from longer durations, then the proper longitudinal design for comparison would also call for systematic long-term direct instruction. We can grant that performance on measures of spontaneous use, requiring automaticity, fluency and native-speaker like accuracy reflects implicit competence. But performance on tests is not necessarily *only* an index of learned explicit knowledge. With competence alone and no relevant metalinguistic knowledge, speakers (of L1 and of L2) can respond correctly on discrete-point items, and performance on the same items by beginner level interlanguage speakers will on average be inferior for lack of both tacit competence and explicit knowledge. Results from assessments with well-designed test items can reveal complete or incomplete competence in specific domains of language knowledge and associated language-related skills. Test data, like all data, suffer from specific and usually well-understood shortcomings. But if results are reliable, they need to be explained. If we discarded research findings that cannot eliminate all margin of limitation, there would be nothing left standing, including findings from "contextualized" research with high ecological validity.

In classroom studies, of both qualitative and quantitative varieties, a different set of advantages and defects (some of the advantages and defects are the same) have to be balanced against each other. The principal limitation so far has been how to ensure clearly contrasting applications of the comparison treatments — input-only immersion without FFI, and more problematically, FFI without enriched comprehensible input now that traditional rule explanation in students' L1 followed by non-communicative drill is no longer an alternative model of interest to anyone. Also, systematically structured input and different kinds of inductive method can fall under either paradigm, depending on subtle distinctions that are not easy to make; see the discussion of these problems in DeKeyser (2005b).

In Chapter 3 of *Lectures*, which critically reviews previous studies, Krashen correctly raises a related issue — in a comparison to a structured instructional program in which learners are engaged face-to-face, everyday with a lesson plan-equipped and task-oriented second language educator, the comprehensible input/whole-language alternative better be of comparable engagement and richness in processible Primary Linguistic Data. If the non-FFI whole language instructional style is too hands-off or radically constructivist, all bets are off. Indications from a number of studies that in some of the input-only conditions instruction was not sufficiently acquisition rich, in fact, is one of the important criticisms of the research reviewed in Krashen's Chapter 3. The point is well taken, and surely rings true to many educators from experience conducting informal observations of teaching that eschews direct instruction.

But readers will be excused for becoming suspicious of this argument upon encountering it in the concluding section of *Lectures* Chapter 3. Citing the seminal studies of early French immersion from Canada that called attention to broad deficiencies in students' grammatical competence (Swain, 1996), the not-sufficiently-acquisition-rich explanation is proposed again — perhaps reading and listening materials were not "interesting" enough, and that "we haven't yet given comprehensive input a real chance" (p. 65). But this suggestion fails on all counts. Comprehensive input in the French immersion programs was nothing less than massive, for early immersion students, starting in kindergarten, spanning all elementary grades and extending into secondary school. Through 6th grade, up to a major fraction, more than 50%, of total instructional time would typically be in the target language. Engagement with both content and language objectives in this variety of comprehensive CLT should be a given for all program completers. With French as medium of instruction, *motivation* to understand messages in the target language must have been uniformly high among students who remained in immersion as they complied, on average, year after year, with all academic subject area expectations, with the only exception being that of L2 grammar in expressive tasks. Refer to Swain and Lapkin (2005) and related citations in Chapter 7 for a summary of this assessment. What is meant by "interesting" in Krashen's critique isn't always well defined; but in this case the objections clearly don't stand up to what we know about these immersion programs.

For one last time, it's important to emphasize that the research problems outlined in this chapter have not yet been settled. Thus, the arguments presented here in favor of an integration of meaning-focused and form-focused language teaching should be taken as alternative hypotheses that might help us design better experiments and naturalistic classroom studies.

9.4 Looking back — Main ideas

This last point about further investigation brings us to the final conclusion, concentrating the discussion on our fourth overarching theme: a contrast between two lines of theory and practice in second language teaching. Enough has been said about the debate on pedagogical issues in this chapter and Chapters 5, 6 and 7. Truly, the contrast between holistic/incidental and direct instruction approaches has been one of the most enduring in the fields of language and literacy learning. Why that is should be a topic of serious reflection in its own right, for example why the research biases of one tendency and the other turn out to be remarkably consistent from one domain of language ability to another. This is probably a good thing in this case, as it should allow for the confrontation of hypotheses at a higher level.

Our third theme, if the reader recalls, fed into the very same debate. Starting off with the idea that reading ability can be broken down into component competencies and skills, this approach led to a proposal for research about universal underpinnings shared by all literate cultures. One of the universals of reading may be about how phonology plays a role, that it cannot be by-passed in decoding text; that it cannot be by-passed in alphabetic systems nor in morphosyllabic systems. If this hypothesis turns out to be correct, the development of decoding skills that correspond to the linguistic components of the language would appear to be essential, essential for children in literacy learning, for example. That is, proficient reading is more than just predicting and constructing meaning. Even in reading Chinese (where it might be tempting to propose a direct and exclusive orthography-semantics route), it appears that comprehension processes cannot normally by-pass phonology. A componential, or modular, approach to understanding reading ability also favors the view that in processing written language, some (so-called lower level) computations are obligatory. This is the opposite of a strong top-down view that higher-level processes predominate and can freely override bottom-up processes. Interestingly, whole-language approaches tend to be strongly top-down, and de-emphasize the importance of direct instruction that fosters efficient word decoding skills that attend to linguistic components (e.g., fast and automatic mapping of orthographic forms to phonological patterns). The discussion here is entirely parallel to the one we just covered in the field of second language acquisition, an example of the theoretical consistency just mentioned.

Working backwards to recapitulate Chapters 3 and 2, it was the underlying architecture of bilingual competence and ability that concerned us. Again, the idea of componential design came forward as a useful tool of analysis. Two kinds of imbalance in bilingualism helped us think about the relevant research problems more analytically — the typical imbalance of stronger and weaker language (by far the most common type of bilingualism), and the imbalances occasioned by impairment of different kinds. One of the main ideas in these chapters was that asymmetry reveals internal diversity more clearly, better than when systems and subsystems are in equilibrium.

On the topic of bilingual mental architecture the lines of debate are not as clearly drawn as in the area of literacy and language teaching, the research being much more complex, more cross-disciplinary, and about phenomena that are hard to observe directly. For this reason, trying to draw the lines sharply is not a good idea. Investigators should consider what appear to be opposing viewpoints with an open mind, and in general proceed cautiously because things are often not what they initially seem to be, to put it plainly. Proceeding with caution isn't the same as avoiding controversy; but in this still new area of research the best way forward is to first establish a common platform from which further discussion can go forward. The introduction to this chapter started with this idea. Sometimes this can begin with agreement on the facts of an empirical finding, say, about an aspect of performance in which the two language subsystems of the bilingual are involved. Candidates for broad agreement might include:

- The ability of young bilingual children to separate in usage the two languages that they know is demonstrated early in development. The achievement is impressive, and still not well understood.
- One of the languages often develops as the dominant/stronger language, the other as the weaker, even when bilinguals are exposed to both. It's still a mystery why this happens.
- Language attrition in normally developing bilinguals is evidenced only in one language or the other. Attrition or long-term delay in both is evidence of pathology.
- At the same time, balanced bilingualism, with equal competence in both languages is possible, and widely observed.
- Bilingualism does not cause language deficiency, and it does not result in cognitive impairment of any kind. Knowledge of only one language doesn't either.
- Second languages do not develop in the same way, in all respects, as first languages.
- Nevertheless, bilinguals can attain very high levels of proficiency in their second language.
- All modern writing systems, cross-linguistically and cross-culturally, appear to share certain properties. The way that readers process them also shows parallels.

- Digital technology has changed the way we process language in the most profound way ever. The way it has changed how we understand written language processing cross-culturally, and across writing systems, is new and very important.

While consensus on a short list of plausible explanations for any of these observations is not yet possible, excluding the most implausible ones should be. Because all researchers in the cognitive sciences work with the same rules of evidence, agreement on what the competing hypotheses are and on the kinds of assessment that can be implemented as valid tests of one or the other hypothesis charts a path for real progress. Work on the resulting shorter list of explanations would go forward as we build a broader common platform of concepts and proposals. Such methods assume an optimistic view of the power of scientific inquiry. So it is with an assumption that we are concluding this book, even though that's how discussions usually begin, or begin again.

Notes

1. An important concept from psychology comes to the field of language learning in the distinction between declarative and procedural knowledge. Perhaps the clearest example of declarative knowledge we would find in traditional foreign language teaching in which a grammar rule is learned and understood (e.g., it can be explained) and illustrative examples provided by the learner. Applying the rule to a variety of grammatical patterns and receiving relevant positive and negative evidence, leading to extensive practice in situations where performance can be monitored easily (as in writing) and in spontaneous interaction, declarative knowledge is automatized — proceduralized. In similar and analogous scenarios of deliberate learning, this kind of transformation of one kind of explicit knowledge to another is probably a correct portrayal, more or less, of some aspects of L2 learning. But at the same time, it should also be clear that there are other kinds of language development. Also of the explicit knowledge type would be purely inductive learning. And most importantly is the kind of acquisition that is characteristic of child L1 development, resulting in tacit competence — in this case, declarative knowledge of grammar is not an issue at all. Then, neither would be the idea of proceduralizing this kind of knowledge. Lastly, if we accept that some domains of L2 grammar can and do develop in a manner guided and constrained by UG to some extent (still a controversial claim), the declarative → procedural progression would not apply either. See DeKeyser's informative chart in (2005, Figure 11.1) for an explanation of how "deductive" does not always correspond to declarative procedural. For example, UG-constrained acquisition mechanisms can be thought of as "deductive."

Glossary

Ability: synonymous with *proficiency*. A network of knowledge structures, processing mechanisms and different kinds of sub-skill comes together in performance. For example, reading ability brings together different knowledge components and processing components necessary for skilled performance — some are linguistic and others are non-linguistic.

Additive bilingualism: in sequential bilingualism, the second language develops without resulting in any erosion of the first language. In contrast, *subtractive bilingualism* results in the development of one strongly dominant language and the early stabilization or loss of the other. It is important to emphasize that subtractive bilingualism is a normal language development outcome among children exposed to two languages.

Aphasia: Impairment or disruption of language ability as a result of trauma to the brain. Impairment may be partial and/or temporary and may affect only specific domains or functions.

Assessment: see *discrete-point, formative*.

Awareness: Attention that is brought to bear on mental activity. Perception that undergoes processing and is subject to deliberate reflection.

Bilingual: Refers to knowledge of two languages. The two language systems may be of: (1) equivalent completeness (in balanced bilingualism), or (2) one dominant language system, characterized by native-speaker completeness, with the other being weaker and manifestly non-native (imbalanced bilingualism).

Bootstrapping: from the metaphor "pulling yourself up by your bootstraps." Refers to carrying out a task by relying on one's own resources. In language development, the idea is that children call upon existing knowledge and ability to intervene in the learning of new competencies and abilities. One that is more highly developed "pulls up" another.

Bottom-up processing: see *top-down*.

Codeswitching: see *mixing*.

Coherence: The characteristic of a discourse or *text* in which its elements are organized in a logical or structured manner. The different parts are connected in a meaningful way, for example chronologically in the case of narrative. In argumentative discourse, points and counterpoints are pertinent. Meanings in the text or discourse are linked to form an integrated object of understanding.

Competence: A knowledge structure. Competence is revealed indirectly in performance, when executing an ability or skill that deploys the competence component in question.

Componential: refers to cognitive components or structures. In this book, a "componential approach" to studying language is the same as a "modular approach." See *modularity*.

Concurrent translation: in second language teaching, the practice of providing L2 learners with a translation to their L1 of instructional content that they receive in L2. Considered today to be counterproductive to the goal of learning the L2, the practice might be observed, for example, in *submersion* (see Glossary entry) situations where L2 learners do not understand the teacher.

Connectionism: A theory of mental architecture in which mental operations can be described by the structure of interconnected networks and how they interact and change (e.g., as a result of learning). The units that comprise these networks tend to be considered as basic and uniform, as opposed to the components of a modular architecture in which many of these components are thought to be specialized. Learning involves modifying the strength of connections within and among networks. Related terms: *ability, domain, double dissociation, higher order, integrativist model, language-specific, modularity, representation, top-down.*

Content-based language instruction (CLI): Synonymous with *immersion*. The second language of students is the medium of instruction (in a bilingual program, of course, CLI methods need only be implemented in the second language learning component). Comprehensibility of content teaching in a language students are still learning as beginners is ensured by applying systematic modifications in instructional discourse and provision of additional context support. Second language medium instruction that does not implement these CLI methods is not considered to be an example of immersion. Related terms: *Context-embedded, Language Learner Sensitive Discourse.*

Context-embedded: refers to comprehension, for example, that depends to a significant degree on the physical situation in which the message occurs. Another kind of context-embedded communication is when prior knowledge, background information, or shared assumptions are so complete that comprehension of the message may require relatively little processing of new information in the message or text itself.

Creole: The development of a *pidgin* into the primary language of a speech community. The creole becomes the L1/native language of children acquiring their mother tongue. Whereas creoles are fully formed languages, pidgins are "streamlined" systems with a reduced grammar, used by speakers who already have knowledge of a complete primary language (i.e., normally a person would not be a monolingual speaker of a pidgin; in cases of extreme language deprivation a person could be). Pidgins emerge from the need to construct a system for intercultural and interlinguistic communication by simplifying a target language.

Deficit: impairment, disability, or other kind of internal dysfunction that affects ability and performance, e.g., in speech comprehension or production, literacy learning, etc. Does not apply to learning difficulties (of extrinsic origin) that are amenable to instructional treatment and can be remediated completely. Deficits are intrinsic handicapping conditions. Should not to be confused with the use of the term "deficient," which does not necessarily describe an intrinsic impairment or disability.

Dialect: variation in language, among speakers of a language, associated with regional, ethnic, or social differences. Contrast to the kind of variation in *register* and *interlanguage*. The term *dialect* is not meant to refer to separate (minority or indigenous) languages that are not standard, official or national languages of a country, although this incorrect usage is common (often for the purpose of suggesting a lower social status for the language considered to be a "dialect"). For example, a vernacular language that has never been written or lacks a standardized form described in a published grammar or dictionary, does not become a "dialect" by virtue of this circumstance.

Diglossia: the term bilingualism is used to describe how two languages interact within an individual (mentally) or socially (in groups of speakers). Diglossia only refers to the second sense — the relationship between two languages in society. For example the concept is applied to situations where it is likely that one language is associated with certain social functions and the other with different functions, uses, circumstances and/or purposes. In this way it is said that the uses of the two languages are "distributed" in a speech community. The term *triglossia* extends this concept to the use of three languages in society.

Discourse: Speech or writing about a topic, subject, or theme that is treated at some length; typically speech or writing beyond the sentence level. Discourse can be interactive, as in a conversation, or produced by a single speaker or writer. The critical feature of discourse is that the sequence of sentences or utterances forms an integrated whole. They are related to one another in some coherent way. In this book, the term is restricted to the narrow technical sense indicated here. Related terms: *coherence, context-embedded, register*.

Discrete point assessment: evaluation of an instance of performance (e.g., response to a prompt or question) that focuses on a specific aspect of mastery, a pointed and focused aspect of knowledge. Thus, the knowledge or skill that is evaluated in this way is "discrete" — narrowly confined, to one "point" — as opposed to evaluation that is "holistic." An example would be an assessment of grammar that focuses on the ability of learners to supply in writing the correct plural affix for nouns and adjectives in a language that so marks them. Typically, discrete point tests can be scored quantitatively, marking responses as correct or incorrect.

Domain: in this book, refers to mental structures and processes in the cognitive sphere, as in the case of a distinctly delimited component of knowledge, a processing mechanism, or a network of structures and processors that underlie a specific ability.

Dominant language: in bilinguals and multilinguals the language subsystem that has attained native-speaker completeness (or in the case of young children, is marking the typical developmental milestones on schedule toward completeness). This would be in contrast to the language subsystem that has either stabilized in development at a stage short of native-speaker attainment or which has undergone attrition. In normally developing bilingual children: either (1) one language is dominant, or (2) development in both language subsystems indicates balanced acquisition and equivalent ability.

Double dissociation: is characteristic of a relationship between two cognitive structures that are autonomous one from the other. For example, if in a given individual one language ability is disrupted due to brain damage, another language ability may be spared, while a different affected individual may suffer a pattern of disruption that shows the reverse condition.

Dyslexia: a specific reading disability independent of general learning difficulty. An intrinsic *deficit* related to specific cognitive and/or linguistic dysfunction. Thus, it is also independent of extrinsic factors such as inadequate literacy instruction. At the same time, children suffering from a dyslexic condition often do not receive adequate instruction in reading and writing.

Focus on form (FonF), Focus on forms (FonFs), Focus on Meaning (FonM): In the opinion of this author, these three terms do not lend clarity to the discussion on teaching grammar objectives in content-based language instruction, despite their widespread usage in the research literature. In the first place, today, content-based language instruction (immersion) that includes a form-focused component strives to be (should strive to be) thoroughly communicative and *meaning focused.* Thus, FonM is no longer clearly counterposed to a focus on grammar in immersion teaching. Secondly, the distinction between FonF (incidental focus, integrated into content lessons) and FonFs (deliberate, specific and planned focus) is not clearly delineated either (for different reasons). Especially in practice, the proposed distinction may turn out not to be important. In this book, the more overarching term, *Form-focused Instruction* (encompassing both FonF and FonFs), is preferred.

Form-focused instruction (FFI): in language teaching, methods that draw learners' attention to grammatical forms or discourse patterns and promote metalinguistic awareness, either systematically and directly or indirectly. FFI encompasses both planned, direct instruction approaches to grammar teaching and spontaneous/incidental approaches. FFI is the more general category covering all types of teaching approach that include attention to language (grammar) learning objectives. Most second language educators who favor direct instruction of grammar learning objectives would maintain that it is most effective when it is part of a meaning-based approach that includes a strong communicative component. Thus, FFI can be clearly contrasted to second language acquisition models that reject grammar teaching or strongly minimize its importance.

Formative assessment: is a kind of evaluation of learning objectives that emphasizes feedback to the learner on his or her progress in mastering these objectives. For example, a learning program that systematically provides learners with focused corrective feedback (in addition to information about performance that shows mastery) during engagement in learning activities would be considered formative. Contrast to summative assessment, which does not provide feedback on specific points of learning during the learning activity (in summative assessment, for example, learners receive a grade indicating the percentage of correct responses upon completion of a task).

Fossilization: an outcome of language acquisition or learning that applies to second languages or attriting languages; when development in certain domains of linguistic competence fails to advance despite adequate exposure, relevant instruction, etc. "Stabilization" is preferred by some authors to avoid the connotation that such a plateau in development remains permanent.

Higher-order: refers to language ability in comprehension and production that requires the integration of knowledge structures, processing mechanisms, and other necessary component subskills. For example, in problem solving, language serves as a tool to direct attention to pertinent aspects of the task, and facilitates awareness of thinking and learning strategies. "Higher-order" also refers to processing of larger units of language involving sentence-level and discourse-level comprehension in contrast to language processing below the sentence level. Word and letter recognition (e.g. in reading) and phonological processing would be examples of processing at a "lower-order" level.

Immersion: see *Content-based language instruction (CLI).*

Indigenous language (IL): a language that is native to a region, spoken by a people that has been incorporated into a larger nation-state or has become a minority language by colonization. Indigenous typically implies that it is not the national or official language of the new nation-state. Indigenous languages are not necessarily of few speakers or endangered; and they can have a writing system and a literary heritage. In exceptional cases an IL could be the most widely spoken language of a country.

Input: language data to which a language learner is exposed. Input can be visual or auditory. Implicit in the definition is that input is potentially processible; that the learner can actually use the data in some way (for example: utilize the information received to build up knowledge of a language). See *Primary Linguistic Data.*

Integrativist model: an approach to the study of cognition that would reject any notion of specialized components, autonomous mental structures, or modules. While some approaches to modularity conceive of domains or mental operations that may be highly interactive and non-specialized together with others that are autonomous and self-contained, an integrativist model proposes an unconstrained integration of mental representations and processes through and through. In the study of language ability related to literacy, strong versions of the "whole language" philosophy tend to be integrativist in this sense.

Interference: see *transfer* (cross-linguistic influence); typically in the literature *interference* indicates a kind of cross-linguistic influence that results in grammatical error or the participation of L1 phonological features in L2 language production (as in "accented speech").

Interlanguage (synonym: learner language): the linguistic system that develops in second language learning. The second language competence that learners construct which approaches in a systematic way the target language. "Approaching" implies incompleteness in comparison to the fully formed grammar of normal first language acquisition. Interlanguage is different from approximative systems in L1 child acquisition because of the prior existence of, and continuing interaction with, the L2 learner's primary language.

Language Acquisition Device (LAD): the set of processing mechanisms specialized for language acquisition, in children especially, that allows them to build up a complete native-speaker competence in their primary language. Acquisition is guided by the principles of Universal Grammar, and does not require deliberate analysis of language forms, awareness of grammatical patterns, corrective feedback or any other kind of *negative evidence*. It was proposed in Chapter 2 that in second language learning the mechanisms of the LAD are still available for processing language input for the purpose of constructing implicit grammatical knowledge. They have not atrophied or been dissolved, even if their deployment might come to be blocked or deflected under certain circumstances. Related term: *parameter-setting*.

Language awareness: see *metalinguistic awareness*.

Language contact: a situation when two or more languages or dialects of the same language come into contact in a community or society. One possibility is that the languages are spoken by different people, and no one is bilingual. More typically, when languages interact, bilingualism is common. This interaction, results in mutual influences between the languages. For example, two dialects of the same language that were once "far apart" may evolve toward a relationship where they converge and speakers of each dialect find that the other is easier to understand than it was before. Another example is where a minority or subordinate language borrows heavily (words and even grammatical patterns) from a majority language.

Language Learner Sensitive Discourse (LLSD): speech and writing that is modified temporarily for the purpose of making it more comprehensible to the beginner second language learner. For example, teachers provide additional context support (including relevant background knowledge), graphic organizers, examples, etc. Pronunciation is clearer and complex syntax is initially avoided, while at the same time always striving to ensure that phrases and sentences are grammatical (no "Tarzan-talk").

Language-specific: refers to a cognitive structure that is associated with or linked to the specific linguistic representation of one language subsystem or another (in a bilingual speaker, the specific language subsystems of L1 and L2). This idea assumes that each language subsystem of a bilingual is a separate cognitive entity.

Language shift: language erosion or loss socially. Shift refers to the displacement of one language by another at the level of a community. The expanding language is almost always a language of wider communication. Not to be confused with other kinds of language change such as the evolution of a language over time.

Lingua franca: typically, a language used to make communication possible between people not sharing a common primary language. In some cases, the lingua franca might be a language that is not the mother tongue of any of the speech communities in contact. Often, a language of wider communication, also the mother tongue of a numerically populous and or expanding nation, serves this communicative function. The language of wider communication may be especially useful in the realm of literacy, for publishing, and for sharing information widely across borders.

Metacognition: see: *metalinguistic awareness.*

Metalinguistic awareness: the awareness (or explicit knowledge) of language itself, especially attention to its outward forms and observable patterns in speech and writing. More specifically, viewing language as an object of reflection in which the learner deliberately manipulates or attends to the forms of the language. Children appear to spontaneously manifest the beginnings of this kind of awareness or knowledge when they experiment with rhymes and engage in word play, or when they make reference to knowledge of different languages in bilingual situations. Metalinguistic awareness can be observed in any of the subsystems of language, as when readers pay attention to correspondences between units of sound (e.g., phonemes or syllables) and units of writing (e.g., letters or characters). Metacognition is a more general concept that refers to thinking about and reflection upon mental processes. In this way, metalinguistic awareness is a kind of metacognition. In this book: *language awareness* = metalinguistic awareness. Related terms: *Form-focused instruction, phonological awareness.*

Metaphonological knowledge: see *metalinguistic awareness.*

Mixing: in this book, language mixing should be taken as a blanket term referring to the use of two languages in the same sentence or same unit of discourse. Grammatical constituents, words, or morphemes from two languages appear together in different ways. For example, a phrase or a word from one language might be *inserted* into a grammatical pattern of the other language. Alternatively, a *switch* may occur at a certain point in the sentence from one language to the other (a switch from the grammatical pattern of the one to the other).

Modularity: a theory of cognitive architecture that proposes that domains of knowledge and skill networks can be independent one from the other; that mental faculties and abilities are made up, at least in part, of specialized component structures. For example, the component modules and specialized processing mechanisms that come together to form an ability (e.g., reading ability, conversational ability) are separate and autonomous and that interface connections make it possible for them to be deployed in a coordinated and efficient way. Interaction among components is necessary for a network of modules and their associated interfaces to be put to use in performance. Sarva (2010) is a comprehensive explanation of the properties of modular organization.

Morphosyllabic: is the characterization of the Chinese writing system that is the most precise (as opposed to "logographic," for example). Typically, characters map onto a monosyllabic morpheme. In this way the mapping links units of pronunciation (syllables) to units of meaning (morphemes) (Xue, 2011). See Note 4 in Chapter 4.

Negative evidence: provides information to the learner calling attention to a grammatical pattern that does not conform to the target language system. Corrective feedback is one kind of negative evidence. When learners reflect on their own language production they might provide themselves with negative evidence.

Parameter-setting: in language acquisition a hypothesis about how the "learning burden" may be reduced, especially for young cognitively immature children. In some proposals, Universal Grammar provides parameters (sets of options) for how grammatical principles are realized in each language a person acquires.

Phonological awareness: see *metalinguistic awareness*. Importantly, phonological awareness refers to explicit knowledge at any level of phonology — e.g., of phonemes or of syllables as these correspond to different units of writing. For example, *phonemic awareness* (not to be confused with the more general category of phonological awareness) refers to awareness of phonemes and how they might be represented by letters in an alphabetic writing system.

Phonology: refers to the component of grammar dedicated to mentally representing the sound patterns of a language.

Pidgin: see *creole*.

Poverty of Stimulus (PoS): in reference to language acquisition, the evidence that children receive in the input is not sufficient for them to be able to construct a complete grammar. In particular, information about which patterns do not conform to the target language is not available in any reliable way from experience alone. Nevertheless, children do not have to learn the grammar of their primary language by trial and error, forming hypotheses, trying them out with native-speakers, and receiving usable corrective feedback. Young children appear to be able to construct the grammar of their L1 with positive evidence alone. An important discussion in the field of second language learning is whether the PoS problem applies to interlanguage development in second languages.

Primary Linguistic Data: linguistic input that a child or second language learner receives that contains positive evidence of the structure of the language. This evidence consists of examples of well-formed sentences in the target language. From these examples the acquirer or learner constructs a mental grammar of the language.

Proficiency: (synonymous with *ability)* while knowledge (synonymous with *competence*) might be revealed indirectly in some aspect of language use, proficiency itself is revealed more or less directly by performance on a given set of tasks. A specific proficiency, or ability, is made up of a network of closely interacting components: competence structures and processing mechanisms.

Putonghua: (translated as "common speech") synonymous with Modern Standard Chinese. Based on the northern Mandarin dialects, it is the lingua franca of China, the national language and official language of schooling for all children. Since the establishment of the Republic of China in 1912, the promotion of a common national language has been the goal of language planning and policy. The same official Mandarin (*Guoyu*, translated as "national language") policy has been widely implemented in Taiwan. The modern Chinese writing system (using both "simplified" and "traditional" characters) corresponds closest to the linguistic subsystems of Putonghua/Mandarin.

Register: A situationally determined discourse variety (e.g., reflecting degrees of formality), or variation according to specific communicative purpose — not to be confused with dialectical variation. Also, a speaker of a language may develop proficiency in uses of language (registers) related to different fields or endeavors (e.g., academic discourse ability). Related terms: *discourse, coherence, context-embedded.*

Representation: a mental entity or structure that forms part of a competence component or a larger network of components that correspond to an ability. Examples could be a: knowledge structure, module, schema, processing module, or interface.

Schema: a mental *representation* of complex patterns of events, scenes, different kinds of knowledge, and so forth. Knowledge that is stored, or represented, in the mind and which is connected to networks of related categories of knowledge.

Semantics: the cognitive domain, separate from syntax, morphology and phonology, responsible for the organization of thoughts and concepts that can be expressed linguistically. When we ask about the meaning of a word, a phrase or a sentence, we are referring to semantics.

Semilingualism: an abnormal condition that may affect children exposed to two languages in which neither language attains a complete native-speaker level of *competence*. Circumstances that may lead to this condition include: brain damage, severe deprivation during the critical period of language acquisition, denial of access to processible language input during the critical period (as in the case of some deaf children), an intrinsic language deficit such as *Specific Language Impairment* that would typically affect ability on both languages of a bilingual child. Not to be confused with *subtractive bilingualism*, which is a different concept altogether. In addition, the concept of semilingualism should not be applied to failed or below average achievement in literacy-related language abilities which might be manifested "in both languages" if a bilingual student is evaluated for these abilities in L1 and L2.

Simultaneous bilingualism: in the research on child bilingualism, usually refers to the acquisition of two languages during the critical period of primary language development. As such, both languages would be considered as primary L1, sometimes designated L_a and L_b (as in this book) to avoid the misleading indication of a L1 and a L2. Simultaneous bilingualism may evolve toward either balanced competence in two languages or an imbalanced relationship between the language subsystems in which only one may come to be primary. See entries for related terms: *bilingual, additive bilingualism, dominant language,* and *semilingualism.*

Skill: in this book synonymous with "ability." Sometimes *skill* has the connotation of referring to a component part of a more complex ability. A skill implies having access to a specific domain, or specific domains of knowledge together with processing mechanisms that make it possible to put the skill to use in the performance of a specific task.

Specific Language Impairment (SLI): a deficit in grammatical competence or basic-level processing functions specific to language production and comprehension. As an intrinsic handicapping condition, bilingual children afflicted with SLI manifest the disability in both languages. Should be considered independently from *dyslexia* which involves dysfunctions related to the decoding of written language, although SLI by itself can negatively affect literacy learning depending on which subcomponents of grammatical competence and processing have been impaired and which have been spared.

Submersion: The use of a second language as medium of instruction for beginner learners of the language without implementing any of the standard teaching practices for beginner second language learners. Students are not provided with teaching modifications to help make instruction comprehensible (typically occurring when L2 learners are integrated into classes of native speakers of the target language without any systematic plan for differentiated instruction). As such, submersion is completely contrary to the accepted pedagogical practices of immersion teaching.

Subtractive bilingualism: see *additive bilingualism.*

Syntax: the component of grammar that determines how words and morphemes combine in such a way that a speaker/listener is able to construct phrases, clauses and sentences that are grammatical and interpretable. It serves as a "way-station between phonology and semantics making the mapping between them more articulate and precise" (Jackendoff 2001, 126).

Text: a meaningful instance of language, beyond the single word level. In this book the term text is used to refer to written language. For example, expository text is a prose genre, usually associated with the general category of non-fiction, for the purpose of communicating ideas, transmitting information, explaining concepts, relating events, analyzing phenomena, ideas, propositions, and so forth.

Top-down: refers to processing. Top-down processes progress from larger units and proceed "downward" toward smaller units. For example in reading, word recognition might be affected (e.g., facilitated) by sentence-level grammar patterns involving semantic and syntactic information. In listening, one might be able to make use, to a certain degree, of previous knowledge ("higher-level" knowledge structures) in processing information that is received. "In the other direction," bottom-up processes progress from lower-level units "upward" toward larger units.

Transfer: in this book, synonymous with cross-linguistic influence. In the research literature the term *transfer* is often used more broadly to encompass interactions and interfaces among linguistic and non-linguistic components alike.

Triglossia: see *diglossia.*

Universal Grammar (UG): general principles specific to linguistic knowledge that are not violated by any particular language; also, design features common to all languages. For example: operations of movement and ordering that language systems allow are structure-dependent. According to UG, there are certain constraints on language variation, which are universal, set down by the human genetic endowment. In this sense, UG is a kind of innate knowledge that allows language acquirers to deduce a grammar from language input.

Universal Writing System Constraint: all modern writing systems encode spoken language; they do not encode meaning independently of language. In no writing system today does reading implement a direct visual-to-meaning interface that allows the reader to by-pass language. The related Universal Phonological Principle proposes that for skilled readers the activation of word pronunciation occurs across all writing systems. Phonology is activated at the lowest level specified by the script, e.g., phonemes in an alphabetic system, syllables in a morphosyllabic system (Perfetti and Liu, 2005).

References

Abrahamsson, N. and Hyltenstam, K. (2009). Age of onset and nativeness in a second language: Listener perception versus linguistic scrutiny. *Language Learning*, 59, 249–306.

Adamson, B. and Feng, A. (2009). A comparison of trilingual education policies for ethnic minorities in China. *Compare*, 39, 321–333.

Allen, S. E. M. (2006). Formalism and functionalism working together? Exploring roles for complementary contributions in the domain of child null arguments. In R. Salbakova, S. Montrul and P. Prévost (Eds.), *Inquiries in linguistic development: In honor of Lydia White* (pp. 233–255). Amsterdam: John Benjamins.

Allen, S. E. M., Crago, M. and Pesco, D. (2006). The effect of majority language exposure on minority language skills: The case of Inuktitut. *International Journal of Bilingual Education and Bilingualism*, 9, 578–596.

Ammar, A. and Spada, N. (2006). One size fits all? Recasts, prompts and L2 learning. *Studies in Second Language Acquisition*, 28, 543–574.

Anderson, R. T. (2001). Lexical morphology and verb use in child first language loss: A preliminary case study investigation. *International Journal of Bilingualism*, 5, 377–401.

Anderson, S. and Lightfoot, D. (2002). *The language organ: Linguistics as cognitive physiology.* Cambridge: Cambridge University Press.

Ansaldo, A. I. and Joanette, Y. (2002). Language mixing and language switching following aphasia. In F. Fabbro (Ed.), *Advances in the neurolinguistics of bilingualism: Essays in honor of Michel Paradis* (pp. 261–274). Udine: Forum.

Archer, N. and Bryant, P. (2001). Investigating the role of context in learning to read: A direct test of Goodman's model. *British Journal of Psychology*, 92, 579–591.

Argyri, E. and Sorace, A. (2007). Cross-linguistic influence and language dominance in older bilingual children. *Bilingualism: Language and Cognition*, 10, 79–99.

Au, T. K.-F.; Oh, J. S.; Knightly, L. M.; Jun, S.-A. and Romo, L. F. (2008). Salvaging a childhood language. *Journal of Memory and Language*, 58, 998–1011.

Baker, C. (2011). *Foundations of bilingual education and bilingualism, 5th edition.* Bristol: Multilingual Matters.

Baker, J. R.; Luo, Y. W. and Hung, Y. Y. (2007). Helping daunted low level adult EFL learners get a fresh start with a literature ladder. *Asian EFL Journal*, 9, 254–279.

Bar-Shalom, E. and Zaretsky, E. (2008). Selective attrition in Russian-English bilingual children: Preservation of grammatical aspect. *International Journal of Bilingualism*, 12, 281–302.

Barry, A. K. (2008). *Linguistic perspectives on language and education.* Columbus: Pearson.

Batstone, R. and Ellis, R. (2009). Principled grammar teaching. *System*, 37, 194–204.

Beaser, D. (2006). The outlook for Taiwanese language preservation. *Sino-Platonic Papers*, 172, 1–18.

Berent, G. (2004). Sign language—Spoken language bilingualism: Code mixing and mode mixing by ASL-English bilinguals. In T. Bhatia and W. R. Ritchie (Eds.), *The handbook of bilingualism* (pp. 312–335). Oxford: Blackwell.

Bernal, S.; Dehaene-Lambertz, G.; Millotte, S. and Christophe, A. (2010). Two-year-olds compute syntactic structure on-line. *Developmental Science*, 13, 69–76.

Bernardini, P. and Schlyter, S. (2004). Growing syntactic structure and code-mixing in the weaker language: The Ivy Hypothesis. *Bilingualism: Language and Cognition*, 7, 49–69.

Bi, Y.; Han, Z.; Weekes, B. and Shu, H. (2007). The interaction between semantic and the nonsemantic systems in reading: Evidence from Chinese. *Neuropsychologia*, 45, 2660–2673.

Bialystok, E. (2007). Cognitive effects of bilingualism: How linguistic experience leads to cognitive change. *International Journal of Bilingual Education and Bilingualism*, 10, 210–223.

Bialystok, E. (2009). Bilingualism: The good, the bad and the indifferent. *Bilingualism: Language and Cognition*, 12, 3–11.

Bialystok, E. and Feng, X. (2010). Language proficiency and its implications for monolingual and bilingual children. In A. Durgunoglu and A. Goldberg (Eds.), *Language and literacy development in bilingual settings* (pp. 121–138). New York: Guilford Press.

Bialystok, E.; Craik, F. and Luk, G. (2008). Cognitive control and lexical access in younger and older bilinguals. *Journal of Experimental Psychology*, 34, 859–873.

Bigelow, M.; Ranney, S. and Dahlman, A. (2006). Keeping the language focus in content-based ESL instruction through proactive curriculum planning. *TESL Canada Journal*, 24, 40–58.

Birch, B. (2002). *English L2 reading: Getting to the bottom.* Mahwah: Lawrence Erlbaum.

Bitchener, J.; Young, S. and Cameron, D. (2005). The effect of different types of corrective feedback on ESL student writing. *Journal of Second Language Writing*, 14, 191–205.

Bley-Vroman, R. (1996). What we have to explain in foreign language learning. *Behavioral and Brain Sciences*, 19, 718.

Bolonyai, A. (1998). In-between languages: Language shift/maintenance in childhood bilingualism. *International Journal of Bilingualism*, 2, 21–43.

Bolonyai, A. (2007). (In)vulnerable agreement in incomplete bilingual L1 learners. *International Journal of Bilingualism*, 11, 3–23.

Bosch, L. and Sebastián-Gallés, N. (2001). Early language differentiation in bilingual infants. In J. Cenoz and F. Genesee (Eds.), *Trends in bilingual acquisition* (pp. 71–93). Amsterdam: John Benjamins.

Boudreault, P. and Mayberry, R. (2006). Grammatical processing in American Sign Language: Age of first-language effects in relation to syntactic structure. *Language and Cognitive Processes*, 21, 608–635.

Bouffard, L. and Sarkar, M. (2008). Training 8-year-old French immersion students in metalinguistic analysis: An innovation in form-focused pedagogy. *Language Awareness*, 17, 3–24.

Brashear, H.; Henderson, V.; Park, K.-H. and Lee, S. (2006). American Sign Language recognition in game development for deaf children. *Proceedings of the Eighth International ACM SIGACCESS Conference on Computers and Accessibility*, 79–86.

Brinton, D. M.; Snow, M. A. and Wesche, M. B. (2003). *Content-based second language instruction*. Ann Arbor: University of Michigan Press.

Buckwalter, J. and Lo, Y. H. (2002). Emergent biliteracy in Chinese and English. *Journal of Second Language Writing*, 11, 269–293.

Burling, R. (2003). Review of R. Jackendoff, Foundations of language: Brain, meaning, grammar, evolution. *Language in Society*, 32, 415–445.

Bylund, E.; Abrahamsson, N. and Hyltenstam, K. (2010). The role of language aptitude in first language attrition: The case of pre-pubescent attriters. *Applied Linguistics*, 31, 443–464.

Calabretta, R. and Parisi, D. (2005). Evolutionary connectionism and mind/brain modularity. In W. Callebaut and D. Rasskin-Gutman (Eds.), *Modularity: Understanding the development and evolution of natural complex systems* (pp. 309–330). Cambridge: MIT Press.

Callebaut, W. (2005). The ubiquity of modularity. In W. Callebaut and D. Rasskin-Gutman (Eds.), *Modularity: Understanding the development and evolution of natural complex systems* (pp. 11–28). Cambridge: MIT Press.

Carpenter, H.; Seon Jeon, K.; MacGregor, D. and Mackey, A. (2006). Learners' interpretations of recasts. *Studies in Second Language Acquisition*, 28, 209–236.

Castles, A. and Coltheart, M. (2004). Is there a causal link from phonological awareness to success in learning to read? *Cognition*, 93, 77–111.

Catts, H. W. and Hogan, T. P. (2003). Language basis of reading disabilities and implications for early identification and remediation. *Reading Psychology*, 24, 223–246.

Chan, C. K. K. and Siegel, L. (2001). Phonological processing in reading Chinese among normally achieving and poor readers. *Journal of Experimental Child Psychology*, 80, 23–43.

Chan, D. W.; Ho, C. S.-H.; Tsang, S.-M.; Lee, S.-H. and Chung, K. K. H. (2006). Exploring the reading-writing connection in Chinese children with dyslexia in Hong Kong. *Reading and Writing*, 19, 543–561.

Chan, M.-L. (2010). *Notions of language dominance, language preference and language choice in the study of bilingual first language acquisition (BFLA)*. Master's thesis, University of Hong Kong.

Chelliah, S. and de Reuse, W. (2011). *Handbook of descriptive linguistic fieldwork*. New York: Springer.

Chen, H.-C. (1996). Chinese reading and comprehension: A cognitive psychology perspective. In M. Bond (Ed.), *The handbook of Chinese psychology* (pp. 43–62). Oxford: Oxford University Press.

Chen, H.-J. (2006). Examining the scoring mechanism and feedback quality of MyAccess. Paper presented at the *Tamkang International Conference on Second Language Writing*, Tamkang University, Taipei, December 2, 2006.

Chen, S.-C. (2010). Multilingualism in Taiwan. *International Journal of the Sociology of Language*, 205, 79–104.

Chen, X.; Shu, H.; Wu, N. and Anderson, R. (2003). Stages in learning to pronounce Chinese characters. *Psychology in the Schools*, 40, 115–124.

Cheng, L. (2008). The key to success: English language testing in China. *Language Testing*, 25, 15–37.

Cheng, L. Y.; Li, M.; Kirby, J. R.; Qiang, H. Y. and Wade-Woolley, L. (2010). English language immersion and students' academic achievement in English, Chinese and mathematics. *Evaluation and Research in Education*, 23, 151–169.

Cheung, H. and Lin, A. M. Y. (2005). Differentiating between automatic and strategic control processes: Toward a model of cognitive mobilization in bilingual reading. *Psychologia*, 48, 39–53.

Cheung, H.; Chen, H.-C.; Lai, C. Y.; Wong, O. C. and Hills, M. (2001). The development of phonological awareness: Effects of spoken language experience and orthography. *Cognition*, 81, 227–241.

Chireac, S.-M. (2010). *La adquisición del catalán y del castellano por los escolares inmigrantes de origen rumano y chino: Un análisis sistemático de los usos correctos y erróneos en la expresión oral*. Doctoral thesis, Universitat de Lleida.

Chow, B. W.-Y.; McBride-Chang, C. and Burgess, S. (2005). Phonological processing skills and early reading abilities in Hong Kong Chinese kindergartners learning to read English as a second language. *Journal of Educational Psychology*, 97, 81–87.

Christophe, A. (2002). L'apprentissage du langage: Une capacité innée? *Intellectica*, 34, 189–210.

Chung, K. H.; Ho, C. S.-H.; Chan, D. W.; Tsang, S.-M.; Lee, S.-H. (2011). Cognitive skills and literacy performance of Chinese adolescents with and without dyslexia. *Reading and Writing*, 24, 835–859.

Clahsen, H. and Felser, C. (2006). How native-like is non-native language processing? *Trends in Cognitive Science*, 10, 564–570.

Clahsen, H. and Muysken, P. (1996). How adult second language learning differs from child first language development. *Behavioral and Brain Sciences*, 19, 721–723.

Clark, E. (2003). Critical periods, time, and practice. *University of Pennsylvania Working Papers in Linguistics*, 9, 39–48.

Clothey, R. (2005). China's policies for minority nationalities in higher education: Negotiating national values and ethnic identities. *Comparative Education Review*, 49, 389–409.

Coltheart, M. (1999). Modularity and cognition. *Trends in Cognitive Science*, 3, 115–120.

Coltheart, M. (2005). Analysing developmental disorders of reading. *Advances in Speech-Language Pathology*, 7, 49–57.

Crain, S.; Goro, T. and Thornton, R. (2006). Language acquisition is language change. *Journal of Psycholinguistic Research*, 35, 31–49.

Culicover, R. and Jackendoff, R. (2006). The simpler syntax hypothesis. *Trends in Cognitive Science*, 10, 413–418.

Cummins, J. (1991). Language development and academic learning. In L. Malavé and G. Duquette (Eds.), *Language, culture and cognition* (pp. 161–175). Clevedon: Multilingual Matters.

Cummins, J. (2000). *Language, power and pedagogy: Bilingual children in the crossfire*. Clevedon: Multilingual Matters.

Cummins, J.; Brown, K. and Sayers, D. (2007). *Literacy, technology and diversity: Teaching for success in changing times*. Boston: Pearson.

Cutler, A. (2002). Native listeners. *European Review*, 10, 27–41.

Daigle, D. and Armand, F. (2004). L'approche bilingue et l'apprentissage de a lecture chez les sourds. *Revue Canadienne de Linguistique Appliquée*, 7, 23–38.

Davies, A. (1990). *Principles of language testing*. Oxford: Blackwell.

De Graaff, S.; Bosman, A.; Hasselman, F. and Verhoeven, L. (2009). Benefits of systematic phonics instruction. *Scientific Studies of Reading*, 13, 318–333.

De Groot, A. M. B. and Christoffels, I. (2006). Language control in bilinguals: Monolingual tasks and simultaneous interpreting. *Bilingualism: Language and Cognition*, 9, 189–201.

De Houwer, A. (2007). Parental language input patterns and children's bilingual use. *Applied Psycholinguistics*, 28, 411–424.

De Houwer, A. (2009). *Bilingual first language acquisition*. Bristol: Multilingual Matters.

DeFrancis, J. (1989). *Visible speech: The diverse oneness of writing systems*. Honolulu: University of Hawaii Press.

DeFrancis, J. (1996). How efficient is the Chinese writing system? *Visible Language*, 30, 6–44.

Dehaene, S. (2009). *Reading in the brain: The new science of how we read*. New York: Penguin.

DeKeyser, R. (1998). Beyond focus on form: Cognitive perspectives on learning and practicing second language grammar. In C. Doughty and J. Williams (Eds.), *Focus on form in classroom second language acquisition* (pp. 42–63). Cambridge: Cambridge University Press.

DeKeyser, R. (2005a). What makes learning second language grammar difficult? A review of issues. *Language Learning*, 55, 1–25.

DeKeyser, R. (2005b). Implicit and explicit learning. In C. J. Doughty and M. Long (Eds.), *The handbook of second language acquisition* (pp. 313–348). Oxford: Blackwell.

DeKeyser, R. and Juffs, A. (2005). Cognitive considerations in L2 learning. In E. Hinkel (Ed.), *Handbook of research in second language teaching and learning* (pp. 437–454). Mahwah: Lawrence Erlbaum.

Delgado, R. (2010). Common underlying proficiency and its role in the American bilingual education debate. *The Journal of Kanda University of International Studies*, 22, 199–219.

Diab, N. M. (2010). Effects of peer- versus self-editing on students' revision of language errors in revised drafts. *System*, 38, 85–95.

Ding, Y. (2007). Text memorization and imitation: The practices of successful Chinese learners of English. *System*, 35, 271–280.

Domínguez, L. (2007). Knowledge of features in fossilized second language grammars. *Second Language Research*, 23, 243–260.

Doughty, C. J. (2003). Instructed SLA: Constraints, comprehension, and enhancement. In C. J. Doughty and M. H. Long (Eds.), *The handbook of second language acquisition* (pp. 256–310). Oxford: Blackwell.

Dubuisson, C.; Bastien, M.; Berthiaume, R.; Parisot, A.-M. and Villeneuve, S. (2004). Création du logiciel d'alphabétisation bilingue pour les sourds《Le français sur le bout des doigts》: Évaluation de l'outil et de la démarche de développement. *ReCALL*, 16, 360–376.

Dufour, R. (1997). Sign language and bilingualism: Modality implications for bilingual language representation. In A. M. B. de Groot and J. F. Kroll (Eds.), *Tutorials in bilingualism: Psycholinguistic perspectives* (pp. 301–329). Mahwah: Lawrence Erlbaum.

Dussias, P. (2004). Parsing a first language like a second: The erosion of L1 parsing strategies in Spanish-English bilinguals. *International Journal of Bilingualism*, 8, 355–371.

Dutro, S. and Moran, C. (2003). Rethinking English language instruction: An architectural approach. In G. García (Ed.), *English learners: Reaching the highest level of English literacy* (pp. 227–258). Columbus: Pearson.

Echevarría, J. and Graves, A. (2011). *Sheltered content instruction: Teaching English language learners with diverse abilities*. Boston: Pearson.

Ehri, L. (2005). Learning to read words: Theory, findings, and issues. *Scientific Studies of Reading*, 9, 167–188.

Ehri, L. (2009). Learning to read in English: Teaching phonics to beginning readers from diverse backgrounds. In L. Morrow, R. Rueda and D. Lapp (Eds.), *Handbook of research on literacy and diversity* (pp. 292–319). New York: Guilford.

Ellis, R. (2005). Principles of instructed language learning. *System*, 33, 209–224.

Ellis, R. (2006). Current issues in the teaching of grammar: An SLA perspective. *TESOL Quarterly*, 40, 83–107.

Ellis, R. and Sheen, Y. (2006). Reexamining the role of recasts in second language acquisition. *Studies in Second Language Acquisition*, 28, 575–600.

Ellis, R.; Loewen, S. and Erlam, R. (2006). Implicit and explicit corrective feedback and the acquisition of L2 grammar. *Studies in Second Language Acquisition*, 28, 339–368.

Evans, S. (2011). Hong Kong English and the professional world. *World Englishes*, 30, 293–316.

Evans, S. and Green, C. (2007). Why EAP is necessary: A survey of Hong Kong tertiary students. *Journal of English for Academic Purposes*, 6, 3–17.

Fabbro, F. (2001). The bilingual brain: Bilingual aphasia. *Brain and Language*, 79, 201–210.

Fabiano, L. and Goldstein, B. (2005). Phonological cross-linguistic effects in bilingual Spanish-English speaking children. *Journal of Multilingual Communication Disorders*, 3, 56–63.

Fang, G. (2011). Linguistic capital: Continuity and change in educational language policies for South Asians in Hong Kong primary schools. *Current Issues in Language Planning*, 12, 251–263.

Ferguson, A.; Harding, E.; Helmer, K. and Suh, S. J. (2003). Miscue analysis of native and non-native speakers. *Arizona Working Papers in SLAT*, 10, 51–67.

Ferris, D. (2010). Second language writing research and written corrective feedback in SLA: Intersections and practical applications. *Studies in Second Language Acquisition*, 32, 181–201.

Fitch, W. T.; Hauser, M. and Chomsky, N. (2005). The evolution of the language faculty: Clarifications and implications. *Cognition*, 97, 179–210.

Fletcher, P. (1999). Specific language impairment. In M. Barrett (Ed.), *The development of language* (pp. 349–371). East Sussex: Psychology Press.

Francis, D. J. (2006). Language of instruction. In D. August and T. Shanahan (Eds.), *Developing literacy in second-language learners: Report of the National Literacy Panel on Language-Minority Children and Youth* (pp. 365–414). Mahwah: Lawrence Erlbaum.

Francis, N. (2007). Corrective feedback in L2 assessment: Negative evidence and interactive practice. In Y.-N. Leung (Ed.), *Selected papers from the 16th International Symposium on English Teaching* (pp. 376–386). Taipei: English Teachers' Association.

Francis, N. (2008). Modularity in bilingualism as an opportunity for cross-discipline discussion. In J. Cummins and N. Hornberger (Eds.), *Encyclopedia of language and education: Bilingual education, Volume 5* (pp. 105–116). New York: Springer.

Francis, N. (2012). *Bilingual competence and bilingual proficiency in child language development*. Cambridge: MIT Press.

Francis, N. and Navarrete Gómez, P. R. (2009). Documentation and language learning: Separate agendas or complementary tasks? *Language Documentation and Conservation*, 3, 176–191.

Francis, N. and Paciotto, C. (2004). Bilingüismo y diglosia en al Sierra Tarahumara: Fundamentos de la evaluación del lenguaje. *Pueblos Indígenas y Educación*, 55, 57–82.

Fusellier-Sousa, I. (2003). Apprentissage institutionnel d'une troisième langue par les apprenants sourds: Discussion autour d'une approche bilingue dans l'enseignment d'une langue vivante. *Langue Française*, 137, 86–104.

Gajo, L. (2007). Linguistic knowledge and subject knowledge: How does bilingualism contribute to subject development? *International Journal of Bilingual Education and Bilingualism*, 10, 563–581.

Gass, S. and Mackey, A. (2006). Input, interaction and output. *AILA Review*, 19, 3–17.

Genesee, F. (2002). Portrait of the bilingual child. In V. Cook (Ed.), *Portraits of the L2 user* (pp. 170–196). Clevedon: Multilingual Matters.

Genesee, F. (2003). Rethinking bilingual acquisition. In J.-M. Dewaele, A. Housen and L. Wei (Eds.), *Bilingualism: Beyond basic principles: Festschrift in honor of Hugo Baetens Beardsmore* (pp. 204–228). Clevedon: Multilingual Matters.

Genesee, F.; Lindholm-Leary, K.; Saunders, W. and Christian, D. (2005). English language learners in U.S. schools: An overview of research findings. *Journal of Education for Students Placed at Risk*, 10, 363–385.

Gentil, G. (2011). A biliteracy agenda for genre research. *Journal of Second Language Writing*, 20, 6–23.

Geva, E. and Wang, M. (2001). The development of basic reading skills in children: A cross-language perspective. *Annual Review of Applied Linguistics*, 21, 182–204.

Gleitman, L.; Cassidy, K.; Nappa, R.; Papafragou, A. and Trueswell, J. (2005). Hard words. *Language Learning and Development*, 1, 23–64.

Goldberg, A. (2001). Patient arguments of causative verbs can be omitted: The role of information structure distribution. *Language Sciences*, 23, 503–524.

Goldin-Meadow, S. (2005). What language creation in the manual modality tells us about the foundations of language. *The Linguistic Review*, 22, 199–225.

Gollan, T. and Kroll, J. (2001). Bilingual lexical access. In B. Rapp (Ed.), *The handbook of cognitive neuropsychology: What deficits reveal about the human mind* (pp. 321–345). Philadelphia: Psychology Press.

Goodman, K. (2005). Making sense of written language: A lifelong journey. *Journal of Literacy Research*, 37, 1–24.

Goodman, Y. (1997). Reading diagnosis: Qualitative or quantitative? *The Reading Teacher*, 50, 534–538.

Goral, M.; Levy, E. and Obler, L. (2002). Neurolinguistic aspects of bilingualism. *International Journal of Bilingualism*, 6, 411–440.

Goswami, U. (2002). Phonology, reading development, and dyslexia: A cross-linguistic perspective. *Annals of Dyslexia*, 52, 141–163.

Grabe, W. and Stoller, F. (2002). *Teaching and researching reading*. London: Longman.

Green, D. (2002). Representation and control: Exploring recovery patterns in bilingual aphasics. In F. Fabbro (Ed.), *Advances in the neurolinguistics of bilingualism: Essays in honor of Michel Paradis* (pp. 239–259). Udine: Forum.

Grosjean, F. (2010). Bilingualism, biculturalism, and deafness. *International Journal of Bilingual Education and Bilingualism*, 13, 133–145.

Groves, J. (2010). Language or dialect, topolect or regiolect? A comparative study of language attitudes toward the status of Cantonese in Hong Kong. *Journal of Multilingual and Multicultural Development*, 31, 531–551.

Guo, Y.; Peng, D. and Liu, Y. (2005). The role of phonological activation in the visual semantic retrieval of Chinese characters. *Cognition*, 98, B21–B34.

Gupta, A. and Jamal, G. (2007). Reading strategies of bilingual normally progressing and dyslexic readers in Hindi and English. *Applied Psycholinguistics*, 28, 47–68.

Gürel, A. (2004). Selectivity in L2-induced L1 attrition: A psycholinguistic account. *Journal of Neurolinguistics*, 17, 53–78.

Hakuta, K.; Bialystok, E. and Wiley, E. (2003). Critical evidence: A test of the critical-period hypothesis for second-language acquisition. *Psychological Science*, 14, 31–38.

Hall, J. K.; Cheng, A. and Carlson, M. T. (2006). Reconceptualizing multicompetence as a theory of language knowledge. *Applied Linguistics*, 27, 220–240.

Halmari, H. (2005). 'I'm forgetting both': L1 maintenance and codeswitching in Finnish-English language contact. *International Journal of Bilingualism*, 9, 197–433.

Hamel, R. E. (2010). Hacia la construcción de un proyecto escolar de EIB. La experiencia p'urhepecha: Investigación y acción colaborativa entre escuelas e investigadores. In L. E. Pincén and G. Duarte (Eds.), *VIII Congreso Latinoamericano de Educación Intercultural Bilingüe* (pp. 113–135). Buenos Aires: Ministerio de Educación and UNICEF.

Hamel, R. E. and Francis, N. (2006). The teaching of Spanish as a second language in an indigenous bilingual intercultural curriculum. *Language, Culture and Curriculum*, 19, 171–188.

Han, Z.-H. (2004). Fossilization: Five central issues. *International Journal of Applied Linguistics*, 14, 212–239.

Han, Z.-H. and Bi, Y. (2009). Oral spelling and writing in a logographic language: Insights from a Chinese dysgraphic individual. *Brain and Language*, 110, 23–28.

Hatta, T.; Kawakami, A. and Hatasa, Y. (1997). Kanji writing errors in Japanese college students and American Japanese students. In H.-C. Chen (Ed.), *Cognitive processing of Chinese and related Asian languages* (pp. 410–416), Hong Kong: The Chinese University Press.

Hayashi, Y. and Murphy, V. (2011). An investigation of morphological awareness in Japanese learners of English. *Language Learning Journal*, 39, 105–120.

He, Y.; Wang, Q. and Anderson, R. C. (2005). Chinese children's use of subcharacter information about pronunciation. *Journal of Educational Psychology*, 97, 572–579.

Heift, T. (2004). Corrective feedback and learner uptake in CALL. *ReCALL*, 16, 416–431.

Henao Alvarez, O.; Ramírez Salazar, D. A. and Medina Medina, M. (2004). Potenciando la capacidad lectora de los sordos con el apoyo de nuevas tecnologías. *Lectura y Vida*, 25, 18–25.

Henderson-Summet, V.; Grinter, R. E.; Carroll, J. and Startner, T. (2007). Electronic communication: Themes from a case study of the deaf community. *Proceedings of INTERACT '07, V. 4662 of LNCS*, 347–360. New York: Springer.

Hernández, A. (2005). Making content instruction accessible for English language learners. In G. García (Ed.), *English learners: Reaching the highest level of English literacy* (pp. 125–149). Newark, DE: International Reading Association.

Herschensohn, J. (2009). Fundamental and gradient differences in language development. *Studies in Second Language Acquisition*, 31, 259–289.

Herschensohn, J.; Stevenson, J. and Waltmunson, J. (2005). Children's acquisition of L2 Spanish morphosyntax in an immersion setting. *International Review of Applied Linguistics*, 43, 193–217.

Hidalgo, M. (2001). Sociolinguistic stratification in New Spain. *International Journal of the Sociology of Language*, 149, 55–78.

Ho, C. S.-H. and Fong, K.-M. (2005). Do Chinese dyslexic children have difficulties learning English as a second language. *Journal of Psycholinguistic Research*, 34, 603–618.

Ho, C. S.-H. and Ma, N.-L. (1999). Training in phonological strategies improves Chinese dyslexic children's character reading skills. *Journal of Research in Reading*, 22, 131–142.

Ho, C. S.-H.; Chan, D. W.-O.; Lee, S.-H.; Tsang, S.-M. and Luan, V. H. (2004). Cognitive profiling and preliminary subtyping in Chinese developmental dyslexia. *Cognition*, 91, 43–75.

Ho, C. S.-H.; Chan, D. W.; Tsang, S.-M.; Lee, S.-H. and Chung, K. K. H. (2006). Word learning deficit among Chinese dyslexic children. *Journal of Child Language*, 33, 145–161.

Hu, C.-F. (2003). Phonological memory, phonological awareness, and foreign language word learning. *Language Learning*, 53, 429–462.

Hu, C.-F. (2004). The development of phonological representations among Chinese-speaking children. *Taiwan Journal of Linguistics*, 2, 103–130.

Hu, C.-F. and Catts, H. W. (1998). The role phonological processing in early reading ability: What we can learn from Chinese. *Scientific Studies of Reading*, 2, 55–79.

Hu, G. (2008). The misleading academic discourse on Chinese-English bilingual education in China. *Review of Educational Research*, 78, 195–231.

Hu, G. and Alsagoff, L. (2010). A public policy perspective on English medium instruction in China. *Journal of Multilingual and Multicultural Development*, 31, 365–382.

Huang, T.-C. (2010). The application of translingualism to language revitalization in Taiwan. *Asian Social Science*, 6, 44–59.

Hudelson, S. (1994). Literacy development of second language children. In F. Genesee (Ed.), *Educating second language children: The whole child, the whole curriculum, the whole community* (pp. 129–158). Cambridge: Cambridge University Press.

Hyltenstam, K.; Bylund, E.; Abrahamsson, N. and Park, H.-S. (2009). Dominant-language replacement: The case of international adoptees. *Bilingualism: Language and Cognition*, 12, 121–140.

Jackendoff, R. (1997). *The architecture of the language faculty*. Cambridge: MIT Press.

Jackendoff, R. (2002). *Foundations of language: Brain, meaning, grammar, evolution*. Oxford: Oxford University Press.

Jackendoff, R. (2007). *Language, consciousness, culture: Essays on mental structure*. Cambridge: MIT Press.

Janhunen, J. (2005). Tungusic: An endangered language family in Northeast Asia. *International Journal of the Sociology of Language*, 173, 37–54.

Jessner, U. (2008). Multicompetence approaches to language proficiency development in multilingual education. In J. Cummins and N. Hornberger (Eds.), *Encyclopedia of language and education: Bilingual education, Volume 5* (pp. 91–104). New York: Springer.

Julbe-Delgado, D. (2010). *Spanish spelling errors of emerging bilingual writers in middle school*. Doctoral dissertation, University of South Florida.

Kang, H. (2011). *Computer-based writing and paper-based writing: A study of beginning-level and intermediate-level Chinese learners' writing*. Doctoral dissertation, Ohio State University.

Kasule, D. and Lunga, V. (2010). How effective are students' self-editing endeavours? —Evidence from L2 writing tasks. *International Journal for Cross-Disciplinary Subjects in Education*, 1, 103–112.

Kaufman, D. (1998). Children's assimilatory pattern and L1 attrition. In A. Greenhill, M. Hughes, H. Littlefield and H. Walsh (Eds.), *Proceedings of the 22nd Annual Boston University Conference on Language Development* (pp. 409–420). Somerville: Cascadilla Press.

Kaufman, D. (2001). Tales of L1 attrition: Evidence from pre-puberty children. In T. Ammerlaan, M. Hulsen, H. Strating and K. Yagmur (Eds.), *Sociolinguistic and psycholinguistic perspectives on maintenance and loss of minority languages* (pp. 185–202). Münster: Waxmann.

Kegl, J.; Senghas, A. and Coppola, M. (1999). Creation through contact: Sign language emergence and sign language change in Nicaragua. In M. DeGraff (Ed.), *Language creation and language change* (pp. 179–237). Cambridge: MIT Press.

Ki, W.-W.; Lam, H.-C.; Chung, A. L.-S.; Tse, S.-K.; Ko, P.-Y.; Lau, E. C.-C.; Chou, P. W.-Y.; Lai, A. C.-Y. and Lai, S. M.-S. (2003). Structural awareness, variation theory and ICT support. *Educational Studies in Language and Literature*, 3, 53–78.

Kinsella, A. (2009). *Language, evolution and syntactic theory*. Cambridge: Cambridge University Press.

Kinsella, A. and Marcus, G. (2009). Evolution, perfection, and theories of language. *Biolinguistics*, 3, 186–212.

Klöter, H. (2004). Language policy in the KMT and DPP eras. *China Perspectives*, 56, 2–12.

Ko, H. and Tzeng, O. J. L. (2000). Learning to read Chinese: The role of phonological awareness in a phonetically opaque script. *Studies in the Linguistic Sciences*, 30, 119–132.

Kohnert, K. (2010). Bilingual children with primary language impairment: Issues, evidence and implications for clinical actions. *Journal of Communication Disorders*, 43, 456–473.

Kohnert, K.; Windsor, J. and Ebert, K. D. (2009). Primary or "specific" language impairment and children learning a second language. *Brain and Language*, 109, 101–111.

Köpke, B. (2004). Neurolinguistic aspects of attrition. *Journal of Neurolinguistics*, 17, 3–30.

Köpke, B. and Schmid, M. (2004). Language attrition: The next phase. In M. Schmid, B. Köpke, M. Keijzer and L. Weilemar (Eds.), *First language attrition: Interdisciplinary perspectives on methodological issues* (pp. 1–43). Amsterdam: John Benjamins.

Krashen, S. (1996). A gradual exit, variable threshold, model for limited English proficient children. *NABE News*, 19, 1–17.

Krashen, S. (1998). Comprehensible output? *System*, 26, 175–182.

Krashen, S. (2002). Defending whole language: The limits of phonics instruction and the efficacy of whole language instruction. *Reading Improvement*, 39, 32–42.

Krashen, S. (2003). *Explorations in language acquisition and use: The Taipei lectures*. Portsmouth, NH: Heinemann.

Krashen, S. (2004). False claims about literacy development. *Educational Leadership*, 61 (6), 18–21.

Krashen, S. (2008). Language education: Past, present and future. *RELC Journal*, 39, 178–187.

Krashen, S. and Biber, D. (1988). *On course: Bilingual education's success in California*. Sacramento: California Association for Bilingual Education.

Kubota, M. (2005). Spelling correction strategies employed by learners of Japanese. *Australian Journal of Applied Linguistics*, 28, 67–80.

Lai, M. L. (2011). Cultural identity and language attitudes—Into the second decade of postcolonial Hong Kong. *Journal of Multilingual and Multicultural Development*, 32, 249–264.

Lam, H. C.; Ki, W. W.; Law, N.; Chung, A. L. S.; Ko, P. Y.; Ho, A. H. S. and Pun, S. W. (2001). Designing CALL for learning Chinese characters. *Journal of Computer Assisted Learning*, 17, 115–128.

Laplante, B. (2001). French education in Canada. *Language, Culture and Curriculum*, 14, 91–97.

Laufer, B. (2006). Comparing focus on form and focus on forms in second language vocabulary learning. *Canadian Modern Language Review*, 63, 149–166.

Law, S.-P. (2004). Writing errors of a Cantonese dysgraphic patient and their theoretical implications. *Neurocase*, 10, 132–140.

Law, S.-P. and Or, B. (2001). A case of acquired dyslexia and dysgraphia in Cantonese: Evidence for nonsemantic pathways for reading and writing Chinese. *Cognitive Neuropsychology*, 18, 729–748.

Law, S.-P.; Wong, W. and Chiu, K. M. Y. (2005). Preserved reading aloud with semantic deficits: Evidence for a non-semantic lexical route for reading Chinese. *Neurocase*, 11, 167–175.

Law, S.-P.; Wong, W. and Kong, A. (2006). Direct access from meaning to orthography in Chinese: A case study of superior written to oral naming. *Aphasiology*, 20, 565–578.

Lazaruk, W. (2007). Linguistic, academic, and cognitive benefits of French immersion. *Canadian Modern Language Review*, 63, 605–628.

Le Pichon, E. (2010). *What children know about communication: A language biographical approach of the heterogeneity of plurilingual groups*. Utrecht: Landelijke Onderzoekschool Taalwetenschap.

Le Pichon, E.; de Swart, H.; Vorstman, J. and van den Bergh, H. (2010). Influence of the context of learning a language on the strategic competence of children. *International Journal of Bilingualism*, 14, 447–465.

Lee, I. (2004). Error correction in L2 secondary writing classrooms: The case of Hong Kong. *Journal of Second Language Writing*, 13, 285–312.

Lee, J. R.; Hung, D. L. and Tzeng, O. J. L. (2006). Cross-linguistic analysis of developmental dyslexia: Does phonology matter in learning to read Chinese? *Language and Linguistics*, 7, 573–594.

Lei, L.; Pan, J.; Liu, H.; McBride-Chang, C.; Li, H.; Zhang, Y.; Chen, L.; Tardiff, T.; Liang, W.; Zhang, Z. and Shu, H. (2011). Developmental trajectories of reading development and impairment from ages 3 to 8 years in Chinese children. *Journal of Child Psychology and Psychiatry*, 52, 212–220.

Leikin, M.; Share, D. and Schwartz, M. (2005). Difficulties in L2 Hebrew reading in Russian-speaking second graders. *Reading and Writing*, 18, 455–472.

Levy, B.; McVeigh, N.; Marful, A. and Anderson, M. (2007). Inhibiting your native language: The role of retrieval-induced forgetting during second language acquisition. *Psychological Science*, 18, 29–34.

Li, D. C. S. (2006). Chinese as a lingua franca in Greater China. *Annual Review of Applied Linguistics*, 26, 149–176.

Li, D. C. S. (2009). Towards "biliteracy and trilingualism" in Hong Kong (SAR): Problems, dilemmas and stakeholders' views. *AILA Review*, 22, 72–84.

Li, H. and Rao, N. (2005). Curricular and instructional influences on early literacy attainment: Evidence from Beijing, Hong Kong and Singapore. *International Journal of Early Years Education*, 13, 235–253.

Li, V. W. K. and Majhanovich, S. E. (2010). Marching on a long road: A review of the effectiveness of the mother-tongue education policy in post-colonial Hong Kong. *GIST Education and Learning Research Journal*, 4, 1–29.

Li, W.; Anderson, R. C.; Nagy, W. and Zhang, H. (2002). Facets of metalinguistic awareness that contribute to Chinese literacy. In W. Li, J. S. Gaffney and J. Packard

(Eds.), *Chinese children's reading acquisition: Theoretical and pedagogical issues* (pp. 87–106). Boston: Kluwer.

Liberman, A. (1999). The reading researcher and the reading teacher need the right theory of speech. *Scientific Studies of Reading*, 3, 95–111.

Liceras, J. (2010). Second language acquisition and syntactic theory in the 21st century. *Annual Review of Applied Linguistics*, 30, 248–269.

Lidz, J. (2010). Language learning and language universals. *Biolinguistics*, 4, 201–217.

Lin, A. M.-Y. and Akamatsu, N. (1997). The learnability and psychological processing of reading in Chinese and reading in English. In H.-C. Chen (Ed.), *Cognitive processing of Chinese and related Asian languages* (pp. 369–387). Hong Kong: The Chinese University Press.

Lin, A. M.-Y. and Man, E. Y.-F. (2009). *Bilingual education: Southeast Asian perspectives*. Hong Kong: Hong Kong University Press.

Lin, C. M.-C.; Gerner de García, B. and Chen-Pichler, D. (2009). Standardizing Chinese Sign Language for use in post-secondary education. *Current Issues in Language Planning*, 10, 327–337.

Lin, H. and Chen, T. (2006). Decreasing cognitive load for novice EFL learners: Effects of questions and descriptive advance organizers in facilitating EFL learners' comprehension of an animation-based content lesson. *System*, 34, 416–431.

Lin, H.-F. and Morrison, B. (2010). The impact of the medium of instruction in Hong Kong secondary schools on tertiary students' vocabulary. *Journal of English for Academic Purposes*, 9, 255–266.

Liu, P. D. and McBride-Chang, C. (2010). What is morphological awareness? Tapping lexical compounding awareness in Chinese third graders. *Journal of Educational Psychology*, 102, 62–73.

Loewen, S. and Erlam, R. (2006). Corrective feedback in the chatroom: An experimental study. *Computer Assisted Language Learning*, 19, 1–14.

Long, M. (2005). Problems with supposed counter-evidence to the Critical Period Hypothesis. *International Review of Applied Linguistics*, 43, 287–317.

Lust, B. (2010). Acquisition of language. In P. Hogan (Ed.), *The Cambridge encyclopedia of the language sciences* (pp. 56–64). Cambridge: Cambridge University Press.

Lyster, R. (2004). Differential effects of prompts and recasts on form-focused instruction. *Studies in Second Language Acquisition*, 26, 399–432.

Lyster, R. (2004). Research on form-focused instruction in immersion classrooms: Implications for theory and practice. *French Language Studies*, 14, 321–341.

Lyster, R. and Mori, H. (2006). Interactional feedback and instructional counterbalance. *Studies in Second Language Acquisition*, 28, 269–300.

Ma, Q. (2007). From monitoring users to controlling user actions: A new perspective on the use-centered approach to CALL. *Computer Assisted Language Learning*, 20, 297–321.

MacSwan, J. (2000). The architecture of the bilingual language faculty: Evidence from intrasentential codeswitching. *Bilingualism: Language and Cognition*, 3, 37–54.

MacSwan, J. and Pray, L. (2005). Learning English bilingually: Age of onset of exposure and rate of acquisition among English language learners in a bilingual education program. *Bilingual Research Journal*, 29, 653–678.

MacWhinney, B. (2005). Extending the competition model. *International Journal of Bilingualism*, 9, 69–84.

Mahon, M. and Crutchley, A. (2006). Performance of typically-developing school-age children with English as an additional language on the British Picture Vocabulary Scales II. *Child Language Teaching and Therapy*, 22, 333–351.

Marcus, G. (2006). Cognitive architecture and descent with modification. *Cognition*, 101, 443–465.

Marcus, G. and Fisher, S. (2003). FOXP2 in focus: What can genes tells us about speech and language? *Trends in Cognitive Sciences*, 7, 257–262.

Marshall, J.; Atkinson, J.; Woll, B. and Thacker, A. (2005). Aphasia in a bilingual user of British Sign Language and English: Effects of cross-linguistic cues. *Cognitive Neuropsychology*, 22, 719–736.

Masumi, N. (2006). Changes in Japanese EFL writing through a native English reader's feedback. Paper presented at the *Tamkang International Conference on Second Language Writing*, Tamkang University, Taipei, December 1, 2006.

Matthews, S. and Yip, V. (2011). Unbalanced bilingual acquisition as a mechanism of grammatical change. *Bilingualism: Language and Cognition*, 14, 159–161.

Mayberry, R. (2007). When timing is everything: Age of first-language acquisition effects on second-language learning. *Applied Psycholinguistics*, 28, 537–549.

Mayberry, R. and Lock, E. (2003). Age constraints on first versus second language acquisition: Evidence for linguistic plasticity and epigenesis. *Brain and Language*, 87, 369–384.

Mayer, C. (2007). What really matters in the early literacy development of deaf children. *Journal of Deaf Studies and Deaf Education*, 12, 411–431.

McBride-Chang, C. and Ho, C. S.-H. (2000). Developmental issues in Chinese children's character acquisition. *Journal of Educational Psychology*, 92, 50–55.

Meisel, J. (2001). The simultaneous acquisition of two first languages: Early differentiation and subsequent development of grammars. In J. Cenoz and F. Genesee (Eds.), *Trends in bilingual acquisition* (pp. 11–41). Amsterdam: John Benjamins.

Meisel, J. (2004). The bilingual child. In T. Bhatia and W. R. Ritchie (Eds.), *The handbook of bilingualism* (pp. 91–113). Oxford: Blackwell.

Meisel, J. (2007). The weaker language in early child bilingualism: Acquiring a first language as a second language. *Applied Psycholinguistics*, 28, 495–514.

Meisel, J. (2009). Second language acquisition in early childhood. *Zeitschrift für Sprachwissenschaft*, 28, 5–24.

Menéndez, B. (2010). Cross-modal bilingualism: Language contact as evidence of linguistic transfer in sign language education. *International Journal of Bilingual Education and Bilingualism*, 13, 201–223.

Miao, Y.; Badger, R. and Zhen, Y. (2006). A comparative study of peer and teacher feedback in a Chinese EFL writing class. *Journal of Second Language Writing*, 15, 179–200.

Miles, E. (2000). Dyslexia may show a different face in different languages. *Dyslexia*, 6, 193–201.

Min, H.-T. (2006). The effects of trained peer review on EFL students' revision types and writing quality. *Journal of Second Language Writing*, 15, 118–141.

Mohanty, A.; Panda, M. and Pal, R. (2010). Language policy in education and classroom practices in India: Is the teacher a cog in the policy wheel? In K. Menken and O. García (Eds.), *Negotiating language policies in schools: Educators as policymakers* (pp. 211–231). New York: Routledge.

Montrul, S. (2004). Convergent outcomes in L2 acquisition and L1 loss. In M. Schmid, B. Köpke, M. Keijzer and L. Weilemar (Eds.), *First language attrition: Interdisciplinary perspectives on methodological issues* (pp. 259–279). Amsterdam: John Benjamins.

Montrul, S. (2005). Second language acquisition and first language loss in adult early bilinguals: Exploring some differences and similarities. *Second Language Research*, 21, 199–249.

Montrul, S. (2006). Incomplete acquisition as a feature of bilingual and L2 grammars. In R. Slabakova, S. Montrul and P. Prévost (Eds.), *Inquiries in linguistic development: In honor of Lydia White* (pp. 335–359). Amsterdam: John Benjamins.

Montrul, S. (2008). *Incomplete acquisition in bilingualism: Re-examining the age factor*. Amsterdam: John Benjamins.

Morais, J. and Kolinsky, R. (2001). The literate mind and the universal human mind. In E. Dupoux (Ed.), *Language, brain, and cognitive development: Essays in honor of Jacques Mehler* (pp. 463–480). Cambridge: MIT Press.

Morgan, G. and Kegl, J. (2006). Nicaraguan Sign Language and theory of mind: The issue of critical periods and abilities. *Journal of Child Psychology and Psychiatry*, 47, 811-819.

Mori, Y.; Sato, K. and Shimizu, H. (2007). Japanese language students' perceptions on kanji learning and their relationship to novel kanji word learning ability. *Language Learning*, 57, 57–85.

Morris, F. (2005). Child-to-child interaction and corrective feedback in a computer mediated L2 class. *Language, Learning and Technology*, 9, 29–46.

Morrison, L. (2004). Comprehension monitoring in first and second language reading. *The Canadian Modern Language Review*, 61, 77–106.

Mumtaz, S. and Humphreys, G. W. (2001). The effects of bilingualism on learning to read English: Evidence from the contrast between Urdu-English bilingual and English monolingual children. *Journal of Research in Reading*, 24, 113–134.

Muysken, P. (2000). *Bilingual speech: A typology of code-mixing*. Cambridge: Cambridge University Press.

Myers-Scotton, C. (2004). Precision tuning of the Matrix Language Frame (MLF) model of codeswitching. *Sociolinguistica*, 18, 106–117.

Myers-Scotton, C. (2006). *Multiple voices: An introduction to bilingualism*. Oxford: Blackwell.

Myles, F. (2004). From data to theory: The over-representation of linguistic knowledge in SLA. *Transactions of the Philosophical Society*, 102, 139–168.

Navarra, J.; Sebastián-Gallés, N. and Soto-Faraco, S. (2005). The perception of second language sounds in early bilinguals: New evidence from an implicit measure. *Journal of Experimental Psychology*, 31, 912–918.

Neville, H. (2005). Development and plasticity of human cognition. In U. Mayr, E. Ahw and S. Keele (Eds.), *Developing individuality in the human brain: A tribute to Michael I. Posner* (pp. 209–235). Washington DC: American Psychological Association.

Newmeyer, F. (2003). Grammar is grammar and usage is usage. *Language*, 79, 682–707.

Newport, E. L. (1990). Maturational constraints on language learning. *Cognition*, 14, 11–29.

Nicoladis, E. and Grabois, H. (2002). Learning English and losing Chinese: A case study of a child adopted from China. *International Journal of Bilingualism*, 6, 441–454.

Niederberger, N. and Frauenfelder, U. (2005). Linguistic proficiency of the deaf bilingual child in French Sign Language and written French: What is the relation between the two? In A. Burgos, M. R. Clark-Cotton and S. Ha (Eds.), *Proceedings of the 29th Boston University Conference on Language Development* (pp. 413–423). Somerville: Cascadilla Press.

Norris, D. (1990). Connectionism: A case for modularity. In D. Balota, G. Flores d'Arcais and K. Rayner (Eds.), *Comprehension processes in reading* (pp. 331–343). Hillsdale: Lawrence Erlbaum.

Norris, J. and Ortega, L. (2000). Effectiveness of L2 instruction: A research synthesis and quantitative meta-analysis. *Language Learning*, 50, 417–528.

Norris, J. and Ortega, L. (2001). Does type of instruction make a difference? Substantive findings from a meta-analytic review. *Language Learning*, 51, 157–213.

Oller, D.; Jarmulowicz, L.; Pearson, B. and Cobo-Lewis, A. (2010). Rapid spoken language shift in early second language learning: The role of peers and effects on the first language. In A. Durgunoğlu and C. Goldenberg (Eds.), *Language and literacy development in bilingual settings* (pp. 94–120). New York: Guilford Press.

Oller, J. (2008). *El coneixement de la llengua catalana i la llengua castellana per part de l'alumnat estranger escolaritzat a l'educació primària de Catalunya: Factors explicatius i relacions d'interdependència lingüística.* Doctoral thesis, Universitat de Girona.

Oller, J. and Vila, I. (2011). Interdependencia entre conocimiento de catalán y castellano y efectos de la lengua familiar en la adquisición de las lenguas escolares. *Cultura y Educación*, 23, 3–22.

Ong, W. J. (1982). *Orality and literacy: The technologizing of the word.* London: Methuen.

Oren, R. and Breznitz, Z. (2005). Reading processes in L1 and L2 among dyslexic as compared to regular bilingual readers: Behavioral and electrophysiological evidence. *Journal of Neurolinguistics*, 18, 127–151.

Packard, J. (2000). *The morphology of Chinese: A linguistic and cognitive approach.* Cambridge: Cambridge University Press.

Packard, J. (2002). Metalinguistic awareness as a critical factor. In W. Li, J. S. Gaffney and J. Packard (Eds.), *Chinese children's reading acquisition: Theoretical and pedagogical issues* (pp. 107–111). Boston: Kluwer.

Paivio, A. (1991). Mental representation in bilinguals. In A. Reynolds (Ed.), *Bilingualism, multiculturalism, and second language learning* (pp. 113–125). Mahwah: Lawrence Erlbaum.

Pallier, C. (2007). Critical periods in language acquisition and language attrition. In B. Köpke, M. Schmid, M. Keijzer and S. Dostert (Eds.), *Language attrition: Theoretical perspectives* (pp. 155–168). Amsterdam: John Benjamins.

Pallier, C.; Colomé, A. and Sebastián-Gallés, N. (2001). The influence of native-language phonology on lexical access. *Psychological Science*, 12, 445–449.

Paradis, J.; Crago, M. and Genesee, F. (2005). Domain-general versus domain-specific accounts of specific language impairment: Evidence from bilingual children's acquisition of object pronouns. *Language Acquisition*, 13, 33–62.

Paradis, M. (2004). *A neurolinguistic theory of bilingualism*. Amsterdam: John Benjamins.

Perfetti, C. (1992). The representation problem in reading acquisition. In P. Gough, L. Ehri and R. Treiman (Eds.), *Reading acquisition* (pp. 145–174). Mahwah: Lawrence Erlbaum.

Perfetti, C. (1999). Comprehending written language: A blueprint of the reader. In C. Brown and P. Hagoort (Eds.), *The neurolinguistics of language* (pp. 167–208). Oxford: Oxford University Press.

Perfetti, C. (2003). The Universal Grammar of reading. *Scientific Studies of Reading*, 7, 3–24.

Perfetti, C. (2010). Decoding, vocabulary, and comprehension: The golden triangle of reading skill. In M. G. McKeon and L. Kucan (Eds.), *Bringing reading research to life* (pp. 291–303). New York: The Guilford Press.

Perfetti, C. and Liu, Y. (2005). Orthography to phonology and meaning: Comparisons across and within systems. *Reading and Writing*, 18, 193–210.

Peter, L.; Hirata-Edds, T. and Montgomery-Anderson, B. (2008). Verb development by children in the Cherokee language immersion program, with implications for teaching. *International Journal of Applied Linguistics*, 18, 166–187.

Pettito, L. and Holowka, S. (2002). Evaluating attributions of delay and confusion in young bilinguals: Special insights from infants acquiring a signed and a spoken language. *Sign Language Studies*, 3, 4–33.

Petitto, L.; Holowka, S.; Sergio, L.; Levy, B. and Ostry, D. (2004). Baby hands that move to the rhythm of language: Hearing babies acquiring sign languages babble silently on the hands. *Cognition*, 93, 43–73.

Pettito, L. and Kovelman, I. (2003). The bilingual paradox: How signing-speaking bilingual children help us resolve bilingual issues and teach us about the brain's mechanisms underlying all language acquisition. *Learning Languages*, 8, 5–18.

Pettito, L.; Katerelos, M.; Levy, B. G.; Gauna, K.; Tétreault, K. and Ferraro, V. (2001). Bilingual signed and spoken language acquisition from birth: Implications for the mechanisms underlying early bilingual language acquisition. *Journal of Child Language*, 28, 453–496.

Pfaff, C. (1999). Changing patterns of language mixing in a bilingual child. In G. Extra and L. Verhoeven (Eds.), *Bilingualism and migration* (pp. 97–121). New York: Mouton de Gruyter.

Pi, W. B. (2004). *Zhongxue shuangyu jiaoxue de shijian yu sikao [Bilingual education in secondary schools and reflections]*. Master's thesis, East China Normal University, Shanghai, China.

Pica, T. (2008). SLA in the instructional environment. *Working Papers in Educational Linguistics*, 23, 1–27.

Pietrandrea, P. (2002). Iconicity and arbitrariness in Italian Sign Language. *Sign Language Studies*, 2, 296–321.

Pinker, S. (1990). Language acquisition. In D. Osherson and H. Lasnik (Eds.), *Language: An invitation to cognitive science* (pp. 199–241). Cambridge: MIT Press.

Pinker, S. (1999). *Words and rules: The ingredients of language*. New York: Harper Collins.

Pinker, S. (2004). Clarifying the logical problem of language acquisition. *Journal of Child Language*, 31, 949–953.

Pinker, S. and Jackendoff, R. (2005). The faculty of language: What's special about it? *Cognition*, 95, 201–236.

Pinker, S. and Ullman, M. (2002). The past and future of the past tense. *Trends in Cognitive Science*, 6, 456–472.

Poole, A. (2005). Focus on form instruction: Foundations, applications, and criticisms. *The Reading Matrix*, 5, 47–56.

Proctor, C. P.; Carlo, M.; August, D. and Snow, C. (2005). Native Spanish-speaking children reading in English: Toward a model of comprehension. *Journal of Educational Psychology*, 97, 246–256.

Pugh, K.; Sandak, R.; Frost, S.; Moore, D. and Menel, E. (2005). Examining reading development and reading disability in English language learners: Potential contributions from functional neuroimaging. *Learning Disabilities Research and Practice*, 20, 24–30.

Pyun, D. O. and Lee-Smith, A. (2011). Reducing Korean language learners' orthographic errors: The contribution of online and in-class dictation and form-focused instruction. *Language, Culture and Curriculum*, 24, 141–158.

Qiang, H.-Y.; Huang, X.-D.; Siegel, L. and Trube, B. (2011). English immersion in Mainland China. In A. Feng (Ed.), *English language education across greater China* (pp. 169–188). Bristol: Multilingual Matters.

Rajagopalan, K. (2009). Exposing young children to English as a foreign language: The emerging role of World English. *Trabalhos em Linguística Aplicada*, 48, 185–196.

Raman, I. and Weekes, B. (2005). Acquired dyslexia in a Turkish-English speaker. *Annals of Dyslexia*, 55, 79–104.

Rao, Z. (2006). Understanding Chinese students' use of language learning strategies from cultural and educational perspectives. *Journal of Multilingual and Multicultural Development*, 27, 491–508.

Rayner, K.; Foorman, B.; Perfetti, C.; Pesetsky, D. and Seidenberg, M. (2001). How psychological science informs the teaching of reading. *Psychological Science in the Public Interest*, 2, 31–74.

Read, J. (2004). Research in teaching vocabulary. *Annual Review of Applied Linguistics*, 24, 146–161.

Reed, C. and Delhorne, L. (1995). A study of the tactual reception of sign language. *Journal of Speech, Language and Hearing*, 38, 477–489.

Reich, S.; Chou, T.-L. and Paterson, K. (2003). Acquired dysgraphia in Chinese: Further evidence on the links between phonology and orthography. *Aphasiology*, 17, 585–604.

Rollinson, P. (2005). Using peer feedback in the ESL writing class. *ELT Journal*, 59, 23–30.

Rothenberg, C. and Fisher, D. (2007). *Teaching English language learners: A differentiated approach*. Upper Saddle River, NJ: Pearson.

Ruan, J. (2004). Bilingual Chinese/English first-graders developing metacognition about writing. *Literacy*, 38, 106–112.

Russell, J. and Spada, N. (2006). The effectiveness of corrective feedback for the acquisition of L2 grammar. In J. Norris and L. Ortega (Eds.), *Synthesizing research on language learning and teaching* (pp. 133–163). Amsterdam: John Benjamins.

Sánchez, L.; Camacho, J. and Ulloa, J. E. (2010). Shipibo-Spanish: Differences in residual transfer at the syntax-morphology and the syntax-pragmatics interfaces. *Second Language Research*, 26, 329–354.

Sandler, W. (1993). Sign language and modularity. *Lingua*, 89, 315–351.

Sandler, W. and Lillo-Martin, D. (2001). Natural sign languages. In M. Aronoff and J. Rees-Miller (Eds.), *Handbook of linguistics* (pp. 533–562). Oxford: Blackwell.

Sandler, W.; Meir, I. and Aronoff, M. (2005). The emergence of grammar: Systematic structure in a new language. *Proceedings of the National Academy of Sciences*, 102, 2661–2665.

Sarva, A. (2010). *The concept of modularity in cognitive science*. Saarbrücken: VDM Verlag.

Sauro, S. (2009). Computer-mediated corrective feedback and the development of L2 grammar. *Language Learning and Technology*, 13, 96–120.

Schachter, J. (1996). Maturation and the issue of Universal Grammar in second language acquisition. In W. C. Ritchie and T. J. Bhatia (Eds.), *Handbook of second language acquisition* (pp. 159–193). New York: Academic Press.

Schachter, J. (1998). Recent research in language learning studies: Promises and problems. *Language Learning*, 48, 557–589.

Schleppegrell, M. J.; Achugar, M. and Oteíza, T. (2004). The grammar of history: Enhancing content-based instruction through a functional focus on language. *TESOL Quarterly*, 38, 67–93.

Schlyter, S. (1993). The weaker language in bilingual Swedish-French children. In K. Hyltenstam and A. Viberg (Eds.), *Progression and regression in language: Sociocultural, neuropsychological, and linguistic perspectives* (pp. 289–308). Cambridge: Cambridge University Press.

Schmitt, E. (2000). The lost word: Language attrition among children. *Boston University Conference on Language Development Proceedings*, 24, 645–656.

Schwartz, B. (1998). The second language instinct. *Lingua*, 106, 133–160.

Schwartz, B. (2003). Child L2 acquisition: Paving the way. *Boston University Conference on Language Development Proceedings*, 27, 26–50.

Sebastián-Gallés, N. and Bosch, L. (2001). On becoming and being bilingual. In E. Dupoux (Ed.), *Language, brain, and cognitive development: Essays in honor of Jacques Mehler* (pp. 379–393). Cambridge: MIT Press.

Seidel, K. and Moritz, J. (2009). Changes in Ethiopia's language policy—Pioneering reforms. In S. Ege, H. Aspen, B. Teferra and S. Bekele (Eds.), *Proceedings of the 16th International Conference of Ethiopian Studies* (pp. 1125–1138). Trondheim: Department of Social Anthropology, Norwegian University of Science and Technology.

Seidenberg, M. S. (2005). Connectionist models of word reading. *Current Directions in Psychological Science*, 14, 238–242.

Seliger, L. (1996). Primary language attrition in the context of bilingualism. In W. Ritchie and T. Bhatia (Eds.), *Handbook of second language acquisition* (pp. 605–625). New York: Academic Press.

Senghas, A. (2003). Intergenerational influence and ontogenetic development in the emergence of spatial grammar in Nicaraguan Sign Language. *Cognitive Development*, 18, 511–531.

Senghas, A.; Kita, S. and Özyürek, A. (2008). Children creating core properties of language: Evidence from an emerging sign language in Nicaragua. In K. Lindgren, D. DeLuca, B. Reynolds and D. Napoli (Eds.), *Signs and voices* (pp. 90–99). Washington DC: Gallaudet University Press.

Senghas, A.; Sotaro, K. and Özyürek, A. (2004). Children creating core properties of language: Evidence from an emerging sign language in Nicaragua. *Science*, 305, 1779–1782.

Shankweiler, D. and Fowler, A. (2004). Questions people ask about the role phonological processes in learning to read. *Reading and Writing*, 17, 483–515.

Share, D. L. and Leikin, M. (2004). Language impairment at school entry and later reading disability: Connections at lexical versus supralexical levels of reading. *Scientific Studies of Reading*, 8, 87–110.

Sharwood-Smith, M. (1991). Language modules and bilingual processing. In E. Bialystok (Ed.), *Language processing in bilingual children* (pp. 10–24). Cambridge: Cambridge University Press.

Sharwood-Smith, M. and Van Buren, P. (1991). First language attrition and the parameter setting model. In H. Seliger and R. Vago (Eds.), *First language attrition* (pp. 17–30). Cambridge: Cambridge University Press.

Shatil, E. and Share, D. L. (2003). Cognitive antecedents of early reading ability: A test of the modularity hypothesis. *Journal of Experimental Child Psychology*, 86, 1–31.

Sheen, R. (2003). Focus on form: A myth in the making. *ELT Journal*, 57, 225–233.

Sheen, Y. (2004). Corrective feedback and learner uptake in communicative classrooms across instructional settings. *Language Teaching Research*, 8, 263–300.

Shehadeh, A. (2003). Learner output, hypothesis testing, and internalizing linguistic knowledge. *System*, 31, 155–171.

Shen, H. H. and Ke, C. (2007). Radical awareness and word acquisition among nonnative learners of Chinese. *The Modern Language Journal*, 91, 97–111.

Shu, H. (2003). Chinese writing system and learning to read. *International Journal of Psychology*, 38, 274–284.

Shu, H.; Chen, X.; Anderson, R. C.; Wu, N. and Xuan, Y. (2002). Properties of school Chinese: Implications for learning to read. *Child Development*, 74, 27–47.

Shum, M. S. K.; Gao, F.; Tsung, L. and Ki, W.-W. (2011). South Asian students' Chinese language learning in Hong Kong: Motivations and strategies. *Journal of Multilingual and Multicultural Development*, 32, 285–297.

Shwartz, M.; Leikin, M. and Share, D. (2005). Bi-literate bilingualism versus mono-literate bilingualism: A longitudinal study of reading acquisition in Hebrew (L2) among Russian-speaking (L1) children. *Written Language and Literacy*, 8, 179–206.

Siguán, M. (1998). *La escuela y los inmigrantes*. Barcelona: Paidós.

Silva-Corvalán, C. (2003). Linguistic consequences of reduced input in bilingual first language acquisition. In N. Montrul and F. Ordóñez (Eds.), *Linguistic theory and language development in Hispanic languages* (pp. 375–397). Somerville: Cascadilla Press.

Singleton, C. (2005). Dyslexia and oral reading errors. *Journal of Research in Reading*, 28, 4–14.

Singleton, J. L. and Newport, E. L. (2004). When learners surpass their models: The acquisition of American Sign Language from inconsistent input. *Cognitive Psychology*, 49, 370–407.

Siok, W. T. and Fletcher, P. (2001). The role of phonological awareness and visual-orthographic skills in Chinese reading acquisition. *Developmental Psychology*, 37, 886–899.

Snow, M. A. (2005). A model of academic literacy for integrated language and content instruction. In E. Hinkel (Ed.), *Handbook of research in second language teaching and learning* (pp. 693–712). Mahwah: Lawrence Erlbaum.

Snow, M. A.; Met, M. and Genesee, F. (1989). A conceptual framework for the integration of language and content in second/foreign language instruction. *TESOL Quarterly*, 23, 201–218.

Song, B. (2006). Content-based ESL instruction: Long-term effects and outcomes. *English for Specific Purposes*, 25, 420-437.

Sorace, A. (2003). Near nativeness. In C. J. Doughty and M. H. Long (Eds.), *The handbook of second language acquisition* (pp. 130–151). Oxford: Blackwell.

Sorace, A. (2005). Selective optionality in language development. In L. Cornips and K. Corrigan (Eds.), *Syntax and variation: Reconciling the biological and the social* (pp. 55–80). Amsterdam: John Benjamins.

Sperber, D. and Wilson, D. (2002). Pragmatics, modularity and mind-reading. *Mind and Language*, 17, 3–23.

Stanovich, K. (2000). *Progress in understanding reading: Scientific foundations and new frontiers*. New York: Guilford.

Stanovich, K. (2003). Understanding the styles of science in the study of reading. *Scientific Studies of Reading*, 7, 105–126.

Stanovich, K. and Stanovich, P. (1999). How research might inform the debate about early reading acquisition. In J. Oakhill and R. Beard (Eds.), *Reading development and the teaching of reading: A psychological perspective* (pp. 12–41). Oxford: Blackwell.

Su, Y.-F. and Samuels, S. J. (2010). Developmental changes in character-complexity and word-length effects when reading Chinese script. *Reading and Writing*, 23, 1085–1108.

Sunuodula, M. and Feng, A. (2011). Learning English as a third language by Uyghur students in Xinjiang. In A. Feng (Ed.), *English language education across greater China* (pp. 260–283). Bristol: Multilingual Matters.

Sutton-Spence, R. (1999). The influence of English on British Sign Language. *International Journal of Bilingualism*, 4, 363–394.

Swain, M. (1996). Integrating language and content in immersion classrooms: Research perspectives. *Canadian Modern Language Review*, 52, 529–548.

Swain, M. and Lapkin, S. (2005). The evolving sociopolitical context of immersion education in Canada: Some implications for program development. *International Journal of Applied Linguistics*, 15, 169–186.

Taft, M. and van Graan, F. (1998). Lack of phonological mediation in a semantic categorization task. *Journal of Memory and Language*, 38, 203–224.

Tager-Flusberg, H. and Zukowski, A. (2009). Putting words together: Morphology and syntax in the preschool years. In J. Berko Gleason and N. Bernstein Ratner (Eds.), *The development of language, 7th edition* (pp. 139–191). Boston: Pearson.

Tam, A. C. F. (2011). Does the switch of medium of instruction facilitate the language learning of students? A case study of Hong Kong from teachers' perspective. *Language and Education*, 25, 399–417.

Tan, L. H.; Spinks, J.; Eden, G.; Perfetti, C. and Siok, W. T. (2005). Reading depends on writing, in Chinese. *Proceedings of the National Academy of Sciences*, 102, 8781–8785.

Taylor, I. (2002). Phonological awareness in Chinese reading. In W. Li, J. S. Gaffney and J. Packard (Eds.), *Chinese children's reading acquisition: Theoretical and pedagogical issues* (pp. 39–58). Boston: Kluwer.

Thomas, M. and Karmiloff-Smith, A. (2005). Can developmental disorders reveal the component parts of the human language faculty? *Language Learning and Development*, 1, 65–92.

Thomason, S. (2001). *Language contact*. Washington DC: Georgetown University Press.

Thordardottir, E. (2010). Towards evidence-based practice in language intervention for bilingual children. *Journal of Communication Disorders*, 43, 523–537.

Tong, X.; McBride-Chang, C.; Wong, A. M.-Y.; Shu, H.; Reitsma, P. and Rispens, J. (2011). Longitudinal predictors of very early Chinese literacy acquisition. *Journal of Research in Reading*, 34, 315–332.

Towell, R. (2004). Representational modularity and second language acquisition research. *Transactions of the Philological Society*, 102, 281–305.

Truscott, J. (2010). Some thoughts on Anthony Bruton's critique of the correction debate. *System*, 38, 329–335.

Truscott, J. and Hsu, A. Y.-P. (2008). Error correction, revision, and learning. *Journal of Second Language Writing*, 17, 292–305.

Tsai, J. L.; Lee, C. Y.; Tzeng, O.; Hung, D. L. and Yen, N. S. (2004). Use of phonological codes for Chinese characters: Evidence from processing of parafoveal preview when reading sentences. *Brain and Language*, 91, 235–244.

Tse, S.-K. and Tan, W.-X. (2011). Catering for primary school pupils with different Chinese language proficiencies in Singapore through differentiated curricula and instructional materials. In L. Tsung and K. Cruikshank (Eds.), *Teaching and learning Chinese in global contexts: Multimodality and literacy in the New Media Age* (pp. 29–44). London: Continuum.

Tse, S.-K.; Lam, J. W.-I.; Loh, E. K.-Y. and Lam, R. Y.-H. (2007). The influence of the language that Hong Kong primary school students habitually speak at home on their Chinese reading ability in school. *Journal of Multilingual and Multicultural Development*, 28, 400–417.

Tzeng, O. J. L. (2002). Current issues in learning to read Chinese. In W. Li, J. S. Gaffney and J. Packard (Eds.), *Chinese children's reading acquisition: Theoretical and pedagogical issues* (pp. 3–16). Boston: Kluwer.

Tzeng, O. J. L.; Zhong, H. L.; Hung, D. L. and Lee, W. L. (1995). Learning to be a conspirator: A tale of becoming a good Chinese reader. In B. de Gelder and J. Morais (Eds.), *Speech and reading: A comparative approach* (pp. 227–246). East Sussex: Taylor and Francis.

Ullman, M. (2001). The neural basis of lexicon and grammar in first and second language: The declarative/procedural model. *Bilingualism: Language and Cognition*, 4, 105–122.

Ullman, M. and Gopnik, M. (1999). Inflectional morphology in a family with inherited language impairment. *Applied Psycholinguistics*, 20, 51–117.

Van Der Lely, H. K. J. (2005). Domain specific cognitive systems: Insight from grammatical-SLI. *Trends in Cognitive Science*, 9, 53–59.

Ventureyra, V.; Pallier, C. and Yoo, H.-Y. (2004). The loss of first language phonetic perception in adopted Koreans. *Journal of Neurolinguistics*, 17, 79–91.

Verhoeven, L. (2000). Components of early second language reading and spelling. *Scientific Studies of Reading*, 4, 313–330.

Vermeerbergen, M. (2006). Past and current trends in sign language research. *Language and Communication*, 26, 168–192.

Vygotsky, L. (2004). Imagination and creativity in childhood. *Journal of Russian and East European Psychology*, 42, 7–89.

Walter, C. (2004). Transfer of reading comprehension skills to L2 is linked to mental representations of text and to L2 working memory. *Applied Linguistics*, 25, 315–339.

Wan, M. and Zhang, S. (2007). Research and practice of Tibetan-Chinese bilingual education. In A. Feng (Ed.), *Bilingual education in China: Practices, policies and concepts* (pp. 127–144). Clevedon: Multillingual Matters.

Wang, L. (2003). Switching to first language among writers with differing second-language proficiency. *Journal of Second Language Writing*, 12, 347–375.

Wang, M.; Koda, K. and Perfetti, C. (2003). Alphabetic and nonalphabetic L1 effects in English word identification: A comparison of Korean and Chinese English L2 learners. *Cognition*, 86, 129–149.

Wang, M.; Liu, Y. and Perfetti, C. (2004). The implicit and explicit learning of orthographic structure and function of a new writing system. *Scientific Studies of Reading*, 8, 357–379.

Wang, M.; Yang, C. and Cheng, C. (2009). The contributions of phonology, orthography, and morphology in Chinese-English biliteracy acquisition. *Applied Psycholinguistics*, 30, 291–314.

Wannagat, U. (2007). Language through L2: Content and language integrated learning (CLIL) and English as medium of instruction. *International Journal of Bilingual Education and Bilingualism*, 10, 663–682.

Weekes, B. S.; Yin, W.; Su, I. F. and Chen, M. J. (2006). The cognitive neuropsychology of reading and writing in Chinese. *Language and Linguistics*, 7, 595–617.

Wei, L. and Hua, Z. (2006). The development of code-switching in early second language acquisition. *Birkbeck Studies in Applied Linguistics*, 1, 68–81.

Wei, L. and Hua, Z. (2010). Voices from the diaspora: Changing hierarchies an dynamics of Chinese multilingualism. *International Journal of the Sociology of Language*, 205, 155–171.

White, L. (2003). Fossilization in steady state L2 grammar: Persistent problems with inflectional morphology. *Bilingualism: Language and Cognition*, 6, 129–141.

White, L. (2011). Second language acquisition at the interfaces. *Lingua*, 121, 577–590.

Wilbur, R. (2001). Sign language and successful bilingual development of deaf children. *Drustvena Istrazivanja*, 10, 1039–1079.

Williams, J. (2005). Form-focused instruction. In E. Hinkel (Ed.), *Handbook of research in second language teaching and learning* (pp. 671–692). Mahwah: Lawrence Erlbaum.

Wong, L.-H.; Chai, C.-S. and Gao, P. (2011). The Chinese input challenges for Chinese as second language learners in computer-mediated writing: An exploratory study. *The Turkish Online Journal of Educational Technology*, 10, 233–248.

Woodall, B. (2002). Language-switching: Using the first language while writing in a second language. *Journal of Second Language Writing*, 11, 7–28.

Wu, X.; Anderson, R.; Li, W.; Wu, X.; Li, H.; Zhang, J.; Zhang, Q.; Zhu, J.; Shu, H.; Jiang, W.; Chen, X.; Wang, Q.; Yin, L.; He, Y.; Packard, J. and Gaffney, J. (2009). Morphological awareness and Chinese children's literacy development: An intervention study. *Scientific Studies of Reading*, 13, 26–52.

Wydell, T. N. and Kondo, T. (2003). Phonological deficit and the reliance on orthographic approximation for reading: A follow-up study on an English-Japanese bilingual with monolingual dyslexia. *Journal of Research in Reading*, 26, 33–48.

Xiang, W. (2004). Encouraging self-monitoring in writing by Chinese students. *ELT Journal*, 58, 238–246.

Xu, Y.; Pollatsek, A. and Potter, M. C. (1999). The activation of phonology during silent word reading. *Journal of Experimental Psychology*, 25, 838–857.

Xue, J. (2011). *Bilingual reading: From the perspective of psycholinguistics*. Beijing: Foreign Languages Press.

Yang, C. (2006). *The infinite gift: How children learn and unlearn the languages of the world*. New York: Scribner.

Yang, M.; Badger, R. and Yu, Z. (2006). A comparative study of peer and teacher feedback in a Chinese EFL writing class. *Journal of Second Language Writing*, 15, 179–200.

Yang, Y. and Lyster, R. (2010). Effects of form-focused practice and feedback on Chinese EFL learners' acquisition of regular and irregular past tense forms. *Studies in Second Language Acquisition*, 32, 235–263.

Yin, W. G. and Weeks, B. S. (2003). Neuropsychological and linguistic framework, reading-related characteristics, screening for dyslexia, and the variant view. *Annals of Dyslexia*, 53, 255–279.

Yip, V. and Matthews, S. (2007). *The bilingual child: Early development and language contact*. Cambridge: Cambridge University Press.

Yip, V. and Matthews, S. (2010). The acquisition of Chinese in bilingual and multilingual contexts. *International Journal of Bilingualism*, 14, 127–146.

Yoshida, R. (2008). Teachers' choice and learners' preference of corrective feedback types. *Language Awareness*, 17, 78–92.

Yoshida, R. (2010). How do teachers and learners perceive corrective feedback in the Japanese language classroom? *The Modern Language Journal*, 94, 293–314.

Yu, L. (2008). English-Chinese bilingual education in China. In J. Cummins and N. Hornberger (Eds.), *Encyclopedia of language and education: Bilingual education, Volume 5* (pp. 175–190). New York: Springer.

Yukawa, E. (1997). *L1 Japanese attrition and regaining: Three case studies of two early bilingual children*. Tokyo: Kurosio Publishers.

Yumoto, K. (2008). Some factors influencing balanced bilingual development: A study of CALP among bilingual Japanese children in Boston. *Japan Journal of Multilingualism and Multiculturalism*, 14, 1–23.

Zhang, J.; Anderson, R.; Li, H.; Dong, Q.; Wu, X. and Zhang, Y. (2010). Cross-language transfer of insight into the structure of compound words. *Reading and Writing*, 23, 311–336.

Zhao, S. and Liu, Y. (2010). Chinese education in Singapore: Constraints of bilingual policy from the perspectives of status and prestige planning. *Language Problems and Language Planning*, 34, 236–258.

Zhou, X. and Marslen-Wilson, W. (1999). Phonology, orthography, and semantic activation in reading Chinese. *Journal of Memory and Language*, 41, 579–606.

Zhou, X. and Marslen-Wilson, W. (2000). The relative time course of semantic and phonological activation in reading Chinese. *Journal of Experimental Psychology*, 26, 1245–1265.

Zuo, X. (2007). China's policy towards minority languages in a globalizing age. *Transnational Curriculum Inquiry*, 4, 80–91.

Zwiers, J. (2008). *Building academic language: Essential practices for content classrooms*. San Francisco: John Wiley and Sons.

Index

D

E

F

N

O

P

T

U

V

W

X

Y

Z